25 Signs We Are Near The End

DON STEWART

25 Signs We Are Near the End
by Don Stewart

© 2017 Don Stewart

Published by EOW (Educating Our World)
www.educatingourworld.com

English Versions Cited

TABLE OF CONTENTS

Don
Stewart +
Daniel
12:10

INTRODUCTION

In this book, we are going to consider twenty-five specific signs that the Bible gives that demonstrate that we are near the "time of the end." By this we mean the time when the Lord Jesus returns from Heaven and sets up His everlasting kingdom.

For the record, we will not involve ourselves in any wild speculation that predicts the exact time the end will occur. This is not biblical, nor is it helpful. Instead, our goal is simply to lay out what the Scripture has to say about the subject, and then observe how its predictions have been literally fulfilled—setting the stage for the return of the Lord.

Not only will we look at what the Bible says—in a number of cases, we will consider the observations of past commentators of Scripture. We will discover that these commentators made certain predictions about the future based upon the Bible and the Bible alone. They did this at such a time when the predicted events looked impossible to ever take place. But they have indeed come to pass just as the Scripture said! In addition, we have included an appendix that provides even further documentation of the predictions of past commentators that have also come to pass.

There are two other appendices in the book. One of them answers a number of objections about predictive prophecy and the "last days." The final appendix looks at the one objective witness throughout the centuries that has continued to prove the truthfulness of the Bible— the miraculous survival of the Jewish people.

We will also consider the present situation of the world to discover how current events line up with the Bible. While we will cite a few stories from today's news, we will resist the temptation of listing endless examples to substantiate what the Scriptures predict will happen. Truth be told, there is so much evidence to back up these signs, each of these twenty-five could become a stand-alone book!

This study should greatly increase the faith of believers who have any doubts as to whether or not God has spoken in the Bible. For unbelievers, this book will provide evidence that a God does exist who knows the future, is in control of the future, and has told us about certain events which will take place in the future. We only ask that all who read this book keep an open mind when examining the evidence that we put forward.

With these thoughts in mind, let us now consider twenty-five signs that we are near the end. . .

The Miracle of
Israel's Survival

As we begin our investigation into the twenty-five specific signs that demonstrate that we are at the time of the end, we must start with the nation of Israel. We do this because it is the key to understanding Bible prophecy.

ISRAEL IS GOD'S PROPHETIC CLOCK

Simply stated, Israel is God's prophetic clock. This has been true in the past, is now true in the present, and will also be true in the future. The evidence for this is as follows.

THE CALL OF ABRAHAM

The nation started some four thousand years ago when a man called Abram, whose name was later changed to Abraham, was told to leave his country and his people, and then to go to a specific land that the Lord had promised him. The Bible explains his call in this way.

> The LORD had said to Abram, "Go from your country, your people and your father's household to the land I will show you. "I will make you into a great nation, and I will bless you; I will make your name great, and you will be a blessing. I will bless those who bless you, and whoever curses you I will curse; and all peoples on earth will be blessed through you" (Genesis 12:1-3 NIV).

God called Abram out of his country and promised to create a great nation from him and his descendants. The Lord also promised that Abram would be blessed and that his name would be made great.

Furthermore, there was another specific promise. God said that those who would bless Abram's descendants would themselves be blessed while those who cursed them would themselves be cursed.

Moreover, the Lord said that the entire world would be blessed through Abram and his descendants.

THERE WERE FURTHER PROMISES MADE TO ABRAM

After Abram obeyed God and left his country, the Lord made more promises to him. The Bible records what was said.

> The LORD said to Abram after Lot had parted from him, "Look around from where you are, to the north and south, to the east and west. All the land that you see I will give to you and your offspring forever. I will make your offspring like the dust of the earth, so that if anyone could count the dust, then your offspring could be counted. Go, walk through the length and breadth of the land, for I am giving it to you" (Genesis 13:14-17 NIV).

The Lord then promised Abram that his offspring were going to inherit a land with specific borders. This land would be their permanent possession. He also told Abram that his descendants would be innumerable.

ABRAM'S NAME IS CHANGED TO ABRAHAM

Later, we read that Abram's name was changed to Abraham ("Father of Many Nations").

> When Abram was ninety-nine years old, the Lord appeared to him and said, "I am God Almighty; walk before me faithfully and be blameless. Then I will make my covenant

between me and you and will greatly increase your numbers." Abram fell facedown, and God said to him, "As for me, this is my covenant with you: You will be the father of many nations. No longer will you be called Abram; your name will be Abraham, for I have made you a father of many nations. I will make you very fruitful; I will make nations of you, and kings will come from you (Genesis 17:1-6 NIV).

The remarkable thing about this renaming of the man Abram to Abraham is that he was childless at this time! Yet, the Lord promised him that he would be "the father of many nations."

AN EVERLASTING COVENANT IS MADE WITH ABRAHAM

There is more. The Lord also promised Abraham that their agreement, or covenant, would be everlasting. He said.

I will establish my covenant as an everlasting covenant between me and you and your descendants after you for the generations to come, to be your God and the God of your descendants after you. The whole land of Canaan, where you now reside as a foreigner, I will give as an everlasting possession to you and your descendants after you; and I will be their God (Genesis 17:7-8 NIV).

The agreement which the Lord made with Abraham is irrevocable—it can *never* be broken.

THE PROMISE MADE TO ISAAC

As the Lord had promised, Abraham and his wife Sarah conceived a son, Isaac. The Lord made it clear that the promises to Abraham would be fulfilled in this particular son of his.

Later, God made the following promise to Isaac:

Stay in this land for a while, and I will be with you and will bless you. For to you and your descendants I will give all these lands and will confirm the oath I swore to your father Abraham. I will make your descendants as numerous as the stars in the sky and will give them all these lands, and through your offspring all nations on earth will be blessed (Genesis 26:3,4 NIV).

God promised that the descendants of Abraham and Isaac would be as numerous as the stars. He also swore that their offspring would inherit the Promised Land.

THE PROMISE MADE TO JACOB

Isaac had two sons, Jacob and Esau. God later promised Isaac's son Jacob that he would be the heir to the promises. The Bible explains what happened in this manner.

> And God said to him, "I am God Almighty; be fruitful and increase in number. A nation and a community of nations will come from you, and kings will be among your descendants. The land I gave to Abraham and Isaac I also give to you, and I will give this land to your descendants after you" (Genesis 35:11,12 NIV).

Many nations were to come from Jacob's descendants. As the Lord promised Abraham, Jacob's descendants would also include kings.

THERE ARE A NUMBER OF SPECIFIC PROMISES MADE TO ABRAHAM AND HIS FAMILY

In these passages where God spoke to Abraham, Isaac, and Jacob, there are a number of very specific promises. They include the following.

Promise 1: A great nation will come from the man Abraham.

Promise 2: Abraham's name shall be blessed.

Promise 3: Abraham shall be a blessing to all nations.

Promise 4: Those who bless Abraham's descendants will be blessed.

Promise 5: Those who curse Abraham's descendants will be cursed.

Promise 6: His descendants, through his son Isaac, will inherit a land with specific boundaries.

Promise 7: This Promised Land will be theirs forever.

Promise 8: Their descendants will be countless.

Promise 9: Among their descendants would be kings.

THERE ARE FURTHER PREDICTIONS AND PROMISES

As God had promised, Abraham's descendants multiplied. Four hundred years later, as they were about to enter the Promise Land, God reconfirmed the covenant with them. The Bible records the Lord saying the following:

> See, I have given you this land. Go in and take possession of the land the LORD swore he would give to your fathers—to Abraham, Isaac and Jacob—and to their descendants after them (Deuteronomy 1:8 NIV).

This land was to belong to them, as well as their descendants, forever. This is what the Lord promised to Abraham, Isaac, and Jacob.

THERE WILL BE BLESSINGS FOR OBEDIENCE

God also told them about the blessings they would receive—if they obeyed Him. The Lord said.

> If you fully obey the LORD your God and carefully follow all his commands I give you today, the LORD your God will set you high above all the nations on earth. All these

> blessings will come on you and accompany you if you obey
> the LORD your God (Deuteronomy 28:1-2 NIV).

Simply put, if they obeyed the Lord, they would be blessed.

THERE WILL BE CONSEQUENCES FOR DISOBEDIENCE

The Lord also warned the people of the consequences of disobedience.
He said the following.

> However, if you do not obey the LORD your God and
> do not carefully follow all his commands and decrees I
> am giving you today, all these curses will come on you
> and overtake you . . . Then the LORD will scatter you
> among all nations, from one end of the earth to the other.
> There you will worship other gods—gods of wood and
> stone, which neither you nor your ancestors have known
> (Deuteronomy 28:15,64 NIV).

While the ownership of the land was theirs forever, their occupancy was
linked with their obedience. Indeed, they would remain in the land as
long as they obeyed the Lord. Disobedience of the commandments of
the Lord would cause the people to be removed from the land.

THE PROMISE TO BRING THEM BACK

However, God promised to bring back the scattered people. We read
the following promises in the Book of Deuteronomy:

> When all these blessings and curses I have set before you
> come on you and you take them to heart wherever the LORD
> your God disperses you among the nations, and when you
> and your children return to the LORD your God and obey
> him with all your heart and with all your soul according to
> everything I command you today, then the LORD your God
> will restore your fortunes and have compassion on you and
> gather you again from all the nations where he scattered you
> (Deuteronomy 30:1-3 NIV).

From these verses, we can observe three further predictions.

Promise 10: If the people would remain faithful to the Lord, He would bless them and give them victory over their enemies.

Promise 11: Yet, God would remove them from the land if they were unfaithful to Him. They would eventually be scattered across the whole earth as strangers in unfamiliar lands and they would find no rest for their wanderings.

Promise 12: However, God in His faithfulness did promise to bring them back into the land.

In sum, from these promises that God made to Abraham and his descendants, we find at least twelve specific things that were predicted for him, as well as for his offspring.

THE FULFILLMENT OF THESE PROMISES

As we look at the verdict of history, we find that each of these promises has been wonderfully and marvelously fulfilled! We can make the following observations.

FULFILLMENT 1: ABRAHAM HAD MANY DESCENDANTS

Many descendants did indeed come from Abraham. This is especially remarkable when we consider that Abraham and his wife Sarah were beyond the age of child bearing when their son, Isaac, was born. Therefore, the nation that sprang from Abraham started with a supernatural beginning.

FULFILLMENT 2: ABRAHAM'S NAME HAS BEEN BLESSED

Abraham was promised that his name would be blessed among the nations. This too has been literally fulfilled. Three of the major religions of the world, Judaism, Christianity, and Islam, all look to Abraham as their human founder. His name is still revered around the world.

FULFILLMENT 3: ABRAHAM HAS BEEN A BLESSING TO ALL NATIONS

God promised Abraham that he would bless the entire world. This has been literally fulfilled, both nationally and individually.

Indeed, the one descendant of Abraham who fulfilled this promise was Jesus Christ. The first verse of the New Testament reads as follows.

> This is the genealogy of Jesus the Messiah the son of David, the son of Abraham (Matthew 1:1 NIV).

The New Testament proclaims Jesus was Israel's Messiah and the Savior of the world. The coming of Jesus Christ is the fulfillment of a specific promise that God made to Abraham. The Apostle Paul wrote to the Galatians.

> The promises were spoken to Abraham and to his seed. Scripture does not say "and to seeds," meaning many people, but "and to your seed," meaning one person, who is Christ (Galatians 3:16 NIV).

Paul says that the prediction to Abraham concerned one particular descendant—that descendant was Jesus Christ. Again, the specific prediction given to Abraham has been fulfilled.

FULFILLMENT 4: THOSE WHO HAVE BLESSED ABRAHAM'S PEOPLE HAVE BEEN BLESSED

The Bible records illustrations of individuals and nations who have helped Israel and found themselves blessed of God.

For example, Scripture records that God spared the woman Rahab because she hid Israel's spies from the people of Jericho. When the city was destroyed, she, and the members of her family, were the only ones that were not killed.

Rahab eventually married one of the Israelites. Among their descendants included King David, and the Lord Jesus Christ. She was indeed blessed by God!

FULFILLMENT 5: THOSE WHO HAVE CURSED ABRAHAM'S PEOPLE HAVE BEEN CURSED

There also is a curse on those peoples who have attempted to destroy Israel. Not only has Israel survived, but the nations that have persecuted them—Moab, Ammon, Amalek, Edom, Philistia—either have been destroyed, or have completely lost their individual identity.

As the Bible predicted, all the nations that have attempted to destroy Israel have been punished, while those who have befriended Israel have prospered (we will have more to say about this in Sign 2).

FULFILLMENT 6: ABRAHAM'S DESCENDANTS INHERITED THE PROMISED LAND

The descendants of Abraham, through his son Isaac, did inherit the land of promise. Four hundred years after God spoke to Abraham, his descendants entered into the Promised Land.

FULFILLMENT 7: THIS LAND IS STILL OCCUPIED BY THEM

Today, they still are there—thousands of years after the initial promise. This is another remarkable fulfillment of the promise—especially given the history of the nation, and the fact that it has been exiled twice from their land, only to later return twice.

FULFILLMENT 8: COUNTLESS NUMBERS OF DESCENDANTS DID COME FROM ABRAHAM

The number of Abraham's descendants has become countless as predicted in Scripture.

FULFILLMENT 9: THE DESCENDANTS OF ABRAHAM DID INCLUDE KINGS

As predicted, Abraham's descendants were royalty. We find that kings such as David and Solomon ruled the nation.

FULFILLMENT 10: THEY WERE BLESSED WHEN THEY OBEYED GOD

God had promised blessings to His people as long as they remained obedient to Him. The Old Testament records times of great prosperity when Israel was faithful to the Lord. During the reigns of David and Solomon, for example, the borders increased and the people were mightily blessed by God.

FULFILLMENT 11: GOD HAS REMOVED THEM TWICE FOR DISOBEYING HIM

If the Israelites were unfaithful, God promised to remove them from the land. This has been literally fulfilled.

In 721 B.C., the Assyrians took the Northern kingdom of Israel, which comprised the ten northern tribes, into captivity.

King Nebuchadnezzar, in three different deportations, took the remaining two tribes, the southern kingdom of Judah, captive to Babylon. Finally, in 588-586 B.C., after a long siege, he burned the city and the temple.

The children of Israel also were scattered in A.D. 70 when Titus, the Roman general, surrounded the city of Jerusalem and burnt the rebuilt city and the temple.

For almost 1900 years, the Jews wandered the earth as strangers—being persecuted from every side. The culmination of their persecution occurred in the Holocaust of World War II, when six million Jews were put to death in concentration camps. The predictions again were literally fulfilled.

FULFILLMENT 12: GOD HAS BROUGHT THEM BACK TWICE

However, as God promised, He allowed the people to return to their land.

In 537-536 B.C., or after seventy years, those who had been taken captive to Babylon were allowed to return to their land from their first exile (Ezra chapter 1).

Though they were removed from their homeland a second time in A.D. 70, once again the people returned. Against all odds, the modern state of Israel was reborn on May 14, 1948, and the Jews began to return to their homeland from all points of the compass. This is the second time in their history they have come back into their land after being forcibly removed.

Since the founding of the modern state of Israel, the Israelis have survived some terrible conflicts. This includes the War of Independence in 1948, the Six-Day War in 1967, and the 1973 Holy Day, Yom Kippur, War. Conflicts continue to this day, yet they still survive. Through all of this, Israel has neither perished nor lost its national identity.

CONCLUSION

From the above evidence, we can conclude that the Jews are a unique people. Indeed, they are different than all of the other nations of the earth. In fact, they have been, and continue to be, a living miracle.

THE LORD HAS GUARANTEED THE CONTINUAL EXISTENCE OF ISRAEL

So, what does all this have to do with the "last days?" Israel, has received a number of predictions with respect to their future. Indeed, there are numerous things predicted about them that have not yet come to pass.

Among those predictions is that they would always exist as a nation. In other words, they would never cease to exist as a unique people, they would never lose their national identity.

Through Jeremiah the prophet, we read the promise of the Lord of their continuing existence.

> The Lord has made a promise to Israel. He promises it as the one who fixed the sun to give light by day and the moon and stars to give light by night. He promises it as the one who stirs up the sea so that its waves roll. He promises it as

the one who is known as the Lord who rules overall. The Lord affirms, "The descendants of Israel will not cease forever to be a nation in my sight. That could only happen if the fixed ordering of the heavenly lights were to cease to operate before me." The Lord says, "I will not reject all the descendants of Israel because of all that they have done. That could only happen if the heavens above could be measured or the foundations of the earth below could all be explored," says the Lord (Jeremiah 31:35-37 NET).

This passage makes it clear—Israel will *never* cease to exist as a nation.

THE BIBLE SAYS THAT ISRAEL WILL EXIST WHEN THE LORD RETURNS

Furthermore, there are many passages in Scripture that specifically predict that the nation of Israel will exist at the time of the end. We will cite merely a few.

THE PEOPLE WILL EXPERIENCE A TIME OF GREAT TROUBLE

In the Book of Daniel, we read of a time of great distress, or tribulation, that the Jewish people will experience.

> At that time Michael, the archangel who stands guard over your nation, will arise. Then there will be a time of anguish greater than any since nations first came into existence. But at that time every one of your people whose name is written in the book will be rescued (Daniel 12:1 NLT).

In this context, "your nation" represents the Jews. The phrase "at that time" is referring to the time of the end, as the context makes clear.

Therefore, this passage clearly teaches that a time of great anguish, or tribulation, will happen to Israel at the time of the end.

JESUS WILL RETURN WHEN THE JEWS ACCEPT HIM AS THEIR MESSIAH

Jesus made it clear that the time will eventually come when the people of Jerusalem, the Jews, eventually accept Him as the Christ, the Messiah. He said the following:

> Jerusalem, Jerusalem, you who kill the prophets and stone those sent to you, how often I have longed to gather your children together, as a hen gathers her chicks under her wings, and you were not willing. Look, your house is left to you desolate. For I tell you, you will not see me again until you say, 'Blessed is he who comes in the name of the Lord' (Matthew 23:37-39 NIV).

In this context, the Lord predicted the destruction of the city of Jerusalem and the Temple. Yet, Jesus also said something hopeful. The nation would see Him again when they acknowledged Him as their Messiah. Since the Lord is returning at the end of this age, the Jewish people must still exist at that time.

THERE WILL BE AN END TO THE EXILE OF THE JEWISH PEOPLE

While Jesus predicted that the people of Jerusalem would be led away as captives, He also predicted that this captivity would not last forever. The Lord said.

> They will fall by the edge of the sword and be led away as captives among all nations. Jerusalem will be trampled down by the Gentiles until the times of the Gentiles are fulfilled (Luke 21:24 NET).

The Jewish people will be taken captive, and Jerusalem will be under the control of Gentile nations for a long time. Yet, according to Jesus, that will come to an end someday. Indeed, the little Greek word translated, "until" tells us that the trampling down of Jerusalem will not l ast forever.

JESUS WILL RETURN AT THE EXACT SPOT WHERE HE DEPARTED

Later, as Jesus ascended into Heaven after His resurrection from the dead, His disciples were told that He would return in the same way in which He left the earth:

> As they were still staring into the sky while he was going, suddenly two men in white clothing stood near them and said, "Men of Galilee, why do you stand here looking up into the sky? This same Jesus who has been taken up from you into heaven will come back in the same way you saw him go into heaven. Then they returned to Jerusalem from the mountain called the Mount of Olives (which is near Jerusalem, a Sabbath day's journey away)" (Acts 1:10-12 NET).

Hence, the exact location of His return to earth has been given to us—the Mount of Olives—which is just outside of the city of Jerusalem.

HIS RETURN WILL BE TO DELIVER THE JEWISH PEOPLE

His return to the Mount of Olives is consistent with an Old Testament prediction of the Messiah's coming.

> On that day his feet will stand on the Mount of Olives which lies to the east of Jerusalem, and the Mount of Olives will be split in half from east to west, leaving a great valley (Zechariah 14:4 NET).

"On that day" refers to a future time—the time of the Messiah's coming. We are told specifically that He will arrive at the Mount of Olives.

Furthermore, this passage assumes that there are Jews in the last days who will live in Jerusalem and witness His coming.

Hence, it is clear from these passages that when the Lord Jesus returns to the earth, He will come to Jerusalem, specifically to the Mount of Olives.

THE JEWS WILL STILL BE CELEBRATING THE SABBATH

When Jesus was answering a question about the time of the end, He made this statement:

> Pray that your flight may not be in winter or on a Sabbath (Matthew 24:20 NET).

Sabbath keeping was a specific commandment for the nation of Israel to observe. Indeed, no other nation does this. The fact that there will be Sabbath observance at the time of the end is another indication that there will be Jews in Israel who are practicing their religion.

CONCLUSION: THE JEWISH PEOPLE WILL EXIST IN THE LAST DAYS ACCORDING TO THE BIBLE

From these passages, to which dozens of others could be added, we discover that the Bible predicts that the Jews will exist in the "last days." There is no doubt about this.

THE PEOPLE OF ISRAEL DO EXIST

To state the obvious, the descendants of Abraham, Isaac, and Jacob, the nation of Israel, still does exist to this day. Hence, the first of our twenty-five signs acknowledges the promises of their existence at the time of the return of the Lord.

Furthermore, as has been true with the past promises and fulfillments, as we look at our twenty-five signs of the end, we will find that Israel will be at the center of these end-time predictions.

ISRAEL, THE LIVING MIRACLE

The continued existence of the nation to this very day has been characterized by one miracle after another. On a natural level, there is really no explanation for this. About one hundred years ago, biblical commentator F.J. Horsefield explained it in this manner:

> Let us begin by thinking of some of those [prophecies] that have reference to the Jewish nation. The entire history of the Jewish race furnishes us with most remarkable examples of literal fulfilment of prophecy. These are far too numerous to be dealt with in detail, but it may safely be asserted that as a people they have borne witness all through the centuries to the authenticity and inspiration of Scripture, and to the certainty of the accomplishment of God's will as revealed by the mouth of His prophets. This testimony cannot possibly be refuted (F.J. Horsefield, *The Return of the King*, Fifth Edition, Good Books Corporation, Harrisburg, Pa., 1920, p. 18).

Indeed, the testimony of the history of the Jews, as well as their survival, cannot be refuted.

Another early 20th century writer put it this way.

> There exists this day in all nations a scattered people, a people without a land or government without metropolis or temple speaking all the principal languages of the world, yet regarding the ancient Hebrew as their sacred tongue; one in race, one in faith, one in religious observances... able to trace their genealogy through 4000 years to one great and good father, as no other people of the earth can do; a people who have exerted more influence over subsequent ages than even Greece or Rome ... a people who have handed down through the ages the sacred books which denounce their own sins, and foretell their own punishment, as well as predicting their ultimate national restoration and salvation. Let unbelievers account for these facts as they may, candour must surely confess that they evidence the hand of God in history and the mind of God in Scripture. Every principal phase of Jewish history was foretold before it came to pass, and has come to pass exactly as it was foretold; except the last; and in this wide analogy of the past we find ground for

confident expectation as to the future of Israel (H. Grattan Guinness, *Light for the last days*, edited and revised by E.P. Cachemaille, Marshall, Morgan and Scott, Ltd. London, 1917, pp. 158,159).

This was written while the Jews were still in their second exile, wandering across the face of the earth. It is an excellent summary of the history of their people.

One line in particular stands out: "Every principal phase of Jewish history was foretold before it came to pass, and has come to pass exactly as it was foretold." This is indeed true, as we have just observed, with the promises made to Abraham, Isaac, and Jacob, as well as their literal fulfillment.

Mark Twain made the following observations about the miraculous history of the Jewish people.

> If the statistics are right, the Jews constitute but one per cent of the human race. It suggests a nebulous dim puff of stardust lost in the blaze of the Milky Way. Properly the Jew ought hardly to be heard of; but he is heard of. He is as prominent on the planet as any other people, and his commercial importance is extravagantly out of proportion to the smallness of his bulk. His contributions to the world's list of great names in literature, science, art, music, finance, medicine . . . are also way out of proportion to the weakness of his numbers. He has made a marvelous fight in this world, in all the ages; and has done it with his hands tied behind him. He could be vain of himself, and be excused for it. The Egyptian, the Babylonian and the Persian rose, filled the planet with sound and splendor, then faded to dream-stuff and passed away; the Greek and the Roman followed, and made a vast noise, and they are gone; other peoples have sprung up and held their torch high for a time, but it burned out, and they

sit in twilight now, or have vanished. The Jew saw them all beat them all, and is now what he always was, exhibiting no decadence, no infirmities of age, no weakening of parts, no slowing of his energies, no dulling of his alert and aggressive mind. All things are mortal but the Jew; all other forces pass, but he remains. What is the secret of his immortality? (Mark Twain, *Concerning the Jews,* 1899).

The secret of the immortality of this ancient people is found in Scripture —and in Scripture alone. In fact, the promises of the living God to this nation have been fulfilled over and over again in the past, and, as we will observe in this book, they are being fulfilled in the present, and will continue to be fulfilled in the future. Israel is indeed a "living miracle," God's clock for time and eternity.

SUMMING UP THE FIRST SIGN OF THE END

As we look at the history of the nation of Israel, we find that no human wisdom could have predicted what we find in Scripture. We noted twelve specific past prophecies that the Lord gave to Abraham, Isaac, and Jacob. All of these have been literally and miraculously fulfilled!

Furthermore, the Bible also predicts that the Jews will always exist. Indeed, there is a passage in Scripture that specifically promises this.

In addition, we cited a number of passages which predict events that will take place at the time of the end. We find Israel is said to be involved in all of these events.

Now, the fact that the nation of Israel still exists to this day is one of the greatest miracles of history. Humanly speaking, they should have ceased to exist long ago. Yet they do exist and, as we will see, they will be center-stage for God's plan for our world in the "last days." The Lord has indeed been faithful to His promises!

Consequently, our first sign, that Israel will still exist as a people in the last days, sets the stage for the remainder of our "25 Signs of the End."

Our next "Sign of the End" will look at another nation that the Bible says will exist in the last days, as well as five nations which Scripture predicted would not survive. We will discover that the predictions made, with respect to these six ancient nations, have proven to be one hundred percent correct.

Jews will always exist + so will Israel
Genesis 17: 7-8
Jeremiah 31: 35-37

Israel will exist in the "last days"
Daniel 12: 1
Acts 1: 10-12
Zech 14: 4
Matt 24: 20

SIGN 2

As Their Enemies Have Done to Israel So God Will Do to Them

While the Bible promises that the nation of Israel will exist until the time the Lord returns, it also contains warnings for those nations who will attempt to destroy God's chosen people.

In fact, as we saw in our previous sign, the Lord has promised punishment, or a curse, upon those who have tried to annihilate Israel. Let's look at this passage again.

> The Lord said to Abram: Go out from your land, your relatives, and your father's house to the land that I will show you. I will make you into a great nation, I will bless you, I will make your name great, and you will be a blessing. I will bless those who bless you, I will curse anyone who treats you with contempt, and all the peoples on earth will be blessed through you (Genesis 12:1-3 CSB).

These promises are very specific. Whoever blesses Israel will be blessed by God. On the other hand, if any nation or individual attempts to treat Israel with contempt, God will curse them.

Simply put, as their enemies have done unto Israel, so the Lord will do to them.

THESE PREDICTIONS HAVE BEEN LITERALLY FULFILLED

Again, we will find that these predictions of God's judgment, upon those who have attempted to destroy Israel, have literally been fulfilled in the past. This is further evidence that the Lord is in control of history.

We will also discover that these warnings are still in effect to this day. In other words, any modern nation—or individual—that treats Israel with contempt, will be cursed by God.

To begin with, let's consider some of the past fulfillments of this promise given to Abraham some four thousand years ago.

EDOM

The Edomites were descendants of Esau, the older brother of the patriarch Jacob. Historically, the descendants of Esau, the Edomites, have been constant enemies of the nation of Israel.

Despite the Edomites continual efforts to rule over the Jews, this prophecy of God was literally fulfilled. Indeed, the descendants of the older child served the descendants of younger. Simply stated, Israel proved stronger than Edom.

When Greek became the international language in the third century B.C., the Edomites were called Idumeans. With the rise of the Roman Empire, an Idumean, whose father had converted to Judaism, was appointed king of Judea. His name was Herod the Great. He was the murderous king who ordered the massacre of the newborns in Bethlehem in an attempt to kill the Christ child. The Bible explains it in this manner:

> When Herod realized that he had been outwitted by the Magi, he was furious, and he gave orders to kill all the boys in Bethlehem and its vicinity who were two years old and under, in accordance with the time he had learned from the Magi. Then what was said through the prophet Jeremiah was fulfilled: "A

voice is heard in Ramah, weeping and great mourning, Rachel weeping for her children and refusing to be comforted, because they are no more" (Matthew 2:16-18 NIV).

After Herod's death, however, the Idumean people slowly disappeared from history. After the destruction of Jerusalem in A.D. 70, the Edomites disappeared altogether.

THE SPECIFIC PROMISE OF THEIR DEMISE

God had foretold the destruction of the Edomites some seven hundred years earlier.

> As you rejoiced over the inheritance of the house of Israel because it was desolate, so will I deal with you—you will be desolate, Mount Seir, and all of Edom—all of it! Then they will know that I am the Lord (Ezekiel 35:15 NET).

Let us not miss this specific prediction. When the descendants of Esau cease to exist, then the people will know that the Lord is God.

To sum up, God predicted that the Edomites, the descendants of Esau who were endlessly at war with Israel, would cease to exist as a nation. This warning was literally fulfilled. Indeed, they have disappeared from history.

AMMON

The Ammonites were a Semitic people who were closely related to the Israelites. As we read the early history of Israel, we find a number of references to the Ammonite people. We can summarize what the Bible has to say about them as follows.

The Ammonites had their beginning with Lot, the nephew of Abraham. After Abraham and Lot separated, Lot settled in the city of Sodom. When God destroyed the evil cities of Sodom and Gomorrah because of their wickedness, Lot and his two daughters fled.

Lot's daughters, seemingly thinking they were the only people left on the earth, got their father drunk on two consecutive nights. Each had incestuous relations with him which produced children. The Bible says:

> In this way both of Lot's daughters became pregnant by their father. ... The younger daughter . . . gave birth to a son and named him Ben-Ammi. He is the ancestor of the Ammonites of today (Genesis 19:37-38 NET).

The Ammonites, the descendants of Ben-Ammi, were a nomadic people who lived in the territory of modern-day Jordan. In fact, the name of the capital city, Amman, reflects the name of those ancient inhabitants.

When Israel left Egypt, the Ammonites refused to assist them in any way. Hence, God punished them for their lack of support. Moses wrote:

> No Ammonite or Moabite or any of their descendants may enter the assembly of the Lord, not even in the tenth generation. For they did not come to meet you with bread and water on your way when you came out of Egypt, and they hired Balaam son of Beor from Pethor in Aram Naharaim to pronounce a curse on you (Deuteronomy 23:3-4 NIV)

Later, however, as the Israelites entered the Promised Land, God instructed them to leave the Ammonites alone:

> When you come to the Ammonites, do not harass them or provoke them to war, for I will not give you possession of any land belonging to the Ammonites. I have given it as a possession to the descendants of Lot (Deuteronomy 2:19 NIV).

God had given the Ammonites a certain amount of land for their possession. Israel was not to provoke them. However, the Ammonites did not stop provoking Israel.

THE PAGANISM OF AMMON

Unfortunately, the Ammonites were a pagan people who worshiped false gods. Consequently, God commanded the Israelites not to intermarry with them, because intermarriage would lead the Israelites to worship these false deities. King Solomon disobeyed this commandment and married Naamah the Ammonite. We later read of this:

> Rehoboam son of Solomon was king in Judah. He was forty-one years old when he became king, and he reigned seventeen years in Jerusalem, the city the Lord had chosen out of all the tribes of Israel in which to put his Name. His mother's name was Naamah; she was an Ammonite (1 Kings 14:21 NIV).

The son of King Solomon had an Ammonite for a mother!

Just as the Lord had warned, Solomon was drawn into idolatry, due to this marriage.

THE CRUELTY OF THE AMMONITES

Molech, one of the false gods of the Ammonites, was a fire-god with the face of a calf. Horrifically, his images had arms outstretched to receive the babies whom the Ammonites sacrificed to him. Like their god, the Ammonites were a cruel people.

After the split of the nation into the two kingdoms Israel and Judah, the Ammonites began to ally themselves with the enemies of Israel.

THE PREDICTION OF THE DESTRUCTION OF THE AMMONITES

After centuries of disobeying God, and trying to thwart Israel, the Lord predicted their destruction.

> The word of the Lord came to me: "Son of man, turn toward the Ammonites and prophesy against them. Say to the Ammonites, 'Hear the word of the sovereign Lord: This

is what the sovereign Lord says: You said "Aha!" about my sanctuary when it was desecrated, about the land of Israel when it was made desolate, and about the house of Judah when they went into exile. So take note, I am about to make you slaves of the tribes of the east. They will make camps among you and pitch their tents among you. They will eat your fruit and drink your milk. I will make Rabbah a pasture for camels and Ammon a resting place for sheep. Then you will know that I am the Lord. For this is what the sovereign Lord says: Because you clapped your hands, stamped your feet, and rejoiced with intense scorn over the land of Israel, take note, I have stretched out my hand against you, and I will hand you over as plunder to the nations. I will cut you off from the peoples and make you perish from the lands. I will destroy you; then you will know that I am the Lord" (Ezekiel 25:1-11 NET).

The Ammonites gloated when the Temple was destroyed, the land of Jerusalem desecrated, and the people exiled to Babylon. Consequently, the Lord pronounced judgment upon them.

Again, we have very specific predictions that have been literally fulfilled. The last mention of Ammonites as a separate people was in the second century by Justin Martyr. Sometime during the Roman period, the Ammonites seem to have been absorbed into Arab society. They no longer exist as a distinct people with their own national identity.

In sum, we find another literal fulfillment of the prediction made to Abraham. The Ammonites, who constantly harassed Israel, cease to exist.

In 1839, Alexander Keith, made the following insightful observation.

> The Ammonites shall not be remembered among the nations. While the Jews, who were long their hereditary

enemies, continue as a distinct people as ever, though dispersed among the nations, no trace of the Ammonites remains; none are now designated by their name nor do any claim their descent from them (Alexander Keith, *Evidence of the Truth of the Christian Religion*, New York, Harper and Brothers, 1839, p. 124).

As we shall see in our next "Sign of the End," while the Ammonites no longer exist, the Jews, miraculously, are no longer dispersed among the nations.

MOAB

Moab was also an offspring of Lot and one of his daughters.

In this way both of Lot's daughters became pregnant by their father. The older daughter gave birth to a son and named him Moab. He is the ancestor of the Moabites of today (Genesis 19:37-38 NET).

Like the Ammonites, the Moabites were constant enemies of Israel. As we just observed, they too did not help Israel when the nation was entering the Promised Land. Judgment was then announced upon them as well as upon Ammon.

MOAB WILL CEASE TO EXIST

After a long history of harassing Israel, the Lord issued the following judgment against Moab:

This is what the sovereign Lord says: 'Moab and Seir say, "Look, the house of Judah is like all the other nations." So look, I am about to open up Moab's flank, eliminating the cities, including its frontier cities, the beauty of the land. . . I will hand it over, along with the Ammonites, to the tribes of the east, so that the Ammonites will no longer be remembered among the nations. I will execute judgments against Moab. Then they will know that I am the Lord" (Ezekiel 25:8-11 NET).

The Lord promised to judge Moab. In fact, Moab was to become non-existent like Ammon. This was literally fulfilled when the nation passed out of existence during the Babylonian Exile.

To sum up, history shows us that none of these three nations, these people-groups, kept their national identity as modern-day authors testify.

> By the time of Roman rule in the Levant around 63 BC, the people of Ammon, Edom and Moab had lost their distinct identities, and were assimilated into Roman culture (LaBianca, Oystein S.; Younker, Randall W. (1995). The Kingdoms of Ammon, Moab, and Edom: The Archaeology of Society in Late Bronze/Iron Age Transjordan (Ca. 1400-500 BCE) in Thomas Levy, *The Archaeology of Society In The Holy Land*, Leicester University Press).

As the Lord predicted, there is no more Ammon, Moab, or Edom!

PHILISTIA

The Philistines were the "sea peoples" who lived on the coast of Israel. Like Edom, Moab, and Ammon, they too detested the Israelites and had continually sought to destroy them (see Judges 13-16; 1 Samuel 4).

THE LORD PRONOUNCES JUDGMENT UPON THEM

The Philistines also had God's judgment pronounced upon them.

> This is what the sovereign Lord says: 'The Philistines have exacted merciless revenge, showing intense scorn in their effort to destroy Judah with unrelenting hostility. So this is what the sovereign Lord says: Take note, I am about to

stretch out my hand against the Philistines. I will kill the Cherethites and destroy those who remain on the seacoast. I will exact great vengeance upon them with angry rebukes. Then they will know that I am the Lord, when I exact my vengeance upon them" (Ezekiel 25:15-17 NET).

The Lord promised that He would take vengeance upon them for their treatment of His chosen people. They would know that the Lord was God when they experienced His judgment.

There is no record of the Philistines' existence after the second century B.C., though the name of their cities remained.

AMALEK

The Amalekites were a tribe first mentioned during the time of Abraham.

Then they turned back and went to En Mishpat (that is, Kadesh), and they conquered the whole territory of the Amalekites, as well as the Amorites who were living in Hazezon Tamar (Genesis 14:7 NIV).

Though the Amalekites are not mentioned in the Table of Nations in Genesis 10, they are referred to as "first among the nations" in the Book of Numbers.

Then Balaam saw Amalek and spoke his message: "Amalek was first among the nations, but their end will be utter destruction" (Numbers 24:20 NIV).

The Amalekites' unrelenting brutality toward the Israelites began with an attack at Rephidim. Later, this is recounted in the Book of Deuteronomy along with the following admonition.

Remember what the Amalekites did to you along the way when you came out of Egypt. When you were weary and worn out, they met you on your journey and attacked all who were lagging behind; they had no fear of God. When the Lord your God gives you rest from all the enemies around you in the land he is giving you to possess as an inheritance, you shall blot out the name of Amalek from under heaven. Do not forget! (Deuteronomy 25:17-19 NIV).

Scripture records the long-lasting feud between the Amalekites and the Israelites and God's direction to wipe the Amalekites off the face of the earth.

These evil people were responsible for the repeated destruction of the Israelites' land as well as their food supply. Finally, the Lord had had enough. He told King Saul,

This is what the Lord Almighty says: 'I will punish the Amalekites for what they did to Israel when they waylaid them as they came up from Egypt. Now go, attack the Amalekites and totally destroy all that belongs to them. Do not spare them . . . (1 Samuel 15:2-3 NIV).

Unfortunately, Saul did not obey the Lord and the escaped Amalekites continued to harass and plunder the Israelites in successive generations that spanned hundreds of years.

Years later, during the reign of King Hezekiah, a group of Simeonites eradicated the last of the Amalekites who had been living in the hill country of Seir.

And five hundred of these Simeonites, led by Pelatiah, Neariah, Rephaiah and Uzziel, the sons of Ishi, invaded the hill country of Seir. They killed the remaining Amalekites who had escaped, and they have lived there to this day (1 Chronicles 4:42-43 NIV).

Interestingly, the last mention of an Amalekite is found in the book of Esther. His name was Haman. He was a descendant of the Amalekite king Agag. This evil man attempted to have all the Jews in Persia anni-hilated by the order of King Xerxes. The Bible records how God mirac-ulously saved the Jews in Persia. In addition, evil Haman, his sons, and the rest of Israel's enemies were themselves destroyed (Esther 9:5-10).

The Amalekites' hatred of the Jews and their repeated attempts to eradicate the entire nation had led to their ultimate doom. Their fate should be a warning to all who would attempt to thwart God's plan, or who would curse the people, Israel, whom God has blessed.

SUMMING UP THE BIBLICAL PREDICTIONS ON THESE PEOPLE GROUPS

The Bible specifically stated that these five particular people-groups continually harassed Israel. Indeed, each of these endlessly attempted to destroy God's chosen people. After years and years of trying to thwart the plans of God, the Lord had had enough with each of them.

He predicted that each of them, as a group, would be destroyed. Their names would be obliterated from history. And, as we observed, these specific predictions were literally fulfilled. Each of these five enemies of Israel have lost their national identity. In other words, they no longer exist as distinct peoples.

There is a valuable lesson in this for all of us. When an individual, or a nation, attempts to thwart the plan of God with respect to the nation of Israel, they will be punished.

Therefore, the Scripture gives us clear precedent that Israel is not to be trifled with.

AN EXCEPTION: EGYPT

Another miraculous prediction of the Bible has to do with the future of Egypt. As one reads the Old Testament, we find that Egypt has histori-cally been an enemy of the people of Israel. Indeed, we read of the years of bondage and suffering Israel spent in Egypt before being set free in the Exodus. The Old Testament records other instances where Egypt warred with the people of God.

Yet, the Lord predicted that Egypt would exist at the time of the end. Moreover, the Bible says that many of the Egyptians will turn to Him in faith:

> At that time there will be an altar for the Lord in the middle of the land of Egypt, as well as a sacred pillar dedicated to the Lord at its border. It will become a visual reminder in the land of Egypt of the Lord who commands armies. When they cry out to the Lord because of oppressors, he will send them a deliverer and defender who will rescue them. The Lord will reveal himself to the Egyptians, and they will acknowledge the Lord's authority at that time. They will present sacrifices and offerings; they will make vows to the Lord and fulfill them. The Lord will strike Egypt, striking and then healing them. They will turn to the Lord and he will listen to their prayers and heal them (Isaiah 19:19-22 NET).

Again, we should appreciate what is predicted here. At the time of the end, in the last days, this ancient nation of Egypt will still exist! Moreover, they will experience a time of spiritual revival. In fact, when they are oppressed by their enemies they will cry out to the Lord and He will listen to their prayers and heal them!

As the Lord has promised, Egypt still does exist. Furthermore, the Christian influence remains in the country to this day. The predictions of the Bible have again been proven to be true.

A WARNING FOR AMERICA

This may answer one of the questions that often gets asked about the Bible and the future—where is the United States of America in the last days?

One possible answer is that it will end up like these five enemies of Israel. In other words, it will cease to exist because of its treatment of Israel. While this is certainly not the only possible answer to the question to the future of America, it is something to be considered. We will look at this question in more detail in Sign 11.

SUMMARY OF SIGN TWO

Our first "Sign of the End" concerned the miraculous existence of the nation of Israel. The Lord promised that they will always exist, and they still do exist to this day. On the other hand, the Lord also promised vengeance on those nations who would attempt to destroy Israel. All of these predictions of Scripture have been literally fulfilled with respect to the nations God has cursed.

There are at least three reasons as to why this sign is so important with respect to the last days.

First, it shows that when the Lord specifies certain nations for punishment, they will indeed be punished. There is no question about this.

In fact, we have given five examples of people-groups that have had judgment pronounced upon them, Edom, Philistia, Amalek, Moab and Ammon. As Scripture predicted, none of these people-groups still exist. They have all lost their national identity. Furthermore, the Bible says that these predictions were made so that the world would recognize that the Lord was God.

Second, while Egypt has been a mortal enemy of Israel from the very beginning, the Bible says that they will not only exist in the last days, they will experience a national conversion. As the Bible predicted, Egypt does exist to this very day.

Thus, coupled with our previous sign, we find that of these seven nations mentioned in Scripture, two of them, Israel and Egypt, as predicted, still exist at the time of the end. On the other hand, these other five evil nations, as the Bible also predicted, no longer exist. This is not a coincidence.

Third, this warning about punishment of those nations, who attempt to destroy Israel, may help us explain why the United States is not a player in the "last days" scenario.

Indeed, if the United States turns its back upon Israel, to the place that it might cause their destruction, then the nation will be punished. This is one of the possible outcomes as to why we do not find the United States in Bible prophecy. Only time will tell.

Our next "Sign of the End" is probably the most marvelous of them all— after almost two thousand years of exile, the miraculous return of the nation of Israel to the Promised Land.

Israel Will Miraculously Return to its Ancient Homeland in the "Last Days"

The Bible is clear that Israel, as a nation, will exist at the time of the end. Scripture also teaches that a number of specific enemies of Israel will cease to exist. We have seen that each of these predictions have literally come true.

Next, we will look at one of the most remarkable predictions that we have in the Bible. Israel, after being gone from its ancient homeland for a long time, will return to their land in the "last days."

PREDICTION 1: THE SCATTERING OF THE PEOPLE

First, we have the predictions that the Lord will scatter His people for this second exile. This prediction, of the scattering of Israel, is found in both testaments.

We read the following prediction in the Old Testament of what would happen to the nation if they turned their back upon the Lord:

> The Lord will raise up a distant nation against you, one from the other side of the earth as the eagle flies, a nation whose language you will not understand, a nation of stern appearance that will have no regard for the elderly or pity for the young. They will devour the offspring of your livestock and the produce of your soil until you are destroyed. They will

not leave you with any grain, new wine, olive oil, calves of your herds, or lambs of your flocks until they have destroyed you. . .

This is what will happen: Just as the Lord delighted to do good for you and make you numerous, he will take delight in destroying and decimating you. You will be uprooted from the land you are about to possess. The Lord will scatter you among all nations, from one end of the earth to the other. There you will worship other gods that neither you nor your ancestors have known, gods of wood and stone. Among those nations you will have no rest nor will there be a place of peaceful rest for the soles of your feet, for there the Lord will give you an anxious heart, failing eyesight, and a spirit of despair (Deuteronomy 28:49-51, 63-65 NIV).

The choices for Israel were simple. God would bless them as long as they obeyed, but He would punish them if they disobeyed. This would include scattering them to the ends of the earth.

After Jesus was rejected by the people of Israel, He predicted the people would be scattered:

When you see Jerusalem being surrounded by armies, you will know that its desolation is near. Then let those who are in Judea flee to the mountains, let those in the city get out, and let those in the country not enter the city. For this is the time of punishment in fulfillment of all that has been written. How dreadful it will be in those days for pregnant women and nursing mothers! There will be great distress in the land and wrath against this people. They will fall by the sword and will be taken as prisoners to all the nations. Jerusalem will be trampled on by the Gentiles until the times of the Gentiles are fulfilled (Luke 21:20-24 NIV).

Note the specifics of Jesus' prediction. Eventually, Jerusalem will be surrounded by armies. When the people view this siege occurring, then it is time for them to get out of the city. For, at that time, the nation will be punished for their rejection of Him as their Messiah.

Christ called it a time of wrath and distress. The Lord predicted that the inhabitants would be carried away as prisoners into all the nations and Jerusalem would be trampled on by the Gentiles.

PREDICTION 2: GOD HAS NOT CAST ISRAEL OFF

While both the Old and New Testament predicted the scattering of the people, Scripture also indicates that God had not entirely cast off His people. In other words, they still have a future in His plan for both time and eternity. The Apostle Paul wrote.

> I am telling the truth in Christ (I am not lying!), for my conscience assures me in the Holy Spirit—I have great sorrow and unceasing anguish in my heart. For I could wish that I myself were accursed—cut off from Christ—for the sake of my people, my fellow countrymen, who are Israelites. To them belong the adoption as sons, the glory, the covenants, the giving of the law, the temple worship, and the promises (Romans 9:1-4 NET).

Note that Paul said these are the people who were given both the "covenants" and the "promises." Later, in chapter 11, the Apostle wrote the following:

> So I ask, God has not rejected his people, has he? Absolutely not! For I too am an Israelite, a descendant of Abraham, from the tribe of Benjamin. God has not rejected his people whom he foreknew! . . . I ask then, they did not stumble into an irrevocable fall, did they? Absolutely not! ... For I do not want you to be ignorant of this mystery, brothers and sisters, so that you may not be conceited: A partial

hardening has happened to Israel until the full number of the Gentiles has come in. And so all Israel will be saved (Romans 11:1-2, 11,25 NET).

The nation has *not* been rejected by the Lord. The fall of Israel is not irrevocable. Paul concluded by saying that a "partial hardening of Israel has happened until" . . . — in other words, it is not forever. Eventually salvation will come to the nation!

Therefore, Israel, as a nation, has not been completely rejected by the Lord.

PREDICTION 3: ISRAEL WILL BE BROUGHT BACK TO THEIR LAND IN THE LAST DAYS

This promise, that Israel has not been completely rejected by the Lord, leads us to our next prediction—they will be brought back to their ancient homeland in the last days. There are numerous promises of this in Scripture.

For example, in Ezekiel 38:8, the Lord is speaking to a future leader who will attack Israel in the "last days":

After many days you will be summoned; in the latter years you will come to a land restored from the ravages of war, with many peoples gathered on the mountains of Israel that had long been in ruins. Its people were brought out from the peoples, and all of them will be living securely (Ezekiel 38:8 NET).

Notice how this situation is described. First, the time frame will be, "after many days," "in the latter years," or "in the future years." These phrases refer to the time of the end.

During these "latter years" the people of Israel will have been gathered from many nations back to their ancient homeland.

The Holy Land, to which they will travel, will have been desolate for a long time. Furthermore, it will be recovering from wars.

The people of Israel, the ones whom have been brought out from these nations, will be living in safety in their ancient homeland.

JEREMIAH

The Lord predicted something similar through Jeremiah.

> The Lord spoke to Jeremiah. "The Lord God of Israel says, 'Write everything that I am about to tell you in a scroll. For I, the Lord, affirm that the time will come when I will reverse the plight of my people, Israel and Judah,' says the Lord. 'I will bring them back to the land I gave their ancestors and they will take possession of it once again'" (Jeremiah 30:1-3 NET).

Here we have another specific promise from the Lord.

We find that the Lord affirmed that a time will come when He will reverse the plight of Israel and Judah, the twelve tribes. Indeed, the Lord will bring the scattered people back to the land of their ancestors and they will take possession of it.

Consequently, Scripture, in a number of passages, speaks of a return of Israel to their ancient homeland in the "last days."

PREDICTION 4: THEY WILL RETURN FROM A SECOND EXILE

In another remarkable prediction, we read the following words that the Lord spoke through the prophet Isaiah.

> In that day the Lord will reach out his hand a second time to reclaim the surviving remnant of his people from Assyria, from Lower Egypt, from Upper Egypt, from Cush, from Elam, from Babylonia, from Hamath and from the islands of the Mediterranean. He will raise a banner for the nations

and gather the exiles of Israel; he will assemble the scattered people of Judah from the four quarters of the earth. (Isaiah 11:11,12 NIV).

Here we have a specific prediction of the return of the people from a "second exile." There are several things that we should observe from this passage.

First, the prophetic words, "on that day," are speaking of that future era before the Lord will return to earth, and then set up His kingdom.

Also, the fact that it is called a "second regathering" assumes that there will be a first. Remarkably, when Isaiah gave this prediction, a first regathering had not yet taken place!

Furthermore, this passage predicts that this will be a worldwide regathering of the people of Israel. In fact, we are specifically told that they will come "from the islands of the sea as well as from the four corners of the earth." In addition, he mentions the specific countries from which the Jews will return. Thus, this will not be merely a local gathering of the people.

Finally, and of utmost importance, it concerns the scattered from both Israel and Judah. The northern kingdom of Israel was taken captive by the Assyrians in 721 B.C, never to return.

The southern kingdom of Judah experienced a seventy-year captivity in Babylon. Some of them returned to their homeland but the northern kingdom did *not* return at that time. This prediction specifically states that both Israel and Judah will return. Therefore, it speaks of a return that was never fulfilled in biblical times.

In 1890, David Baron wrote the following words.

> Now, there has been no second Restoration as yet; neither could the return from Babylon be said to be a gathering from

the "four corners of the earth;" that captivity having been local in its character, and of short duration. Never before the dispersion inaugurated by Titus, could be the *scattering* of the people be said to have been universal; hence could never before have been gathered from the four corners of the earth (David Baron, *The Jewish Problem, It's Solution, or Israel's Present and Future*, 1890, p. 21).

In other words, as of 1890, this prediction of the second restoration had not yet been fulfilled.

PREDICTION 5: THE PEOPLE WILL NEVER BE REMOVED

We learn elsewhere, that once back, the people of Israel will be back to stay. This is their final return to their ancient homeland. Indeed, for once they are in the land, they will not be removed. The prophet Amos recorded the Lord saying.

> I will bring back my people, Israel; they will rebuild the cities lying in rubble and settle down. They will plant vineyards and drink the wine they produce; they will grow orchards and eat the fruit they produce. I will plant them on their land, and they will never again be uprooted from the land I have given them," says the Lord your God (Amos 9:14,15 NIV).

The prediction is clear. Once the people return to their ancient homeland they will never be uprooted.

PREDICTION 6: THE LORD WILL DO THIS FOR HIS SAKE

According to the Lord, this return of the Jewish people to their ancient homeland will be for His sake, not theirs. Ezekiel records Him saying

> Therefore this is what the sovereign Lord says: Now I will restore the fortunes of Jacob, and I will have mercy on the entire house of Israel. I will be zealous for my holy name.

They will bear their shame for all their unfaithful acts against me, when they live securely on their land with no one to make them afraid. When I have brought them back from the peoples and gathered them from the countries of their enemies, I will magnify myself among them in the sight of many nations. Then they will know that I am the Lord their God, because I sent them into exile among the nations, and then gathered them into their own land. I will not leave any of them in exile any longer. I will no longer hide my face from them, when I pour out my Spirit on the house of Israel, declares the sovereign Lord (Ezekiel 39:25-29 NET).

Hence, from this passage, we find the motivation for the return of the people to their ancient homeland. The Lord will cause this to happen so that all the nations will know that He is God. He sent them into exile, He allowed them to return from exile.

Furthermore, a time will come when He will protect them from being destroyed and eventually He will pour out His Spirit upon them.

SUMMARIZING THE VARIOUS PREDICTIONS

These passages contain a number of specific predictions about the future of the nation Israel. They are as follows.

1. The nation of Israel will be removed from their homeland and scattered throughout the world.

2. The Lord, however, made it clear that He had not cast off His people— they will still have a future!

3. In fact, the Lord promised that He would bring them back one day.

4. This return would involve all twelve tribes.

5. This would take place in "the last days."

6. The return in the last days would be from a "second exile."

7. The land to which they are returning has been devastated by war.

8. Once they come back to their land, they would never be uprooted.

9. The Lord will do all of this as a testimony for His holy name.

10. When this marvelous event occurs, the nations will then know that He is the Lord.

11. Once they are back in the land, the time will eventually come when He will pour out His Spirit upon them.

THE FULFILLMENT

As the Lord promised, the people have miraculously returned to their ancient homeland. We can summarize the highlights of their return as follows.

THE SECOND EXILE

When the people of Israel rejected Him, Jesus predicted that the city of Jerusalem, as well as the Temple, would be destroyed.

> Now as Jesus was going out of the temple courts and walking away, his disciples came to show him the temple buildings. And he said to them, "Do you see all these things? I tell you the truth, not one stone will be left on another. All will be torn down!" (Matthew 24:1-2 NET).

WITH THE DESTRUCTION OF JERUSALEM, THE SECOND EXILE BEGINS

In A.D. 70, as the Lord predicted, the city of Jerusalem, as well as the Temple were destroyed. This began the second exile for the Jewish people. While the first one lasted some seventy years, this one would last almost one thousand nine hundred years!

THE WANDERING JEWS

From the time of the destruction of the Second Temple, the Jews, as a people wandered across the face of the earth. With no specific place to call home, they settled in all parts of the globe.

GOD'S MIRACULOUS PRESERVATION

Yet throughout all of this, the Lord has miraculously preserved them. Bible commentators have noted that even with this scattering of the people to the various nations around the world, there has been the remarkable preservation of the Jewish people. One writer put it this way.

> The Apostle Paul said: 'Nevertheless God left not Himself without witness.' What witness of Himself has He given to the Jewish race since the destruction of Jerusalem, in A.D. 70, and the scattering of its inhabitants to the four corners of the globe?

> It might seem that He has kept silent and that His hand has been withheld from them during all these nineteen centuries. This, however, is merely in appearance. His silence has been singularly eloquent, like that of a mother who for a little time turns her face away from the child she adores. God has hidden His face from His people, but in reality His word has never ceased to govern them, or His hand to weigh heavily upon them.

> Israel has ever been the race of miracles. That there should be any Jews alive in the twentieth century is a great miracle in itself. Five times in the course of their history have they been threatened with complete extermination. . .

> No other race subjected to such trials could have resisted. Many nations, indeed, have completely disappeared, though

not one has been so frequently threatened with annihilation. The Jewish nation, after the rage of Titus, was blotted out of the pages of history, but not out of the memory of God and His prophetic scheme. During these nineteen long centuries Israel has witnessed the fulfilling of more than one divine oracle and been unceasingly tormented by misfortunes against which God through Moses had warned them . . .

This historical period of the Jewish race has lasted up to the present time: Israel has lived as predicted, being scattered among all peoples (Paul Perret, *Prophecies I Have Seen Fulfilled*, London, Marshall, Morgan & Scott LTD., 1939, pp. 17,18).

Observe that these words were written while there was no such thing as a state of Israel. In fact, the Holocaust of the Second World War, that would eventually take six million Jewish lives, had already begun and would continue for a number of years. Yet the nation survived.

THEODORE HERZL AND MODERN ZIONISM

It was over eighteen centuries after the destruction of Jerusalem, its Temple, and the scattering of the Jewish people, that the modern push for a state began in earnest.

In January of 1895, a Jewish Austrian journalist named Theodor Herzl, covered the trial in Paris of a French Jew named Dreyfus. Dreyfus was unfairly convicted of a crime that he did not commit. Seeing firsthand the hatred directed against Jews, Herzl determined to begin a process to found a Jewish state.

Later in 1895, Herzl published a book entitled *Der Judenstaat—The Jewish State.* He argued that the only way in which the "Jewish problem" can be resolved was by establishing a Jewish state in the Holy Land. Herzl's writings started the Jews on the road back to their Promised homeland.

At the conclusion of the First Zionist Congress in Basel, Switzerland on September 3, 1897, Theodore Herzl made the following entry into his diary.

In Basel I founded the Jewish State. If I said this aloud, it would be greeted with worldwide derision. In five years, perhaps, and certainly in fifty, everyone will see it.

Herzl's entry in his diary would turn out to be prophetic. The modern state of Israel would be founded about fifty years after he made this statement!

TURKISH RULE ENDS IN THE HOLY LAND

In the early 20th century, the Ottoman Turks four-hundred-year reign over the Holy Land, was about to end. During World War I, the Arabs helped the British fight the Turks. D.E. Lawrence, "Lawrence of Arabia," was instrumental in achieving the victory over the Ottoman Empire.

In October 1917, a British General, Edmund Allenby, launched an invasion in the Holy Land. On Sunday, December 9th, the Turks were driven out of Jerusalem. Two days later, the General made his entry into conquered Jerusalem, on foot. He said no one could enter the Holy City except in humility, on foot. He said upon entering:

> Since your city is regarded with affection by the adherents of three great religions of mankind, and its soil has been consecrated by the prayers and the pilgrimages of devout people of these three religions for many centuries, therefore I do make known to you . . . that all sacred buildings will be maintained and protected according to the existing customs and beliefs of those whose faiths are sacred (*Source Records of the Great War*, Vol. 5, ed. Charles Francis Horne, National Alumni, 1923).

At the conclusion of the First World War, Britain, France, and Russia forged the Sykes-Picot Agreement. This pact carved up the Ottoman Empire which had seen its defeat in the War. Britain gained control of the Holy Land. For the first time in eight hundred years, the Holy sites of Christianity were delivered from the domination of Islam.

THE REQUEST OF CHAIM WEITZMAN

Another step toward the realization of a Jewish homeland came after the First World War. Chaim Weitzman, a Jewish chemist, helped the War effort by developing a technique where synthetic acetone could be manufactured. Acetone was a prime ingredient in the production of explosives. His discovery was given credit by the British government as a main factor in Britain winning the War. The government attempted to personally reward him for his efforts on behalf of the nation. Weitzman asked nothing for himself, but he did make a request for his people—a Jewish homeland in the Promised Land.

THE BALFOUR DECLARATION

In 1917, a monumental event took place. Lord Balfour, the head of the foreign ministry of the British government, wrote a letter to Baron Rothchild—a representative of the Jewish people. In it, he declared the willingness to see a Jewish state established. The letter read as follows.

> Foreign Office
> November 2nd, 1917
> Dear Lord Rothschild,
>
> I have much pleasure in conveying to you, on behalf of His Majesty's Government, the following declaration of sympathy with Jewish Zionist aspirations which has been submitted to, and approved by, the Cabinet.
>
> His Majesty's Government view with favour the establishment in Palestine of a national home for the Jewish people,

and will use their best endeavours to facilitate the achievement of this object, it being clearly understood that nothing shall be done which may prejudice the civil and religious rights of existing non-Jewish communities in Palestine, or the rights and political status enjoyed by Jews in any other country.

I should be grateful if you would bring this declaration to the knowledge of the Zionist Federation.

Yours Sincerely,
Arthur James Balfour

One writer explained what happened like this.

The proclamation was of international importance, as it was solemnly sanctioned by the League of Nations. By this act that body, which is more and more inclined to look upon itself as being invested with the right to control the destiny of the peoples of the world, was obeying the will of Him who really holds the fate of mankind in His hands. How would it be possible to doubt this miracle? God was exercising His sovereign right as King of all nations.

For a long time the diplomats of the various countries, moved to pity by the cruel treatment inflicted upon the Jews during the regularly recurring pogroms and collective murders in Central Europe, had been looking all of the world for some country that would offer this unhappy race a promise of security. One after another Argentina, Brazil, Canada, certain uninhabited regions of Asia, and Uganda have been proposed. But these projects could but come to nought, for they ran counter to a divine promise given to Abraham: "I will give this land to thee and thy seed forever."

On the other hand Palestine had long been coveted by several of the great powers, and these had done their very best to get control of it. Their efforts also came to nought. They were broken against a decree which no human power could shake. What God's lips had proclaimed His hand was accomplishing: "I give thee this land forever" (Paul Perret, *Prophecies I Have Seen Fulfilled*, London, Marshall, Morgan & Scott LTD., 1939, pp. 27, 28).

We again should also observe, that he made this statement in 1939—before the modern state of Israel was reborn.

THE UNITED NATIONS RESOLUTION

The next major event in the establishment of the modern state of Israel was United Nations Resolution 181. This was passed by the UN General Assembly on November 29, 1947. It called for the partition of Palestine into two states—one Arab and one Jewish. The city of Jerusalem was to be a separate entity governed by a special international regime.

On the one hand, this resolution was considered by the Jewish community in the Holy Land to be a legal basis for the establishment of the modern State of Israel. As can be imagined, this resolution was rejected by the Arab community.

THE END OF THE BRITISH MANDATE

In July 1922, the League of Nations had entrusted Britain with the "Mandate For Palestine." The Mandate recognized "the historical connection of the Jewish people with Palestine." In accordance with the Balfour Declaration of 1917, Britain was called upon to facilitate the establishment of a Jewish national home in the Land of Israel.

Interestingly, in September of 1922, the League of Nations and Great Britain decided that the provisions for setting up a Jewish national home would not apply to the area east of the Jordan River. This particular area constituted three-fourths of the territory which was included in the original Mandate. The territory eventually became the Hashemite Kingdom of Jordan..

After the United Resolution 181 was passed in 1947, Britain planned to withdraw from the Holy Land so that a Jewish state could be established. The complete withdrawal would take place on May 14,1948.

THE DECLARATION OF THE STATE OF ISRAEL

On May 14,1948, Israel, as a modern state, came into existence. We have highlighted some of the important points of the text of this declaration that was made by David Ben-Gurion, as well as other Israeli leaders, on that special day:

> The Land of Israel was the birthplace of the Jewish people. Here their spiritual, religious and political identity was shaped. Here they first attained to statehood, created cultural values of national and universal significance and gave to the world the eternal Book of Books.
>
> After being forcibly exiled from their land, the people remained faithful to it throughout their Dispersion and never ceased to pray and hope for their return to it and for the restoration in it of their political freedom. Impelled by this historic and traditional attachment, Jews strove in every successive generation to re-establish themselves in their ancient homeland. . .
>
> In the year 5657 (1897), at the summons of the spiritual father of the Jewish State, Theodore Herzl, the First Zionist Congress convened and proclaimed the right of the Jewish people to national rebirth in its own country. . .
>
> On the 29th November 1947, the United Nations General Assembly passed a resolution calling for the establishment of a Jewish State in Eretz-Israel; the General Assembly required

the inhabitants of Eretz-Israel to take such steps as were necessary on their part for the implementation of that resolution. This recognition by the United Nations of the right of the Jewish people to establish their State is irrevocable.

This right is the natural right of the Jewish people to be masters of their own fate, like all other nations, in their own sovereign State.

ACCORDINGLY, WE, MEMBERS OF THE PEOPLE'S COUNCIL, REPRESENTATIVES OF THE JEWISH COMMUNITY OF ERETZ-ISRAEL AND OF THE ZIONIST MOVEMENT, ARE HERE ASSEMBLED ON THE DAY OF THE TERMINATION OF THE BRITISH MANDATE OVER ERETZ-ISRAEL AND, BY VIRTUE OF OUR NATURAL AND HISTORIC RIGHT AND ON THE STRENGTH OF THE RESOLUTION OF THE UNITED NATIONS GENERAL ASSEMBLY, HEREBY DECLARE THE ESTABLISHMENT OF A JEWISH STATE IN ERETZ-ISRAEL, TO BE KNOWN AS THE STATE OF ISRAEL.

WE DECLARE that, with effect from the moment of the termination of the Mandate being tonight, the eve of Sabbath, the 6th Iyar, 5708 (15th May, 1948), until the establishment of the elected, regular authorities of the State in accordance with the Constitution which shall be adopted by the Elected Constituent Assembly not later than the 1st October 1948, the People's Council shall act as a Provisional Council of State, and its executive organ, the People's Administration, shall be the Provisional Government of the Jewish State, to be called "Israel"...

PLACING OUR TRUST IN THE ALMIGHTY, WE AFFIX OUR SIGNATURES TO THIS PROCLAMATION

AT THIS SESSION OF THE PROVISIONAL COUNCIL OF STATE, ON THE SOIL OF THE HOMELAND, IN THE CITY OF TEL-AVIV, ON THIS SABBATH EVE, THE 5TH DAY OF IYAR, 5708 (14TH MAY, 1948).

This declaration was signed by Ben-Gurion and other Jewish leaders. With it, the modern state of Israel miraculously came into existence!

U.S RECOGNITION UNDER PRESIDENT HARRY TRUMAN

On May 14, 1948, President Harry Truman recognized the newly formed state of Israel with the following telegram.

This Government has been informed that a Jewish state has been proclaimed in Palestine, and recognition has been requested by the provisional Government thereof.

The United States recognizes the provisional government as the de facto authority of the new State of Israel.

We read the following account as to why Truman did this from Clark Clifford—Truman's Secretary of State:

> From our many talks over the past year, I knew that five factors dominated Truman's thinking. From his youth, he had detested intolerance and discrimination. He had been deeply moved by the plight of the millions of homeless of World War II, and felt that alone among the homeless, the Jews had no homeland of their own to which they could return. He was, of course, horrified by the Holocaust and he denounced it vehemently, as, in the aftermath of the war, its full dimensions became clear. Also, he believed that the Balfour Declaration, issued by British Foreign Secretary Arthur Balfour in 1917, committed Great Britain and, by implication, the United States, which now shared a certain global responsibility with the British, to the creation of the Jewish state in Palestine. And

finally, he was a student and believer in the Bible since his youth. From his reading of the Old Testament he felt the Jews derived a legitimate historical right to Palestine, and he sometimes cited such biblical lines as Deuteronomy 1:8: "Behold, I have given up the land before you; go in and take possession of the land which the Lord hath sworn unto your fathers, to Abraham, to Isaac, and to Jacob" (Clark Clifford, *Counsel to the President: A Memoir*, 1991).

Truman, against the wishes of almost all of his advisors, recognized the new state of Israel. Interestingly, among other reasons, we discover that Truman, as a believer in the Bible, accepted the fact that God gave the land of Israel to the descendants of Abraham, Isaac, and Jacob.

THE WAR OF INDEPENDENCE

The declaration of the new State of Israel in Tel Aviv, as well as the recognition by the United States, did not sit well with the Arabs. Fighting immediately broke out. An armistice was declared in 1949.

UN RECOGNITION

Israel became a member of the United Nations on May 11, 1949. The preamble to this resolution admitting Israel to United Nations membership made specific reference to Israel's undertakings to implement General Assembly resolutions 181 and 194 (the right of return).

With this United Nations resolution, the modern state of Israel was officially accepted as one of the nations of the world. However, many problems remained unsolved. This included the borders of the country. In fact, the problem of Israel's borders remains to this day.

LET'S SUM UP WHAT WE HAVE SEEN THUS FAR

1. The Bible says that in the last days, the nation of Israel will still exist while certain of their ancient enemies will not.

2. Jesus had predicted that city of Jerusalem would be destroyed along with the Temple. He also said that the inhabitants would be taken captive and then scattered across all nations. The Old Testament had made similar predictions. *Luke 21: 21-24*

3. Though Israel would be scattered, God was not finished with His people. The Apostle Paul made this clear. *Rom. 11: 1-2, 25*

4. In fact, the people of Israel, all twelve tribes, would miraculously return to their ancient homeland at the time of the end. *Jer 30: 1-10*

5. This return will be from a "second exile." *Isaiah 11: 11-12*

6. This will take place after they have been gone from their land for a long time.

7. The land to which they will return will have been decimated by war. *Ezekiel 38: 8*

8. The newly formed State of Israel will be recognized by the world as a sovereign nation. *UN Resolution 181 p. 55 p. 56, p. 58-59*

9. Once they return to their land, the state of Israel will never be removed. *Amos 9: 14-15*

The Bible says that the Lord will bring them back because of His holy name. It will have nothing to do with them or with their behavior.

Notice that each of these nine predictions have been literally be fulfilled—just as the Scripture says.

PAST BIBLE COMMENTATORS PREDICTED ALL THIS WOULD HAPPEN

While the miracle of the survival of the Jews, and their return to their ancient homeland surprised the world, it did not surprise those who interpreted the prophecies of Scripture literally. In fact, for centuries, this was predicted by students of the Bible who looked forward to this day. We will list a number of examples.

In 1789, the Bible teacher Elhanan Winchester made this statement.

> Nothing need to be more plainly declared than this viz. That
> the Jews shall certainly return to and possess their own land
> again, notwithstanding their long captivity, and utter disper-
> sion—Moses, that great prophet, spake of these events in
> sundry places and expressly declared that they should take
> place in the latter days. See Leviticus 26, Deuteronomy 4:25-
> 31, Deuteronomy 29,30 (Elhanan Winchester, *A Course Of
> Lectures on Prophecies That Remain To Be Fulfilled*, Volume 1,
> London, 1789, p. 165).

Here is a man, writing over two hundred years ago, who predicted from
Scripture, that the Jews would once again return to their ancient land.

About one hundred years later, in 1878, we have the following words
written by William Blackstone:

> But perhaps you say: "I don't believe the Israelites are to be
> restored to Canaan, and Jerusalem rebuilt." Dear reader have
> you read the declarations of God's word about it? Surely noth-
> ing is more plainly stated in Scripture (William Blackstone,
> *Jesus Is Coming*, Fleming H. Revell Company, 1878, p. 162).

Indeed, nothing is more plainly stated in Scripture. We should not miss
the fact that Blackstone wrote this some 1,800 years after Jerusalem was
destroyed, the Temple destroyed, and the people scattered throughout
the world.

In 1855, the great preacher Charles Spurgeon had these words to say
concerning the return of the Jews to their ancient homeland.

> Not long shall it ere be they [the Jews] shall come; shall come
> from distant lands, where'er they rest or roam; and she who
> has been the off-scouring of all things, whose name has been
> a proverb and a bye-word, shall become the glory of all lands.

Dejected Zion shall raise her head, shaking herself from dust, and darkness, and from the dead. Then shall the Lord shall feed his people and make them and the places around them a blessing. I think we do not attach sufficient importance to the restoration of the Jews. We do not think enough of it. But certainly, if there is anything promised in the Bible it is this. I imagine that you cannot read the Bible without seeing clearly that there is to be an actual restoration of the children of Israel. "Thither shall they go up; they shall come with weeping unto Zion, and with supplications unto Jerusalem." May that happy day soon come! (Charles Spurgeon, *The C.H. Spurgeon Collection,* Metropolitan Tabernacle Pulpit 1, no. 28, p. 382).

In 1907, Arno C. Gaebelein wrote.

We shall look first of all to the Harmony of all Prophecy in predicting the . . . restoration of Israel. This topic is one of the most prominent in the prophetic Word. We find it quite a task in the limited space we have to condense all in such a way that the reader will get the correct scriptural view of it, and to show at the same time how the Spirit of God bears witness to this great future of Israel. . . . The present desolation of the land and Jerusalem will have an end (Arno C. Gaebelein, *The Harmony of the Prophetic Word*, New York, Fleming and Revell, 1907, pp.117-118, 141).

Gaebelein also wrote the following a few years later.

The Holy Spirit unfolds . . . the purposes of God concerning the Jewish race. The knowledge of Israel's place and position in God's revealed plan is of incalculable importance. . . Their whole history is outlined. They were to be a people blinded, forsaking God, to be scattered in consequence of it into the corners of the earth. Their whole career of decline and apostasy is prophetically revealed. But alongside of all these prophecies of which should befall them, which were so literally fulfilled, we find prophecies relating to their restoration and future blessing (A.C. Gaebelein, *The Jewish Question,* "Our Hope," New York, 1912, pp. 1, 35).

In each of these instances, these commentators predicted the return of the Jews to their ancient homeland *before* there was any movement for this marvelous event to take place. Some of them made these comments when the Jewish people had been out of their land for some eighteen centuries!

How could they do something like this? It is because they had a Book they could trust, the Bible. As we have observed, their faith in the promises of Scripture was well-founded.

To sum up, we have many predictions in Scripture regarding the return of the Jews to their ancient homeland in the "last days." In addition, we also have Bible commentators, based upon the Bible and the Bible alone, predicting this return would take place.

LET'S RECAP: WHAT HAS HAPPENED?

Against all odds of history, after about 1,900 years away from their homeland, Israel became a modern state on May 14, 1948. Hence, the biblical prophets were right, and the past biblical commentators, who predicted this to occur, were also correct.

How could they know that Israel would even exist in the last days—let alone return their ancient homeland and form a modern state? Simply put, they trusted in the predictions found in the Bible. Their trust proved to be well-placed.

Lance Lambert provides a fitting summary of what has taken place.

God has dealt with no nation as he has dealt with the Jewish people. In their 4,000-year-long history, they have been exiled from their land twice, and have been restored to it twice . . .

No other nation in the history of mankind has twice been uprooted from its land, scattered to the ends of the earth and then brought back again to that same territory. If the first exile and restoration were remarkable, the second is miraculous. Israel has twice lost its statehood and its national sovereignty, twice had its capital and hub of religious life destroyed, its towns and cities razed to the ground, its people deported and dispersed, and then twice had it restored again.

> Furthermore, no other nation or ethnic group has been scattered to the four corners of the earth, and yet survived as an easily identifiable and recognizable group . . . From the Far East to the Far West there is hardly a nation that has not had Jewish citizens within it. The remarkable fact is that the Jewish people have been able to survive as a people, instead of being absorbed and assimilated into the larger Gentile majorities among whom it was scattered. We must remember that we are not considering a period of one generation, or even one century, but nearly two thousand years (Lance Lambert, *Israel,* Wheaton, Illinois, Tyndale, 1981, pp. 55,56).

The miracle of the preservation of Israel, as well as their return to their ancient homeland, is truly *the* major sign of the last days. Indeed, now that they are back in the land, the predictions concerning them, as well as the destiny of the rest of the world, are now able to be fulfilled.

In our next "Sign of the End," we will again discover another fulfillment of Bible prophecy in these last days. This sign is of particular importance because it sets the stage for the monumental events of the last days—the Great Tribulation, the nation of Israel turning to Christ in faith, the Second Coming of Jesus Christ to the earth, and the worldwide return of all of the people of Israel to their ancient homeland.

The Nation Will
Return in Two Stages

After almost two thousand years of being absent, Israel is back in its ancient homeland. This is one of the greatest miracles of all history. Yet, as we have seen, it should not have surprised anyone. Indeed, not only was it clearly predicted in Scripture, it was also predicted by those who took the prophecies of the Bible seriously.

THE TWO-STAGE RETURN

It is important to realize that the Bible says that this return of the people of Israel to their land will be in "two stages."

First, many Jews, but not all of them, will return to the land of Israel on their own. This will be in unbelief of Jesus. As we noted, this has already occurred.

There will also be a later return when the entire nation of Israel, though scattered worldwide, will be brought back to their ancient homeland.

THERE WILL BE THREE INTERVENING EVENTS

However, before this second stage occurs, there will be three intervening events that will take place—the Great Tribulation, the national repentance of Israel, and the Second Coming of Jesus Christ to the earth.

The biblical evidence is as follows:

THE VISION GIVEN TO EZEKIEL

The first prediction we will consider is from the 37th chapter of the Book of Ezekiel. To sum up, the first ten verses record a vision seen by the prophet. The Lord brought him to a valley where there were many dry bones scattered. He then asked Ezekiel if these bones could live. The prophet replied, "You know Lord."

Ezekiel was then told to prophesy toward these bones that they would come to life. He obeyed the Lord and the dry dead bones lived again.

The meaning of this vision is then explained to us in the following verses.

> Then he said to me, "Son of man, these bones are all the house of Israel. Look, they are saying, 'Our bones are dry, our hope has perished; we are cut off.' Therefore prophesy, and tell them, 'This is what the sovereign Lord says: Look, I am about to open your graves and will raise you from your graves, my people. I will bring you to the land of Israel. Then you will know that I am the Lord, when I open your graves and raise you from your graves, my people. I will place my breath in you and you will live; I will give you rest in your own land. Then you will know that I am the Lord—I have spoken and I will act, declares the Lord (Ezekiel 37:11-14 NET).

In verse eleven, the Lord explained to Ezekiel that the bones represented all twelve tribes of Israel. We find that the Israelites were saying that they were like these dry dead bones. Indeed, they had lost all hope of returning to their own land. They had also lost hope of seeing the literal fulfillment of the promises which the Lord had made to them. In fact, the people believed that the Lord had cut them off completely!

However, the Lord said that He would indeed bring them back to the land of Israel. Yet, this restoration will occur in two stages:

First, there will be the physical, or national, restoration of the people. This will take place when many of them, on their own, return to their homeland. This prediction is consistent with what the Lord had promised in the previous chapter of Ezekiel. In fact, the entire context of chapters 36–37 makes it clear that Israel's national restoration will occur at the time of the end.

Next, will be their spiritual restoration. Once they are back in their ancient homeland, after an unknown interval of time, they will be restored spiritually.

THE SEQUENCE OF EVENTS: WHAT WILL HAPPEN AFTER THEIR RETURN?

It is important that we understand what the Bible teaches about the events that will occur after the Jewish people return to their ancient homeland. From a study of Scripture, we can explain the future sequence of events, as far as Israel is concerned, in this manner:

THE FIRST EVENT: THE RETURN OF THE JEWS IN UNBELIEF

First, there will be a return to their ancient homeland in unbelief. We have seen this return predicted in Ezekiel's prophecy. Furthermore, we have also seen the miraculous fulfillment of this prediction. Hence, stage one of their return is complete.

THE SECOND EVENT: THE TIME OF JACOB'S TROUBLE

After the Jews have returned to their ancient homeland in unbelief, there will be an interim period where they are in their land. However, not all Jews from all parts of the earth will return. This second stage of their return is still future; and, before, this can take place, there will be an unprecedented time of trouble for them.

19th century writer, David Baron, describes what will happen next:

> The second item in the Divine programme of the future of
> Israel, as given in this divinely dictated "book," is, to use the

language of inspiration, "the time of Jacob's trouble" (David Baron, *The Jewish Problem, Its Solution, or Israel's Present and Future*, 1890, p. 11)

The Bible indeed says that the nation of Israel will experience a time of unprecedented trouble in the future. This is known by various names in Scripture, one of them being, "the time of Jacob's trouble." Jeremiah recorded the Lord saying the following:

> How awful that day will be! No other will be like it. It will be a time of trouble for Jacob, but he will be saved out of it (Jeremiah 30:7 NIV).

We read about this future time-period in the Book of Daniel:

At that time Michael, the great prince who watches over your people,

> will arise. There will be a time of distress unlike any other from the nation's beginning up to that time. But at that time your own people, all those whose names are found written in the book, will escape. Many of those who sleep in the dusty ground will awake-some to everlasting life, and others to shame and everlasting abhorrence (Daniel 12:1-2 NET)

According to the prophet Daniel, at the time of the end, there will be a time of distress like no other. Indeed, it will be unparalleled.

IT WILL BE A TIME OF GOD'S WRATH

As the prophet Ezekiel explains, the Lord will pour out His wrath upon the people:

> Then the word of the Lord came to me: "Son of man, the people of Israel have become dross to me; all of them are the copper, tin, iron and lead left inside a furnace. They are but the dross of silver. Therefore this is what the Sovereign Lord says: 'Because you have all become dross, I will gather

you into Jerusalem. As silver, copper, iron, lead and tin are gathered into a furnace to be melted with a fiery blast, so will I gather you in my anger and my wrath and put you inside the city and melt you. I will gather you and I will blow on you with my fiery wrath, and you will be melted inside her. As silver is melted in a furnace, so you will be melted inside her, and you will know that I the Lord have poured out my wrath on you (Ezekiel 37:17-22 NIV).

Using the analogy of metals, Israel has become like the dross, the waste, when silver is refined. As the waste is melted down, so will Israel be melted down by the wrath of the Lord. This will take place *after* they have been gathered back to Jerusalem—the first stage of their return.

The predictions of the Old Testament are clear. Once the people return to their ancient homeland they will eventually experience a time of unprecedented trouble.

JESUS CONFIRMED THE COMING "TIME OF JACOB'S TROUBLE" (THE GREAT TRIBULATION)

We find that Jesus Himself acknowledged that there will be a future "Time of Jacob's Trouble," the likes of which the world has never experienced before. He referred to it as "The Great Tribulation."

When He was asked about the signs of His return to earth, He gave this warning:

> For then there will be great tribulation, such as has not been from the beginning of the world until now, no, and never will be. And if those days had not been cut short, no human being would be saved. But for the sake of the elect those days will be cut short (Matthew 24:21,22 ESV).

According to Jesus, unless the Lord intervenes, nobody will be saved. But for the sake of Israel, His chosen people, who will still exist at that time, He will intervene and save them from this unparalleled time of terror known as the "Time of Jacob's Trouble" or "The Great Tribulation."

THE THIRD EVENT: ISRAEL WILL REALIZE THEY REJECTED THEIR MESSIAH, JESUS AND THEN REPENT

It is during this time of the Great Tribulation that the people will realize that Jesus is the Messiah. The Lord gave the following illustration of this through the prophet Hosea:

> I will be like a lion to Israel, like a strong young lion to Judah. I will tear them to pieces! I will carry them off, and no one will be left to rescue them. Then I will return to my place until they admit their guilt and turn to me. For as soon as trouble comes, they will earnestly search for me (Hosea 5:15,16 NLT).

First, the Lord will punish the nation and then depart from them. He will not return until they admit their guilt and turn to Him in belief.

Jesus said something similar:

> For I tell you this, you will never see me again until you say, 'Blessings on the one who comes in the name of the Lord!' (Matthew 23:39 NLT).

Hence, the people will not see Him again until they acknowledge Him as their Messiah. The learned Bible teacher, David L. Cooper explains.

> A careful examination of this passage [Hosea 5:15,16] shows that the prophet was speaking of Israel's confession at the close of the Great Tribulation. The Lord declares that He will not come, in fact, not even leave heaven, until Israel acknowledges her offense against Him and seeks His face earnestly. The repudiation of the national sin is antecedent

to Israel's conversion and the Lord's return to her. This confession presupposes on the part of Jewry, a knowledge of this national sin which is nothing other than her rejection of the Messiah . . . This is confirmed by the language of Matthew 23:39. A study of Matthew, chapters 21 to 23 inclusive, shows that our Lord was talking about those sitting on Moses seat—the elders of Israel—namely, the Great Sanhedrin. He concluded His denunciation of their lives by stating that He often would have gathered Israel together as a hen does her chickens under her wings but they (the leaders) would not. Therefore He declared that their house . . . would be left unto them desolate and that they would see Him no more until they (the leaders) said just what the common people had proclaimed the day before—namely "Blessed *is* he that comes in the name of the Lord" (italics his). From this passage it is evident that the leaders of Israel must repudiate the national sin and apply to Jesus this quotation from the 118th Psalm, which is a virtual acknowledgment of His divinity and Messiahship. "Blessed be he that comes in the name of Jehovah. We have blessed you out of the house of Jehovah" (verse 26).

This confession, according to Jesus, is prerequisite to His coming again as her Messiah (David L. Cooper, *Is the Jew Still First on God's Prophetic Program*, 1935, pp. 18,19).

Once this national repentance takes place, it will begin to fulfill the prediction with respect to the second stage of their return. Isaiah speaks of this future *spiritual* regathering in Israel in the following passage.

At that time you will say: "I praise you, O Lord, for even though you were angry with me, your anger subsided, and you consoled me. Look, God is my deliverer! I will trust in him and not fear. For the Lord gives me strength and protects me; he has become my deliverer." Joyfully you will draw water from the springs of deliverance. At that time you will say: "Praise the Lord! Ask him for help! Publicize his mighty acts among the nations! Make it known that he is unique! Sing to the Lord, for he has done magnificent things, let this be known throughout the earth. Cry out and shout for joy, O citizens of Zion, for the Holy One of Israel acts mightily among you!" (Isaiah 12:1-6 NET).

During this time of great trouble, Israel will turn to the Lord for forgiveness. We read about this in Zechariah:

And I will pour out on the house of David and the inhabitants of Jerusalem a spirit of grace and supplication. They will look on me, the one they have pierced, and they will mourn for him as one mourns for an only child, and grieve bitterly for him as one grieves for a firstborn son. On that day the weeping in Jerusalem will be as great as the weeping of Hadad Rimmon in the plain of Megiddo. The land will mourn, each clan by itself, with their wives by themselves: the clan of the house of David and their wives, the clan of the house of Nathan and their wives, the clan of the house of Levi and their wives, the clan of Shimei and their wives, and all the rest of the clans and their wives (Zechariah 12:10-14 NIV).

When this happens, the people will then be spiritually restored.

THE FOURTH EVENT: THE RETURN OF THE LORD

The next event will be the Second Coming of Jesus Christ to the earth. After Israel repents, the Lord will return to the Mount of Olives in the city of Jerusalem.

Then the Lord will go out and fight against those nations, as he fights on a day of battle. On that day his feet will stand on the Mount of Olives, east of Jerusalem, and the Mount of Olives will be split in two from east to west, forming a great valley, with half of the mountain moving north and half moving south. You will flee by my mountain valley, for it will extend to Azel. You will flee as you fled from the earthquake in the days of Uzziah king of Judah. Then the Lord my God will come, and all the holy ones with him (Zechariah 12:3-5 NIV).

Their spiritual rebirth, as we have just mentioned in our last event, leads to the coming of Christ.

THE FIFTH EVENT: THE FINAL RESTORATION OF ISRAEL, IN BELIEF

The Lord will then gather all remaining people from the twelve tribes of Israel, from all parts of the globe, and bring them to the Promised Land. The prophet Isaiah wrote about this as follows:

At that time the sovereign master will again lift his hand to reclaim the remnant of his people from Assyria, Egypt, Pathros, Cush, Elam, Shinar, Hamath, and the seacoasts. He will lift a signal flag for the nations; he will gather Israel's dispersed people and assemble Judah's scattered people from the four corners of the earth (Isaiah 11:11,12 NET).

Hence, there will be a worldwide gathering of the people of Israel after the Lord returns—the fulfillment of the second stage of Israel's two-stage return.

THE SEQUENCE SUMMARIZED

In sum, the first stage of Israel's future has been fulfilled—they are now back in their ancient homeland. After an indefinite period of time, the next major event for the nation will take place. This time period is known as "The Time of Jacob's Trouble," which Jesus called the "Great Tribulation."

During this tribulation period, the people of Israel will realize that Jesus is their Messiah. This will lead to a national repentance. Jesus will then return to the earth. Christ, at His return to the earth, will then regather the entire nation, all twelve tribes, from all parts of the globe, to the Promised Land.

THE TESTIMONY OF PAST COMMENTATORS TO THE TWO STAGE RETURN

The fact that the return of Israel to its ancient homeland will be in two stages, physical restoration then spiritual restoration, was observed by many past commentators of Scripture.

For example, we read the following from 18th century commentator Elhanan Winchester:

> We may be sure that the Jews will not be converted before their return to their own land. And it has been a very great, though general mistake, to suppose that their conversion would first take place, in order for their return; whereas this terrible calamity that shall fall upon them, supposes the contrary. For is it reasonable to suppose, that God would thus deliver up his beloved people, when they had newly returned to him, into the hands of their cruel foes, who should thus be permitted to exercise such horrible brutality upon them? (Elhanan Winchester, *A Course Of Lectures on Prophecies That Remain To Be Fulfilled*, Volume 1, London, 1789, p. 184).

Winchester's point is well taken. According to Jesus, the Great Tribulation (Matthew 24:21) will occur *when the Israelites are back in the land.* The Lord said this would be the worst time of distress that the world would ever experience. Hence, God would not subject His people to this time of punishment, if they had been newly converted.

In fact, quite the contrary is said. The time of their conversion will be a time of blessing. Thus, they will return in unbelief before their national conversion.

Because of his understanding of Scripture, this 18th century commentator, Elhanan Winchester, believed that a literal Israel would return to their ancient homeland and he also emphasized that their return would be in an "unconverted state."

19th century commentator, B.W. Newton, made a similar observation.

> First, from these chapters [Zechariah 12-14] we learn that the Jews as a nation will be converted and forgiven, *when they are in their own land and city.* Therefore, it follows that they must return to their land and city *when uncoverted* (italics his) (B.W. Newton, *How B.W. Newton Learned Prophetic Truth*, London, Sovereign Grace Advent Testimony, 1880, p. 4).

Newton stressed that the Bible predicted the Jews returning to their ancient homeland in the last days in an unconverted state:

In addition, the great preacher of the 19th century, Charles Spurgeon, gave the following commentary on Ezekiel 37:1-10:

> The meaning of our text, as opened up by the context, is most evidently, if words mean anything, first, that there shall be a political restoration of the Jews to their own land and to their own nationality; and then secondly, there is in the text, and in the context, a most plain declaration that there shall be a spiritual restoration, a conversion in fact, of the tribes of Israel (Charles Spurgeon, *The C.H. Spurgeon Collection,* Metropolitan Tabernacle Pulpit 1, Number 582, 1864, p. 533).

First the political restoration will ensue, then, after an unknown interval, the spiritual restoration.

George Muller, the famed 19th century director of the orphanage in Bristol, England, wrote:

> In Scripture, the glory and resurrection of the Church of the firstborn ones is always connected with the time when Israel (who will have returned to their own land in unbelief)

'shall know the Lord.'"(George Muller, *The Second Coming of Christ*, n.d., p. 64).

In 1867, Bible commentator J.C. Ryle set forth what he believed Scripture taught about the future. He listed a number of points that include the following:

> I believe that the Jews shall ultimately be gathered again as a separate nation, restored to their own land, and converted to the faith of Christ, after going through great tribulation (Jer. 30:10-11; 31:10; Rom. 11:25-26; Dan. 12:1; Zech. 13:8-9). (J.C Ryle, *Coming Events and Present Duties*, Second Edition, London, William Hunt and Company, 1879, p. 6).

Notice that Ryle said that they will be converted to faith in Christ *after* going through the Great Tribulation.

Another past commentator put it this way.

> They will be gathered back in their unconverted state . . . Previous to the coming of the Lord, therefore, it will be still as rejectors of Christ and rebellious to God, that they will occupy their land (Bishop W.R. Nicholson "The Gathering of Israel," in Nathaniel West, *Second Coming of Christ, Premillennial Essays of the Prophetic Conference*, Chicago, F.H. Revell, 1879, p. 231).

We could go on and on but the point is clear. These past commentators, along with many others, anticipated these "last days" circumstances centuries ago.

Furthermore, they made these comments when there was *nothing* happening in the world to suggest these events would ever take place. Yet they correctly predicted that Israel would not only return to their ancient homeland, as the Lord had promised, but also that they would return in unbelief.

This unbelief would only turn to belief in Christ during the end of the Great Tribulation period. Christ will then return to the earth when the people of Israel, especially the leaders, repent of their sins.

THE INITIAL RETURN WILL BE BOTH HUMAN AND DIVINE

Thus, we could say that the first regathering of the people to their ancient homeland, which happened in 1948, was a combination of the human and the divine. Interestingly, Bishop Nicholson observed this in 1879. He wrote:

> It will be effected by both human and divine agency. Partly by human. (Isaiah 49:22,23; 66:19,20). Partly by Divine (Isaiah 11:15,16) . . . for it is the unvarying implication of Scripture that Israel's recovery before the Advent (of Christ) will come about in a natural and ordinary way . . . In this second gathering, as in the first (the return from Babylon) returning Israel will as yet be unconverted (Bishop W.R. Nicholson "The Gathering of Israel," in Nathaniel West, *Second Coming of Christ, Premillennial Essays of the Prophetic Conference*, Chicago, Fleming Revell, 1879, p. 234).

Let's never forget that Bishop Nicholson too was writing this "in faith." There had been no regathering of Israel at this time, nor even a hint of it. Yet this first stage has miraculously happened! The final regathering is still to come.

SUMMING UP SIGN 4

Marvelously, we see Israel back in their land after an absence of about 1,900 years. This return is precisely as the Scriptures have predicted. Indeed, it is a return by the people in unbelief.

We discovered from the prophet Ezekiel that the return will actually be in two stages. First, their restoration to the Land of Promise. This, of course, as we just mentioned, has already occurred.

1948

At some time in the future, at the end of the seven-year Great Tribulation period, the "Time of Jacob's Trouble," the people will fulfill the second stage of Ezekiel's prophecy. According to Scripture, they will experience a time of unparalleled distress. However, not only will the nation survive, they will turn to the Lord and recognize Jesus as their Messiah. After this takes place, the Lord Jesus will return to the earth. When He returns, the Lord will gather the rest of the Jews from all parts of the earth.

We have also observed that careful Bible students of the past understood these predictions. Thus, we documented a number of them predicting Israel's return in the last days while still in unbelief. Their reasoning was clear—God would not return His people to their ancient homeland to punish them if they had been recently converted. To the contrary, the conversion comes afterward.

Again, we want to emphasize the amazing nature of these predictions and their fulfillment which we have seen thus far.

Four thousand years ago, the Lord gave specific promises to a man named Abraham, as well as to his son Isaac, and to Isaac's son Jacob. We saw that there were twelve promises in total. We also discovered that each one of these have been miraculously fulfilled. Furthermore, He specifically promised the nation that they would survive forever.

In addition, the Lord cursed five different "people groups" who attempted to destroy Israel and thwart His promises toward them. These nations no longer exist today. However, Egypt, historically one of Israel's strongest enemies, is not only said to exist in the "last days," but it is also predicted to eventually turn to the Lord. As predicted, Egypt does exist to this day.

Hence, each of these seven specific predictions, with respect to these nations, has been literally fulfilled in these last days.

Add to this what we have considered in Sign 3—Israel has miraculously returned to its ancient homeland after being gone for a long period of time, almost 1,900 years!

With our fourth sign, we see another prediction fulfilled—the people return to the land in unbelief. This sets the stage for the Great Tribulation period, which will lead to a national conversion of the people when they recognize Jesus as their Messiah. This will take place before the Second Coming of Christ. Once they convert, Christ will return and then gather the remaining Jews from the four corners of the earth.

In 1925, David Baron wrote these insightful words before the people had returned to their ancient homeland:

The return in unbelief is, we believe, *the necessary precursor to the resumption of God's dealings with Israel as a nation* (Italics his) (David Baron, *The History of Israel*, London, Morgan and Scott, 1925 p. 153).

The return of the people in unbelief in 1948 was indeed the precursor to the Lord, once again, dealing with Israel as a nation.

We can begin to see a pattern forming. The Lord makes the predictions, the circumstances for fulfillment look impossible, yet the predictions are eventually fulfilled.

If all we had were these four signs, then it should be evidence enough for people to believe in the God of the Bible. However, there are many more signs that we will examine which will further document that the God of Scripture does exist, knows the future, and predicts it accurately.

Indeed, our next sign will look at the Holy City of Jerusalem and some of the predictions which the Bible has made for it. We will discover some modern predictions about the city which were made after the state of Israel was reborn in 1948.

Jerusalem Will be
United Under Israeli Rule

As we continue to observe what the Bible has to say about the nation of Israel in the "last days," we will encounter some important predictions about the Holy City of Jerusalem.

Though rarely appreciated, we will discover that this particular sign, the uniting of Jerusalem under Israeli rule, is actually monumental as far as Scripture is concerned—with respect to prophecies concerning the time of the end. Indeed, the city of Jerusalem is center-stage, or ground zero, in the plan of God for the "last days!"

THE SITUATION ON MAY 14, 1948

As we noted, when the modern state of Israel was born, the exact borders of this new county were not clearly drawn. What made matters worse is that one minute after midnight on May 14, 1948, the newly formed state was attacked by its Arab neighbors. This was known as "The War of Independence."

THE SITUATION AFTER 1948

When the War of Independence ended, the city of Jerusalem was divided right down the middle. West Jerusalem was under Israeli rule, while East Jerusalem was occupied by another country, Transjordan. In 1949, an Armistice was declared. Yet, the precise borders were never officially agreed upon.

THE NEED FOR JERUSALEM TO BE REUNITED

As will be observed with some of the future signs we will consider, the Bible assumes that Jerusalem will be united under Israeli rule in the last days. Indeed, as we will later document in detail, certain events that will take place assume that this will be the case.

This will include the building of a Third Temple, as well as its eventual desecration. Since the coming Temple must be built upon the exact same spot as the previous temples on the Temple Mount, the Israelis must be in control of that geographical area. However, in 1948, after the War of Independence, the Temple Mount was in the hands of Transjordan.

Furthermore, according to Ezekiel 38 and 39, the invading armies come to the "mountains of Israel" in their attack. In 1948, these mountains were not in the hands of Israel at that time.

Therefore, after the miraculous rebirth of the state of Israel in 1948, and the end of the War of Independence, careful Bible students predicted there would have to be another war. In this war, the entire city of Jerusalem would be reunited under Israeli rule.

1967, THE SIX DAY WAR

It took nineteen years, but the predicted unification of Jerusalem did indeed take place. In June of 1967, the Six Day War occurred. The Temple Mount, as well as the "mountains of Israel," were captured by the Israelis. The stage was now set for the eventual building of the Temple, as well as the Ezekiel 38,39 invasion.

A REUNIFIED JERUSALEM WAS PREDICTED BY MANY PAST COMMENTATORS

There is also the fact that a reunified Jerusalem, under Jewish rule, was something that had been expected for a long time by a number of Bible-believing Christians.

In around A.D. 150, the early church father, Justin Martyr, was asked if he believed that . . .

> Jerusalem ... shall be rebuilt; and [the Jews] to be gathered together, and made joyful with Christ and the patriarchs. He responded, "I and many others are of this opinion" (Justin Martyr, *Dialogue with Trypho*, chapter LXXX).

While in the first three hundred years of the Christian era there was an expectation of the restoration of the Jews to their ancient homeland, this all changed with the writings of St. Augustine and the church father Jerome. They spiritualized the promises to Israel and taught that these promises now belonged to the church. For over one thousand years, with a few exceptions, this was the prevailing view.

SIR HENRY FINCH, THE PIONEER

The idea of a literal Israel, being restored to their ancient homeland, began to surface again in the 17th century. Sir Henry Finch was the first person who expounded, in detail, the idea of a literal restoration of the Jews. In 1621, he wrote the following about the Jews returning to their ancient homeland and eventually ruling from Jerusalem.

> Where Israel, Iudah, Tsion, Jerusalem, &c. are named in this argument, the Holy Ghost meaneth not the spiritual Israel, or Church of God collected of the Gentiles, no nor of the Iews and Gentiles both (for each of these haue their promises seuerally and apart) but Israel properly descended out of Iacobs loynes. These and such like are not Allegories . . . but meant really and literally of the Iewes that one day they shall come to Ierusalem againe, and be Kings and chiefe Monarches of the earth, sway, and gouerne all (Sir Henry Finch, *The World's Resurrection or The Calling of the Iewes,* 1621).

While the 17th century English spelling may be a little difficult to follow, the upshot is clear. The Jews, as a people, the actual physical descendants of Jacob, will one day return to their ancient homeland, and its Holy City, Jerusalem. Finch also taught that they would eventually rule the world from there.

It is also sobering to realize what came about from him expressing this idea in print. Finch was the greatest legal mind in England at the time. In fact, the king often sought legal advice from him.

However, arguing for the literal restoration of the Jews to their ancient homeland, as well as maintaining that they would one day rule the world, albeit as Jewish Christians, did not please the king. Finch, along with his publisher, were arrested. He lost everything, and was publicly disgraced.

As can be imagined, the ideas that Finch laid out in his book have been refined through the last four hundred years. Yet, we owe a great debt to this man for insisting on a literal interpretation of Scripture when it comes to the future of the Jews. We also trust that *great* will be his reward in heaven.

In the 19th century, Adolph Saphir, wrote the following.

> When prophecy looks forward to the days of the future, even then it regards Israel being settled in their own country not to leave it, and as having Jerusalem as their capital (Adolph Saphir, *The Divine Unity Of Scripture*, London, Hodder and Stoughton, 1892, p. 92).

So again, we see that certain things can be predicted based upon what the Bible says will happen in the future.

Another early 20th century writer, A.C. Gaebelein, put it this way.

> In connection with this we desire to point out what a witness the Jewish race is to the truth of God's holy Word. It is a supernatural fact, which no infidel can explain, that

thousands of years ago, the entire history of the remarkable race was foretold. The curse which rests upon them, the condition of their land, and the city of Jerusalem, and much else, bear witness that the Bible is the Word of God, that the rejected Jesus is their promised Messiah.

And the Word of God, which has been so literally fulfilled touching the curse, will some blessed day be as literally fulfilled in blessing (A.C. Gaebelein, *The Jewish Question*, "Our Hope," New York, 1912, pp. 39,40).

His words were prophetic. The stage is being set for the Jews to receive that literal blessing. Indeed, they are back in their ancient homeland, and the entire city of Jerusalem is under their control. While a time of great trouble awaits them, after this difficult period will come the greatest blessing the nation has ever known—the national acceptance of Jesus as the Messiah.

THE IMPORTANCE OF JERUSALEM IN THE PLAN OF GOD

In speaking of the prophetic history of the nations, 19th century commentator B.W. Newton wrote these insightful words.

We find another example of this [the importance of Jerusalem] in the method which it has pleased God to adopt in giving the prophetic history of these nations. As soon as they arose, prophets were commissioned but especially Daniel, to delineate their course. We might perhaps have expected that their history would have been given minutely and consecutively from its beginning to its close. *But* (italics his) instead of this, it is only in its connection with Jerusalem; and as soon as Jerusalem was crushed by the Romans, and ceased to retain a national position in the earth, all detailed history of the Gentile Empire is suspended. Many a personage most important in the world's history has since arisen.

Charlemagne has lived, and Napoleon—many a monarch and many a conqueror—battles have been fought, kingdoms raised and kingdoms subverted—yet Scripture passes silently over all these things, however great in the annals of the Gentiles because Jerusalem has nationally ceased to be. Eighteen hundred years ago the detail of Gentile history was suspended—and it is suspended still, nor will it be resumed until Jerusalem re-assumes a national position. Then the history of the Gentiles is minutely given; and the glory and dominion of their last great king described [Antichrist]. He is found to be especially connected with Jerusalem and the land. "He is to glorify himself on Zion, (Isaiah 14:13, Daniel 11:45) and to be broken and trodden under foot in the land, and on the mountains of Israel (Isaiah 14:24-27).

That the Jews while yet unconverted will go back to their land, and there re-assume a national standing, has already been proved from the concluding chapters of Zechariah; for if, as those chapters teach, they are nationally converted *when in their city* (italics his), they must of course have returned to their home unconverted (B.W. Newton, *Aids To Prophetic Enquiry*, London, James Nisbet and Co., Berners Street, 1848, pp. 50,51).

This 19th century author brings up so many important points. They include the following.

First, since the Lord gives us a general outline of the history of the nations, we would expect it to include many details. However, the Gentile nations are only mentioned with reference to the city of Jerusalem. In fact, once Jerusalem was destroyed, and the Jews sent into exile, the Lord became silent as to the history of these nations.

That silence will only end when Jerusalem is again controlled by the chosen people, the Jews. At the time Newton wrote this, there had been almost 1,800 years of the wandering of the Jews, as well as 1,800 years of silence from God, as far as the nations were concerned.

Jerusalem will again come to the forefront when the Jews return to their homeland in an unconverted state. At some unspecified time after this, the final Gentile ruler comes on the scene, the Antichrist.

Hence, when we once again see Jerusalem controlled by the Jews, then we find that the Bible goes into great detail about the events that will take place in the Holy City.

All of this recognizes a profound truth. Jerusalem has been, is, as well as will be, at the center of world events as far as God is concerned. The other nations in the world are only mentioned in reference to the Jews and the city of Jerusalem. This should give us an idea of the importance of the Holy City, as well as the events which will take place there in the future.

The main events of history, as far as the Bible is concerned, revolves around a people, the Jews, and their Holy City, Jerusalem. Therefore, we must appreciate how monumental it was for the Jews to unite the entire city in 1967!

JERUSALEM WILL NEVER BE DIVIDED AGAIN

There is one more thing that we can mention. It seems that once the city of Jerusalem has been united, it will never be divided again. Unhappily, there have been attempts by many in Israel, as well as in the United States of America, to do precisely that.

Since certain events will take place in east Jerusalem in the last days, that will involve Israel, this territory will remain under their authority. This also includes the mountains of Jerusalem. We will have more to say about this as we look at Sign 9—the coming invasion of Israel by certain specified nations as predicted in Ezekiel 38,39.

THE LORD WILL PUNISH THOSE WHO DIVIDE HIS LAND

We should also observe that the Bible says that the Lord will punish those who have divided His Promised Land.

> In those days and at that time, when I restore the fortunes of Judah and Jerusalem, I will gather all nations and bring them down to the Valley of Jehoshaphat. There I will put them on trial for what they did to my inheritance, my people Israel, because they scattered my people among the nations and divided up my land (Joel 3:1-3 NIV).

These are sobering words which speak of a punishment that is still yet to come.

Hence, we cannot overestimate the importance of this particular sign—the re-uniting of the city of Jerusalem under the rule of the Israelis.

SUMMING UP SIGN 5: JERUSALEM IS NOW UNITED UNDER ISRAELI RULE

As we examine what the Bible says about the situation in Israel in the last days, we find that it anticipates that the city of Jerusalem will be united under Israeli rule.

Indeed, certain events, that the Bible predicts will happen in the future, are based upon the idea that Israel controls the entire city. As we shall see in some of our coming "Signs of the End," this includes the building of a Third Temple, along with the invasion of Israel—as predicted in Ezekiel 38,39. Indeed, at the time of this invasion, the "mountains of Israel" are in the hands of the Israelis.

Yet, when the modern state of Israel was founded in 1948, the city of Jerusalem was divided. Israel was in control of west Jerusalem but Transjordan occupied east Jerusalem. While the founding of Israel fulfilled Bible prophecy, it was recognized by careful Bible students that there was still more that had to take place.

Consequently, they predicted, based upon the Biblical scenario of the last days, that another war had to occur. In that war, the city of Jerusalem had to be completely united under Israeli rule.

This is precisely what took place in June 1967. East Jerusalem, the Temple Mount, the Mount of Olives, as well as other territories were liberated by the Israelis. This has set the stage for many Bible prophecies that remain to be fulfilled.

We also observed that past Bible commentators, going all the way back to the second century, looked forward to the day when the Jews would come back to Jerusalem and have the entire city under their control.

How were these Bible commentators able to predict this? It is simple. When we understand Bible prophecy in a literal manner, then we are able to assume that certain things will take place in the future—based upon the predictions of Scripture. This is a case in point.

It is also highly instructive about future things predicted in the Bible which have not yet taken place. Indeed, based upon Scripture, we can predict specific things that will happen simply because the Bible tells us they will happen. In other words, all we are doing is taking the words of Scripture at face-value and then merely stating what it says will happen.

Finally, we have also noted the importance the Bible itself places upon the city of Jerusalem. Indeed, the history of the Gentile nations, as revealed in Scripture, revolve around the city of Jerusalem, as well as the events which take place there. In fact, there was nineteen centuries of silence of Gentile history as far as the Bible was concerned—since the Jews were not back in their land, neither had they united the city of Jerusalem.

Now that the city has been united under Israeli rule, the stage is set for further predictions to come to pass! The "last days" scenario that the biblical prophets predicted so long ago, with respect to Jerusalem, can now be literally fulfilled. Furthermore, Scripture gives us many details as to exactly what will happen there in the future.

In sum, this fifth "Sign of the End," that the Israelis have united Jerusalem under their rule, is monumental as far as Bible prophecy is concerned!

Our next sign fulfills another prediction of Scripture with respect to the nation of Israel in the last days. Not only will they exist, they will be in the spotlight of the world with all eyes upon them.

SIGN 6

Israel Will be
in the World's Spotlight

Though often missed, our sixth sign of the end is significant as well as miraculous.

The Bible says that not only will the Jews exist at the time of the end, return to their ancient homeland, establish a modern state, as well as unite the city of Jerusalem under their rule, they will also be in the world's spotlight. Consider what the Lord stated in the Book of Zechariah.

> I am about to make Jerusalem a cup that brings dizziness to all the surrounding nations; indeed, Judah will also be included when Jerusalem is besieged. Moreover, on that day I will make Jerusalem a heavy burden for all the nations, and all who try to carry it will be seriously injured; yet all the peoples of the earth will be assembled against it (Zechariah 12:2-3 NET).

Let's consider what is precisely stated here.

First, Jerusalem will be a burden for "all the surrounding nations." This tells us that they have become in the crosshairs of the various nations in their region.

But there is much more than this. We then read that, "all the peoples of the earth" will assemble against Israel.

So, they do not merely exist, and have problems with the nations that surround them, they will be at the center of events in our world! In fact, eventually all nations will gather together to seek their destruction.

THE INVASION OF EZEKIEL 38 AND 39

Another illustration, that Israel will be in the spotlight of the world, concerns the predicted invasion recorded in Ezekiel 38 and 39. Rather than being unnoticed by the world, there will be a number of nations that will invade Israel in the last days, as well as other nations issuing a protest to this invasion. In fact, there are at least seven nations mentioned in the invasion as well as several others who protest the invasion.

Among other things, this tells us that Israel, in the last days, will be conspicuous in the eyes of the world.

THE CAMPAIGN OF ARMAGEDDON

We should also include the famous battle, or campaign, of Armageddon. We read about this in the Book of Revelation.

Then the sixth angel poured out his bowl on the great Euphrates River, and it dried up so that the kings from the east could march their armies toward the west without hindrance. And I saw three evil spirits that looked like frogs leap from the mouths of the dragon, the beast, and the false prophet. They are demonic spirits who work miracles and go out to all the rulers of the world to gather them for battle against the Lord on that great judgment day of God the Almighty.

> Look, I will come as unexpectedly as a thief! Blessed are all who are watching for me, who keep their clothing ready so they will not have to walk around naked and ashamed." And the demonic spirits gathered all the rulers and their armies to a place with the Hebrew name Armageddon (Revelation 16:12-16 NLT).

The word Armageddon is a transliteration of the Hebrew "mountain of Megiddo." This refers to a geographical area in Israel where major battles have been previously fought. This includes those of the Judge Deborah, as well as Napoleon.

In this passage, we discover that the armies from the east come to this place to do battle. In other words, this particular territory in Israel will be the scene of a huge war. The fact that it will take place in the land of Israel is another indication that this tiny nation is certainly in the spotlight as far as the world is concerned.

Indeed, of all the places on the earth where this last campaign could have taken place, it is fascinating to observe that it takes place in the land to which the Jews have returned, Israel.

ISRAEL IS PRESENTLY IN THE SPOTLIGHT

Of course, the nation of Israel, in the spotlight of the world, is exactly what we see today. In fact, it seems that this small country Israel is never out of the headlines. They are high-profile as far as the world is concerned. From the Bible, we know that this will continue until the time of the Lord's return.

To sum up, these passages which we have considered predict that Israel will not live in obscurity. Indeed, after their return to the land of promise, the country will live in the spotlight of the world.

In other words, they will never be able to dwell in their land, with any lasting peace, until the Lord Himself comes and establishes it.

GOD WILL FIGHT FOR THEM

While the entire world will be against them in the last days, we must remember that they will have someone watching over them, protecting them, and eventually destroying their enemies—God Himself. The right perspective was stated long ago by the Apostle Paul.

What then shall we say about these things? If God is for us, who can be against us? (Romans 8:31 NET).

The answer, of course, is nobody.

THE RESULT: THE NATIONS WILL KNOW THAT THE LORD IS GOD

Once more we emphasize, though hated, outnumbered, and marked for destruction, Israel will again, miraculously survive through this coming period of Great Tribulation. Indeed, the Lord Himself has stated the eventual outcome of all of these threats against Israel.

I will display my majesty among the nations. All the nations will witness the judgment I have executed, and the power I have exhibited among them. Then the house of Israel will know that I am the Lord their God, from that day forward (Ezekiel 39:21,22 NET).

So, while it would seem like all is lost for Israel, such will not be the case. The Lord will eventually overcome their enemies, and in the process, be glorified by the entire world.

Consequently, this tiny nation of Israel, in the daily spotlight of the world, is certainly something that the Bible assumes will happen in the "last days."

SUMMARY TO SIGN 6: ISRAEL WILL BE IN THE SPOTLIGHT OF THE WORLD

It's one thing to predict Israel will exist at the end of time, its ancient enemies will be destroyed, that the nation will return to its homeland and form a modern state, and that the city of Jerusalem would be reunited.

However, to predict that it would be in the spotlight of the world is another seemingly impossible prediction. Yet, as we have seen, this too has come to pass. Amazingly, it seems that the entire world is against Israel.

In the Book of Zechariah, we are told that at the time of the end, the entire world will indeed be against them.

Furthermore, we also discover two huge skirmishes which will eventually take place on their soil.

First, it is the invasion of seven or eight nations, from the north, south, east, and west, as recorded in Ezekiel 38,39. These armies will be destroyed by the Lord Himself once they enter the Promised Land.

Second, there is the well-known campaign of Armageddon that we read about in the Book of Revelation. The armies gather at the "mountain of Megiddo." This location is also in Israel.

Hence, we have another sign of the end of our age—Israel constantly in the headlines. Indeed, you cannot have the entire world rallying against a country, and two major skirmishes happening in their land, unless that country is well-known to everyone. Israel is in exactly that position.

While this hatred of Israel will lead to a final campaign by their enemies to once-and-for-all destroy the nation, at that point, the Lord will intervene on Israel's behalf—He will once again, rescue them.

Not only will this cause the Israel to turn to the Lord in faith, it will also let all the nations of the world know that the Lord is indeed God!

Our next sign of the end will look at the constant search for peace for the inhabitants of the modern state of Israel. As we will discover, this search for peace fits perfectly with the way Scripture describes the situation of the world in the "last days."

There Will Be a Continual Search for Peace in Israel

As we have observed, the Bible says that Israel will not only exist at the time of the end, it will be back in its ancient homeland, controlling Jerusalem, as well as being in the spotlight of the world.

This brings us to our next sign—one of the main reasons as to why Israel is consistently in the headlines of the world. It is the search for peace for this country, as well as for the entire region.

We can summarize what has taken place as follows.

THE WAR OF INDEPENDENCE

Interestingly, the declaration of independence by the nation of Israel was not the result of winning a war, but instead became the cause of one! Indeed, a few hours after the declaration was made, the newly founded state of Israel was attacked by the countries of Egypt, Iraq Syria, Lebanon, Jordan, and Saudi Arabia. However, the attempt to destroy the new-born nation did not succeed.

THE 1949 ARMISTICE

The armistice of 1949 attempted to draw some temporary borders until agreements could be made between Israel and its neighbors about the exact extent of the country. Yet, to this day, there has been no agreement with respect to the precise borders of Israel.

THE UNIFICATION OF JERUSALEM IN 1967

Furthermore, when Jerusalem was reunited in 1967 after the Six Day War, the world was seemingly unanimous in its condemnation. East Jerusalem became "occupied territory" and the Jewish people "occupiers." Never mind that they only gained the land as they were about to be attacked from all sides!

This constant search for peace, since Israel has become a modern state, was anticipated by Scripture long ago. In fact, it is one of our signs that we are in the last days. We can explain it in this manner.

THE CONFIRMATION OF A PEACE COVENANT

In the Book of Daniel, we read the following prediction of a coming world ruler who will make a covenant with the Jewish people at the time of the end.

> He will confirm a covenant with many for one 'seven.' In the middle of the 'seven' he will put an end to sacrifice and offering. And at the temple he will set up an abomination that causes desolation, until the end that is decreed is poured out on him (Daniel 9:27 NIV).

This passage is crucial to understand the timing of the events of the "last days." It speaks of a ruler who will come on the scene of history at the time of the end. This personage, known as the beast, or the final Antichrist, will confirm a covenant with the Jewish people for a seven-year period. This particular event will start the prophetic clock ticking, and seven years later, Jesus Christ will return to the earth!

THE AGREEMENT IS WITH DANIEL'S PEOPLE

This covenant will be made with "many," that is, with Daniel's people—the majority of the people of the nation of Israel. The one who makes this agreement is called, "the ruler, or prince, who will come" in the previous verse.

And after the sixty-two weeks, an anointed one shall be cut off and shall have nothing. And the people of the prince who is to come shall destroy the city and the sanctuary (Daniel 9:26 ESV).

In other words, a yet-future ruler, this "coming prince," will have the authority to make this agreement with Israel.

In 1858, William Kelly explained what this verse means.

> The death of the Messiah took place long ago; the destruction of Jerusalem thirty or forty years after. After that followed a long period of desolations and wars in connection with Jerusalem. After all this, again, we have a covenant spoken of. Thus, we must examine the passage to see who makes the covenant. . . In verse 26 there is "the people of the prince who shall come," it is to this future Roman prince that verse 27 alludes. He it is that shall confirm a covenant with many, or rather with "the many;" i.e. the mass, or majority (William Kelly, *Notes on the book of Daniel,* London: G. Morrish, 1858, p. 161).

The covenant, which this future ruler will make, will evidently be some type of "peace agreement." In other words, he will supposedly guarantee Israel's safety in the land. This is consistent with what we have already seen. Israel will be in her ancient homeland but will basically have the whole world against her.

Therefore, Israel will need, and indeed welcome, the peacemaking of this future leader. In offering this agreement, this ruler will pose as a "prince of peace." Israel will accept his authority, as well as his ability to make peace.

But in the middle of that "seven," after three and one-half years, he will break the covenant. This will bring the Jewish people into the period known as "the time of Jacob's trouble" or "the Great Tribulation."

IT IS A COVENANT WITH DEATH!

Although the people of Israel will assume that this covenant will guarantee their safety, the Bible calls such agreements as a "covenant with death." We read about such an agreement in the writings of Isaiah.

> Then your covenant with death will be annulled, and your agreement with Sheol will not stand (Isaiah 28:18 ESV).

While this particular passage was speaking of a past agreement that the people of Israel had made with their enemies, the principle is certainly the same here. Having rejected Jesus as their Messiah, they turn to the man who is the essence of evil, the Antichrist, and make an agreement with him.

WILL THERE BE PEACE AND SAFETY?

The Apostle Paul had the following things to say about this "peace treaty" which will characterize the world in the last times.

> Now, brothers and sisters, about times and dates we do not need to write to you, for you know very well that the day of the Lord will come like a thief in the night. While people are saying, "Peace and safety," destruction will come on them suddenly, as labor pains on a pregnant woman, and they will not escape (1 Thessalonians 5:1-3 NIV).

This passage indicates that this period of great tribulation will suddenly come upon them when they believe all is well. In other words, it will happen when they are at peace and are feeling secure.

THE PEOPLE WILL BE DWELLING IN PEACE

The situation at this time, will be one of relative peace as Ezekiel records.

> After many days you will be called to arms. In future years you will invade a land that has recovered from war, whose

people were gathered from many nations to the mountains of Israel, which had long been desolate. They had been brought out from the nations, and now all of them live in safety (Ezekiel 38:8 NIV).

When the nation of Israel thinks that it will be at peace after making this agreement with this final Antichrist, they will discover that they have made an agreement with death and hell!

THE IMPORTANCE OF THIS SIGN

The importance of this sign cannot be overestimated. In fact, it is this agreement, this peace treaty, that starts the seven-year prophetic clock ticking. This will terminate with the return of Jesus Christ to the earth.

For all this to happen, there must be a dire need for peace in this region. This is precisely what we have seen since the modern state of Israel was reborn in 1948.

The continual lack of a lasting peace will eventually cause this treaty to be made. Furthermore, it will give Israel this false hope that they have finally achieved peace with their neighbors.

Instead, this treaty will start the countdown of the Great Tribulation period culminating in the return of Christ to the earth. Consequently, this sign, the continual search for peace, is of the utmost importance.

ISRAEL WILL ONLY HAVE PEACE WHEN THE LORD RETURNS

Though the nation of Israel will never be at peace in the last days, the Bible does indeed predict that a lasting peace is coming. The Lord predicts a time when Israel will be at peace with its neighbors.

This is what Isaiah son of Amoz saw concerning Judah and Jerusalem: In the last days the mountain of the Lord's temple will be established as the highest of the mountains; it will be exalted above the hills, and all nations will stream to it.

Many peoples will come and say, "Come, let us go up to the mountain of the Lord, to the temple of the God of Jacob. He will teach us his ways, so that we may walk in his paths." The law will go out from Zion, the word of the Lord from Jerusalem. He will judge between the nations and will settle disputes for many peoples. They will beat their swords into plowshares and their spears into pruning hooks. Nation will not take up sword against nation, nor will they train for war anymore (Isaiah 2:1-4 NIV).

However, before this time arrives, as we have seen, Israel will go through the darkest period in its history. Sadly, they will enter this period of great distress, great tribulation, when they think they have finally achieved a lasting peace.

In sum, any human-made peace for Israel will only be momentarily at best. Indeed, only the Lord Himself will be able to give the descendants of Abraham, Isaac, and Jacob the peace that they have longed for.

SUMMARY TO SIGN 7: THE CONTINUAL SEARCH FOR PEACE

What are the odds that some two thousand years after the last book of the Bible was written, the Jews, the central people in Scripture, would still exist. Furthermore, the Bible also says that they will return to their land after a second exile, recapture Jerusalem, and then remain in the world's spotlight.

Because of all of this, there is a constant drumbeat of some sort of "peace agreement" that would settle the borders, and also divide Jerusalem between the Israeli's and the Palestinians. We know from Scripture that eventually some sort of peace treaty will be made. However, the Bible calls such an agreement as "a treaty with death."

This peace treaty will be one of the keys to the events of the last days. In fact, it is this particular agreement that will start the prophetic clock ticking. Once signed, the world will have only seven more years until the Lord returns. Before His return, there will be a time of trouble such as this planet has never before seen—the Great Tribulation.

Hence, with the continual conflicts taking place in Israel, the stage is being set for this false peace to be a reality. Therefore, this particular sign of the end, like the others we have considered, is of the utmost importance.

Next, we look at *the* most important sign for the future fulfillment of Scripture—the events surrounding the Temple Mount in Jerusalem as well as the desire to build a Third Temple upon it.

Preparations Will be Made to Build the Third Temple

Of all of the signs we will look at with respect to the last days, this particular one is the most important to consider—as we move ahead toward the time of the end.

Why? It is because this sign foretells events that will culminate in the return of Christ to the earth. Indeed, as we have mentioned, Israel is God's clock. The hour hand is the nation, the minute hand is the city of Jerusalem, but the second hand is the Temple Mount.

BACKGROUND

The Bible does indeed predict another Temple will be built on the Temple Mount. Not only has it been predicted by Scripture, it has also been predicted by Bible commentators of the last two thousand years—those who have literally believed the prophecies of the Scripture.

The evidence for this is as follows.

THE TESTIMONY OF SCRIPTURE

In both the Old and New Testament, we find the anticipation of the construction of another Temple that is yet to be built. Contrary to the previous Temples, this Temple will *not* be blessed by God, because it will be built in unbelief of Him and His Word.

We can make the following observations as to what the Scripture has to say with respect to this future Temple.

THE ABOMINATION OF DESOLATION (MATTHEW 24:15)

In the last week of His life, Jesus pronounced judgment upon the city of Jerusalem, and the Temple, with the following words.

> Jerusalem, Jerusalem, you who kill the prophets and stone those sent to you, how often I have longed to gather your children together, as a hen gathers her chicks under her wings, and you were not willing. Look, your house is left to you desolate. For I tell you, you will not see me again until you say, 'Blessed is he who comes in the name of the Lord' (Matthew 23:37-39 NIV).

This must have confused Jesus' disciples because they had come to believe that He was the promised Messiah. In fact, just a few days previous on Palm Sunday, Jesus acknowledged that He was the Christ:

> As he was drawing near—already on the way down the Mount of Olives—the whole multitude of his disciples began to rejoice and praise God with a loud voice for all the mighty works that they had seen, saying, "Blessed is the King who comes in the name of the Lord! Peace in heaven and glory in the highest!" And some of the Pharisees in the crowd said to him, "Teacher, rebuke your disciples." He answered, "I tell you, if these were silent, the very stones would cry out" (Luke 21: 37-40 ESV).

In addition, Isaiah 2:1-4 tells us that the Messiah will rule from the Temple in Jerusalem.

> This is what Isaiah son of Amoz saw concerning Judah and Jerusalem: In the last days the mountain of the LORD's temple will be established as the highest of the mountains; it will

be exalted above the hills, and all nations will stream to it. Many peoples will come and say, "Come, let us go up to the mountain of the LORD, to the temple of the God of Jacob. He will teach us his ways, so that we may walk in his paths." The law will go out from Zion, the word of the LORD from Jerusalem. He will judge between the nations and will settle disputes for many peoples. They will beat their swords into plowshares and their spears into pruning hooks. Nation will not take up sword against nation, nor will they train for war anymore (Isaiah 2:1-4 NIV).

Jesus acknowledged that He was the promised Messiah, and Scripture says that the Messiah will rule from the Temple in the city of Jerusalem. But now He is talking to His disciples about the destruction of the Temple. How can this be?

We then find the disciples calling attention to the buildings.

As Jesus left the temple courtyard and was walking away, his disciples came to him. They proudly pointed out to him the temple buildings. Jesus said to them, "You see all these buildings, don't you? I can guarantee this truth: Not one of these stones will be left on top of another. Each one will be torn down" (Matthew 24:1-2 God's Word)

This must have really confused them. Consequently, after they walked from the Temple Mount to the Mount of Olives, they had some questions that needed to be answered.

As Jesus was sitting on the Mount of Olives, the disciples came to him privately. "Tell us," they said, "when will this happen, and what will be the sign of your coming and of the end of the age (Matthew 24:3 NIV).

Jesus had spoken of the Temple being made desolate. Consequently, the disciples wanted a specific sign of His coming. Jesus gave them the answer.

So when you see the abomination of desolation spoken of by the prophet Daniel, standing in the holy place (let the reader understand), then let those who are in Judea flee to the mountains. Let the one who is on the housetop not go down to take what is in his house, and let the one who is in the field not turn back to take his cloak. And alas for women who are pregnant and for those who are nursing infants in those days! Pray that your flight may not be in winter or on a Sabbath. For then there will be great tribulation, such as has not been from the beginning of the world until now, no, and never will be. And if those days had not been cut short, no human being would be saved. But for the sake of the elect those days will be cut short (Matthew 24:15-22 ESV).

Jesus spoke of the "abomination of desolation" as *the* sign that would signal the period of "Great Tribulation." We can make the following conclusions from His Words.

1. Jesus was asked for a *specific* sign regarding His return. He gave a definite sign—the abomination of desolation. In other words, He considered Daniel's prophecy as something which was yet to be fulfilled at some time in the future.

2. The abomination of desolation concerns the Temple and its services. The phrase "Holy Place" is a technical term for the Temple.

3. He referred His listeners to the Prophet Daniel who, on three occasions, wrote of a future defiling of the Temple.

4. It is important to realize that Jesus' prophecy was *not* fulfilled with the literal destruction of Jerusalem in A.D. 70. The abomination of desolation has *not yet* occurred.

5. Therefore, the sign of His return revolves around a functioning Temple. Since there is no Temple presently standing, the logical conclusion is that another Temple needs to be built.

THE MAN OF SIN SITS IN THE TEMPLE OF GOD (2 THESSALONIANS 2:3,4)

Another passage of Scripture that anticipates a future Temple is found in Paul's second letter to the Thessalonians. We read.

> Don't let anyone deceive you in any way, for that day will not come until the rebellion occurs and the man of lawlessness is revealed, the man doomed to destruction. He will oppose and will exalt himself over everything that is called God or is worshiped, so that he sets himself up in God's temple, proclaiming himself to be God (2 Thessalonians 2:3,4 NIV).

Several things from this passage add to our knowledge of these future events.

1. Before Jesus Christ returns, there will be a person coming on the scene of history known as the "Man of Sin" or "Man of Lawlessness." He is the "final Antichrist."

2. This man had not yet appeared at the time of Paul's' writing to the Thessalonians (around A.D. 50).

3. The identity of this "man of sin" will be known when he performs an act of abomination in the Temple. He will actually claim to be God while in the Temple itself.

4. This act defines what Jesus referred to as the "abomination of desolation."

5. From the time of Paul's writing, until the destruction of the Second Temple, this event did *not* occur.

6. For this event to occur in the future, another Temple needs to be built.

THE FALSE PROPHET WILL GIVE LIFE TO THE IMAGE OF THE FINAL ANTICHRIST (REVELATION 13:11-15)

The final Antichrist has a cohort known as the "second beast" or the "false prophet." This false prophet gives life to an image of the beast causing the inhabitants of the earth to worship the beast, and his image. The Bible says.

> Then I saw another beast coming up from the earth. He had two horns like a lamb, but was speaking like a dragon. He exercised all the ruling authority of the first beast on his behalf, and made the earth and those who inhabit it worship the first beast, the one whose lethal wound had been healed. He performed momentous signs, even making fire come down from heaven in front of people and, by the signs he was permitted to perform on behalf of the beast, he deceived those who live on the earth. He told those who live on the earth to make an image to the beast who had been wounded by the sword, but still lived. The second beast was empowered to give life to the image of the first beast so that it could speak, and could cause all those who did not worship the image of the beast to be killed (Revelation 13:11-15 NET).

From this passage, we learn more things about the final Antichrist and the coming Temple.

1. This incident further illustrates Paul's words in Thessalonians about the "abomination which causes desolation." The next Temple is defiled by this man of sin who declares himself to be God, and then has his image placed in the Holy of Holies.

2. Consequently, we need not restrict Paul's words to the physical presence of the final Antichrist himself in the Temple. It is an image of the Antichrist that is erected there. The second beast, the "false prophet," who commanded the image to be made, then commanded the people to worship this image of the "first beast." Those who do not worship the beast, or his image, will be put to death. In other words, this act of abomination will cause their desolation.

Therefore, Jesus' reference to the abomination of desolation is fully illuminated by what John says as recorded in the Book of Revelation.

3. This is another indication that another Temple needs to be built since the erection of an image of the final Antichrist has never occurred in history.

THE COMMAND TO MEASURE THE TEMPLE (REVELATION 11:1,2)

A final passage in the New Testament that speaks of a future Temple is also found in the Book of Revelation. It reads as follows.

> I was given a reed like a measuring rod and was told, "Go and measure the temple of God and the altar, with its worshipers. But exclude the outer court; do not measure it, because it has been given to the Gentiles. They will trample on the holy city for 42 months" (Revelation 11:1,2 NIV).

John is told to measure the Temple. He must be referring to a future Temple for the following reasons.

1. It is generally agreed among scholars that John wrote the Book of Revelation at the end of his life (around A.D. 90). If this be the case, then he had to be referring to a Temple that was to be built in the future, for the Second Temple was destroyed in A.D. 70.

2. Even if Revelation was composed before the destruction of the Second Temple, chapter eleven refers to events that are still future. Indeed, the surrounding events of the measuring of the Temple in verses 1 and 2 (the appearance of the two witnesses, the existence of the man of sin, the death and resurrection of these two witnesses, the great earthquake in Jerusalem, and the appearance of the Ark of the Covenant in heaven) are still future. None of these predicted events have happened yet. Hence, the Temple John was told to measure is *yet* to be built.

THE OLD TESTAMENT

This scenario fits well with certain passages in the Old Testament which speak of a Temple that is dishonored. Indeed, there are four passages in the Old Testament, three in the Book of Daniel, and one in Isaiah, that speak of the defiling of a future Temple.

PASSAGE 1: SOMEONE WILL CONFIRM A COVENANT WITH ISRAEL (DANIEL 9:27)

The prophet was told the precise time that this would happen.

> He will confirm a covenant with many for one 'seven.' In the middle of the 'seven' he will put an end to sacrifice and offering. And at the temple he will set up an abomination that causes desolation, until the end that is decreed is poured out on him (Daniel 9:27 NIV).

This passage tells us the following.

1. The coming man of sin will make a covenant with the Jewish people for seven years. Evidently this will involve a "peace agreement" as well as the building of the Temple, and the right to begin their sacrifices.

2. In the middle of the seven-year period, after three and one-half years, this final Antichrist will break the covenant with Israel. He will order the sacrifices stopped, and will desecrate the Temple. This act is known as the "abomination of desolation." The desolation will consist of the attempted annihilation of the Jewish people.

PASSAGE 2: THE SANCTUARY WILL BE DEFILED (DANIEL 11:31)

A second passage is found in Daniel which speaks of a future defiling of the Temple.

> His armed forces will rise up to desecrate the temple fortress and will abolish the daily sacrifice. Then they will set up the abomination that causes desolation (Daniel 11:31 NIV).

From this particular verse, we learn the following.

1. The Temple will be defiled by a future leader and his armed forces.

2. The daily sacrifice will be abolished.

3. An abomination will be put in place of the daily sacrifices.

4. These acts will cause desolation to Jewish people.

> While this passage was initially fulfilled by Antiochus IV, it would prefigure the actions of the final Antichrist actions (see Daniel 9:27; 12:11).

In 167 B.C., Antiochus did away with the regular sacrifice and committed an abomination that caused desolation to the Jewish people. He dedicated the Holy Temple to the god Zeus, and offered a pig on its altar. Antiochus also slaughtered many Jews.

In fact, the apocryphal book of First Maccabees, written before the time of Christ, uses the same Greek phrase "the abomination of desolation" or "desolating sacrilege" to describe this event.

> Now on the fifteenth day of Chislev, in the one hundred forty-fifth year, they erected a desolating sacrilege on the altar of burnt offering. They also built altars in the surrounding towns of Judah (1 Maccabees 1:54 NRSV).

This further indicates that this phrase "the abomination of desolation" was a well-known phrase to the Jews in Jesus' day, as well as exactly what the phrase meant—the desecration of the Temple!

PASSAGE 3: THERE IS A PRECISE TIME LIMIT FOR THE RULE OF THE ANTICHRIST (DANIEL 12:5-7,11)

After these events occur, we find that there is a limited time this final Antichrist will rule. Once more we read from the writings of the prophet Daniel.

> I, Daniel, watched as two others stood there, one on each side of the river. One said to the man clothed in linen who was above the waters of the river, "When will the end of these wondrous events occur?" Then I heard the man clothed in linen who was over the waters of the river as he raised both his right and left hands to the sky and made an oath by the one who lives forever. It is for a time, times, and half a time. Then, when the power of the one who shatters the holy people has been exhausted, all these things will be finished … From the time that the daily sacrifice is removed and the abomination that causes desolation is set in place, there are 1,290 days (Daniel 12:5-7,11 NET).

We learn the following from these verses.

1. This passage again tells us that the daily sacrifice will be taken away.

2. In addition, it is reiterated that an abomination that causes desolation is placed in the Temple.

3. These events will be the work of the future Antichrist.

4. The time frame in which this man of sin will rule is very specific. It is 1290 days, or time, times and half a time—three and one-half years. His power will then be shattered.

5. Once this time period has been completed, the kingdom of God will come to the earth!

PASSAGE 4: THERE ARE UNACCEPTABLE SACRIFICES OFFERED TO GOD (ISAIAH 66:1-4)

The prophet Isaiah also seems to have been speaking of the Third Temple when he recorded God saying.

> This is what the LORD says: "Heaven is my throne, and the earth is my footstool. Where is the house you will build

for me? Where will my resting place be? Has not my hand made all these things, and so they came into being?" declares the LORD. These are the ones I look on with favor: those who are humble and contrite in spirit, and who tremble at my word. But whoever sacrifices a bull is like one who kills a human being, and whoever offers a lamb is like one who breaks a dog's neck; whoever makes a grain offering is like one who presents pig's blood, and whoever burns memorial incense is like one who worships an idol. They have chosen their own ways, and they delight in their abominations; so I also will choose harsh treatment for them and will bring on them what they dread. For when I called, no one answered, when I spoke, no one listened. They did evil in my sight and chose what displeases me (Isaiah 66:1-4 NIV).

Isaiah's passage tells us the following.

1. The Temple built by the Jews will not be honoring to God.

2. This passage stresses there is no need for the people to build a house for God. The Temple is no longer necessary in the plan of God.

SUMMARY OF THE BIBLICAL TEACHING

We can summarize what the Bible says about a future Temple as follows. There are certain events that are predicted which assume the Jews will control Jerusalem and the Temple Mount. These events include the forced stopping of the Temple sacrifices, and the defiling of the Holy of Holies. For these events to occur as prophesied, a new Temple must be built and functioning. There is no reason whatsoever to understand these predictions in a figurative or symbolic sense. Indeed, the next Temple is coming! Scripture demands it.

THE TESTIMONY OF PAST BIBLE COMMENTATORS

The idea that a Third Temple will be built by the Jews, in unbelief of Jesus, is not something new to our day. In fact, since the destruction of the Second Temple there have been Bible commentators who have predicted this event. We will give only a small sampling of what these Bible teachers have said.

Irenaeus (A.D. 140-202) wrote that Antichrist would sit in a rebuilt Jerusalem Temple.

> He will reign a time, times, and half a time (Daniel 7:25) [i.e. three and one-half years] and will sit in the temple at Jerusalem; then the Lord shall come from heaven and cast him into the lake of fire, and shall bring to the saints the time of reigning, the seventh day of hallowed rest, and give to Abraham the promised inheritance (Irenaeus, *Against Heresies*, Book V, Chapter 30, Paragraph 4).

The early Christian writer, Hippolytus (A.D. 220), wrote.

> Which horn (Daniel 7) shows that the one which budded is none other than the Antichrist who will restore the kingdom of the Jews . . . Christ Jesus sprung from the Hebrews; he too will be born a Jew. Christ declared His flesh to be a temple and raised it on the third day, so he (the Antichrist) will restore at Jerusalem the Temple of Stone.

Cyril of Jerusalem, writing in A.D. 360, stated the following.

> Antichrist sits in the temple of God. But what temple is spoken on? The Jewish temple. . . If he came to the Jews as the Messiah, he would surely wish to be worshipped by the Jews, that he may deceive them as much as possible, he will diligently set about building the temple, thus causing it to be believed that he is one of the family of David, who should build the temple originally reared by Solomon.

Gregory the Nazarene was a fourth century theologian, as well as the Archbishop of Constantinople. He wrote the following.

With respect to the abomination of desolation standing in the Holy Place, they say that the temple in Jerusalem will be built by Antichrist being about to be believed by the Jews to be the Messiah, and being about to establish himself and to be acknowledged as king of the whole civilized world. But he shall come for the desolation of the world; for it is "the abomination of desolation."

Sulpicius Severus, a fourth century writer, stated.

But when we enquired of him concerning the end of the age, he said to us, "that the Empire of the East should be seized on by Antichrist, who shall occupy Jerusalem as the seat and head of his kingdom—that by him the city and temple should be repaired."

John of Damascus was a seventh century Christian leader. He stated.

But he (Antichrist) shall come into the temple of God, not ours but the ancient one, that of the Jews—for he will come not to us but to the Jews.

Hence, we have a number of ancient Christian commentators writing about a future Temple which will be built in Jerusalem.

THE PREDICTIONS OF COMMENTATORS FROM THE LAST FEW CENTURIES

We also find these same types of predictions from Bible commentators living in the more recent past.

In 1861, Robert Govett wrote.

The temple in Jerusalem will be yet rebuilt by the Jews in unbelief, and be the scene of wickedness greater than has ever appeared . . . While, then, the temple had been destroyed at the date of the writing of Revelation [approximately A.D. 90], it was hereby predicted that it would be rebuilt . . . Till the Jew is brought back to his own land, and the temple and sacrifices restored, the prophetic part of the Apocalypse does not begin (Robert Govett, *Govett on Revelation*, Volume I, Miami Springs, Florida, 1981, reprint of originally published in London in 1861 titled *The Apocalypse: Expounded by Scripture*, p. 497).

We read the following prediction from Benjamin Wills Newton in 1879.

When therefore the Lord Jesus again used this well-known expression, "abomination of desolation," what could they expect but that a time should come when an Idol should again be established and worshipped in the Temple of Israel? And so it will be. There are three passages in Daniel that refer to this future scene of blasphemous idolatry in the Temple of Jerusalem. We know from various parts of Scripture that the Jews (perhaps soon) will regather themselves to Jerusalem in unbelief. We know that they will restore their Temple: and these passages in Daniel tell us into whose hands that the Temple will fall, and to what use it will be finally applied. . . and seeing that these events are expressly said to be at "the last end of the indignation" against Jerusalem and at the time "when the transgressors are come to the full," it is evident that they are to occur at a time yet future (Benjamin Wills Newton, *The Prophecy of the Lord Jesus as contained in Matthew XXIV. & XXV*, Third Edition, London: Houlston and Sons, 1879, p. 56).

Another 19th century writer, Walter Scott, had this to say.

Prophecy demands the erection of a stone temple, and the reconstruction of the Jewish polity, both secular and religious, during that deeply solemn period between the Translation (1 Thess. 4:16, 17) and the Appearing (Jude 14, 15). The Jews as a nation are restored in unbelief both on their part and on that of the friendly nation who espouse their cause (Isa. 18). They then proceed to build their temple, and restore, so far as they can, the Mosaic ritual. God is not in this Gentile movement for Jewish restoration, which is undertaken for political ends and purposes (Walter Scott, *Exposition of The Revelation* (London, England: Pickering & Inglis, 1860. p. 219)

A famous commentator on the Book of Revelation, Joseph Seiss, wrote the following concerning a future Temple.

What, then, is the implication, but that when this period is once reached, Jerusalem will have been largely repopulated by the children of its ancient inhabitants, its temple rebuilt, and its ancient worship restored (Joseph Seiss, *Lectures on the Apocalypse*, Vol. 2, p. 161, 1870).

Nathaniel West, in his 19th century commentary on Daniel, wrote the following.

That the Jews will build their Temple again is certain. Also revive their bloody sacrifices. (1) Isaiah predicts it. Isa. 66:1-4. (2) Gabriel says it will be the result of a covenant. (3) Jesus Christ predicts the "abomination," Matt. 24:15, "of which that in Daniel 8:13,14; 11:31, was the type. (4) Paul says the "Man of Sin" shall sit in the "temple of God," in the time just preceding the Second Advent, the rebuilt temple in Jerusalem. 2 Thess. 2:4. (5) John exhibits the Anti-Christ's week, the 70th, and the building of the temple, Rev. 11:1-3,7, the very time given in Isaiah 66:1-5 (6) Daniel foretells the period of the reconstruction of the converted Israel's national repentance . . . Zech. 12:10-14, 13:1. The true title of Isaiah chapter 66, and Revelation chapter 11, is *Scenes in Jerusalem under the Anti-Christ* (Nathaniel West, *Daniel's Great Prophecy*, Published by the Hope of Israel Movement, pp. 113,114, 1898).

An early 20ᵗʰ century writer put it this way.

> Students of prophecy are generally agreed that the reference
> here is to a covenant for "one week" —seven years, that this
> great ruler shall make with the Jews to restore their Temple,
> with its sacrifices and ritual; but in the middle of that time he
> will break the covenant cause the daily sacrifices to be taken
> away (Daniel 12:11), blasphemously assume the prerogatives
> of Deity, and cause his image to be set up in the Temple with
> the demand that it should be worshipped. This is to bring
> about the climax of the Great Tribulation, the "time of trou-
> ble" referred to in Daniel 12:1 and elsewhere called the time
> of Jacob's trouble (Jeremiah 30:7), and will ultimately result
> . . . in the War of Armageddon, which will be the immedi-
> ate precursor to the coming of Christ (F.J. Horsefield, *The
> Return of the King*, Fifth Edition, Good Books Corporation,
> Harrisburg, Pa., 1920, p. 79).

The list goes on and on. Clearly, many Christians, for the last two
thousand years, have taught that a Third Temple will be built in unbelief of Jesus before the Lord returns to the earth, and sets up His everlasting kingdom. Accordingly, for this Temple to be built, the Jews will
have returned to their ancient homeland and have taken control over
the entire city of Jerusalem.

WHAT SHOULD WE EXPECT TO SEE BASED UPON WHAT THE BIBLE PREDICTS?

When we examine everything that the Scripture has to say about the
Jews, Jerusalem, and the coming Temple, we can make a number of
observations as to what we should expect to see in the future.

THE KEY PASSAGE!

The key is what we read about in the Book of Daniel. Indeed, Daniel
12:11 tells us that once the daily sacrifice has been removed, and the

abomination that causes desolation takes place, it is 1,290 days until the kingdom of God comes to the earth.

> From the time that the daily sacrifice is removed and the abomination that causes desolation is set in place, there are 1,290 days (Daniel 12:11 NIV).

Once the sacrifices are stopped, and the abomination that causes desolation takes place, then 1,290 days, or three and one-half years later, the Lord Jesus returns to the earth! Consequently, we can see how important is this entire subject of the Third Temple.

NINE THINGS MUST BE IN PLACE

For these events to literally occur, there must be at least nine things in place. They include the following.

1. The Jews Must Still Exist in the Last Days

2. They Will Have Returned to Their Ancient Homeland After Being Scattered Worldwide

3. They are an Actual Nation/State

4. Their Territory Includes East Jerusalem: The Temple Mount

5. They are in Their Land in Unbelief of Jesus

6. They Will Have a Functioning Temple

7. The Temple Will be Built upon the Same Site Where the Previous Temples Stood

8: Israel Will Have Authority Over the Temple Mount

9. The Sacrifices Will be Taking Place

Each of these nine things must be in place before this event can happen.

We will consider them one at a time.

ASSUMPTION 1: THE JEWS MUST STILL EXIST IN THE LAST DAYS

The Scripture assumes that the Jews will still exist in the "last days." In fact, as we have already observed in Sign 1, the Bible contains numerous references of the Jews existing at the time of the end. For example, we read the following in the Book of Daniel.

> At that time Michael, the great prince who protects your people, will arise. There will be a time of distress such as has not happened from the beginning of nations until then. But at that time your people—everyone whose name is found written in the book—will be delivered (Daniel 12:1 NIV).

Daniel's people, the Jews, will still exist when the "last days" arrive.

ASSUMPTION 2: THEY WILL HAVE RETURNED TO THEIR ANCIENT HOMELAND

Not only will these descendants of Abraham, Isaac, and Jacob still exist, they will return to their ancient homeland.

> The Lord spoke to Jeremiah. "The Lord God of Israel says, 'Write everything that I am about to tell you in a scroll. For I, the Lord, affirm that the time will come when I will reverse the plight of my people, Israel and Judah,' says the Lord. 'I will bring them back to the land I gave their ancestors and they will take possession of it once again'" (Jeremiah 30:1-3 NET).

The specific promise given here is that the Lord will bring them back to their land where they will take possession of it once again.

ASSUMPTION 3: THEY WILL BE AN ACTUAL NATION/STATE

These returning Jews will have formed a modern state. In other words, they will be a recognized political entity with a governing body, a military and a land with specific borders.

ASSUMPTION 4: THEIR TERRITORY WILL INCLUDE EAST JERUSALEM: THE TEMPLE MOUNT

The nation of Israel will be in control of East Jerusalem where the Temple Mount stands. In truth, to build a Temple on the Temple Mount, they must have control of this geographic area.

As we have already noted, in 1948, when Israel became a modern state, East Jerusalem and the Temple Mount were not under their control. In fact, the city of Jerusalem was divided in half with the Temple Mount under the control of Transjordan.

Careful Bible students predicted there would have to be another war in which the Israelis would capture East Jerusalem and the Temple Mount. This took place in 1967—the Six Day War. The city was then united, the Temple Mount became under the control of the Israelis.

ASSUMPTION 5: THEY WILL BE IN THEIR LAND IN UNBELIEF OF JESUS

At this time, as a nation, they will be in unbelief of Jesus as their Messiah. Indeed, the fact that they will build a Temple shows that the people have not accepted the sacrifice which Jesus made upon the cross.

The Temple and its sacrifices pointed to the coming of the Messiah and His death. Once Jesus died for the sins of the world the Temple was no longer necessary. Hence, constructing a Temple is a denial of Jesus as the Christ.

Let us not miss the fact that each of these five assumptions of Scripture are in place. There are now four that remain.

ASSUMPTION 6: THEY WILL HAVE A FUNCTIONING TEMPLE

This one is rather obvious. To offer sacrifices there must be a Third Temple that is built and functioning. As we shall see, preparations are now being made for this to happen.

ASSUMPTION 7: THE TEMPLE WILL BE BUILT UPON THE SAME SITE WHERE THE PREVIOUS TEMPLES STOOD

This means the original location of the Temple, on the Temple Mount, will be discovered. There is only one place in which the Jews can build the Third Temple—the exact location where the previous Temples had stood.

Indeed, this is the spot that the Lord directed the first Temple to be built. The Second Temple was built upon exactly the same spot. Someday that location will be discovered and when the circumstances allow, a Third Temple will be built.

ASSUMPTION 8: ISRAEL WILL HAVE COMPLETE AUTHORITY OVER THE TEMPLE MOUNT

Not only does the territory of Israel include East Jerusalem, the nation must have authority over the Temple Mount. The Temple Mount today, though in the territory of Israel, is actually under the control of Islam. This authority was given back to them some ten days after the Temple Mount was liberated by the Israelis in 1967. Hence, Muslims are the presently the custodians of the Mount. According to Scripture, that will change someday.

ASSUMPTION 9: THE SACRIFICES WILL BE TAKING PLACE

Finally, to stop the sacrifices, it is assumed that they have already started. For this to happen, the previous eight assumptions, that we have just considered, must all be in place.

In sum, nine things must be in place for the sacrifices in the Temple to be stopped, and the abomination of desolation to occur. Miraculously, five of them have been literally fulfilled. The preparations are now being made for these final four things to take place. As always, the predictions made in the Bible, the Word of God, come true!

MODERN DAY PREPARATIONS TO BUILD A THIRD TEMPLE

We also find that there are modern day preparations to build the Third Temple. The following statement comes from the website of a group of Jews known as the Temple Institute.

> SHALOM AND WELCOME to the official website of the TEMPLE INSTITUTE in Jerusalem, Israel. The Temple Institute is dedicated to every aspect of the Holy Temple of Jerusalem, and the central role it fulfilled, and will once again fulfill, in the spiritual wellbeing of both Israel and all the nations of the world. The Institute's work touches upon the history of the Holy Temple's past, an understanding of the present day, and the Divine promise of Israel's future. The Institute's activities include education, research, and development. The Temple Institute's ultimate goal is to see Israel rebuild the Holy Temple on Mount Moriah in Jerusalem, in accord with the Biblical commandments (templeinstitute.org).

The expressed desire of the Temple Institute, along with other Jews presently living in Israel, is to build a Third Temple on the Temple Mount.

THE SACRED VESSELS AND THE VESTMENTS

On their website, the Temple Institute has a section on the sacred vessels and vestments that will be used in the Third Temple. They state the following:

> The Temple Institute has likewise called upon Israel's finest craftsmen and artisans, and enlisted them in the historical task of recreating the sacred vessels and vestments. Every vessel produced by the Temple Institute is done in accordance with the precise instructions that were first handed down by G-d to Moses. The vessels you are about to view are all fit and ready for use in the Holy Third Temple, *may it be built speedily, and in our days!* (templeinstitute.org).

Hence, this organization is not only planning to build a Third Temple when circumstances permit, they have already crafted all the necessary vessels, and created all the vestments, that are to be used once the Temple is built.

In 2014, the Temple Institute launched the following campaign to raise money for architectural drawings for the soon-to-be-built Temple as the following article states:

The Temple Institute, an organization in Jerusalem which works toward the rebuilding of the Third Temple, began a revolutionary campaign on Sunday to literally rebuild the Third Temple—through the power of crowdfunding. Headlines under the title, "Don't make history. Make the future. Build the Third Temple," the campaign promises that this generation of children is "ready" to see the center of Jewish worship rebuilt, once and for all.

However, the Temple Institute's campaign aims to bring these speculations to their practical fruition.

"Now is time for one of its most ambitious projects yet: completing architectural plans for the actual construction, fusing ancient texts and modern technology," the campaign's description states. "While strictly adhering to the religious requirements set forth in Biblical texts, the Third Temple will also be equipped with every modern amenity: full computerization, underground parking, temperature control, elevators, docks for public transportation, wheelchair access, and much more."

Obviously, this group is serious about constructing the Third Temple.

These are just some of the modern-day preparations that have been made with respect to building a Third Temple. Indeed, there is so much more that could be said. Our book, *The Jews, Jerusalem, and the Coming Temple*, goes into great detail explaining the Temple past, what is happening today, as well as the Temple in the future.

Hence, the preparations to build the Third Temple is indeed *the* sign which we all want to keep our eyes upon as we draw nearer to the coming of the Lord.

SUMMARY TO SIGN 8: THE PREPARATIONS TO BUILD THE THIRD TEMPLE

The return of the Jews to their ancient homeland has set the stage for the time of the end. The fact that they have returned in unbelief also fulfills what the Bible has predicted.

With Jerusalem united by the Israelis in 1967, and the capturing of the territory of the Temple Mount, the stage is set to fulfill one of the most important signs of the end times—the building of a Third Temple.

In fact, the Bible, in both testaments, speaks of this future Temple being built. Furthermore, when the sacrifices are stopped in this newly built Temple, and then some abominable object is placed in its Holy of Holies, we are told that the Lord will return some 1,290 days later!

In sum, events that take place on the Temple Mount, and the Third Temple, will usher in the Second Coming of Jesus Christ to the earth. This is why we have emphasized that this particular sign is the most important of all the ones that are yet to be fulfilled. Indeed, the Temple Mount is truly the "second hand" on God's prophetic clock.

Our next sign will also deal with the nation Israel and a predicted "last days" invasion of the country as predicted by the prophet Ezekiel some 2,500 years ago.

In the Last Days, Certain Specified Nations Will Invade Israel (Ezekiel 38,39)

The ninth "Sign of the End" is one of the most fascinating to consider—the "last days" invasion of the Holy Land which is predicted by the prophet Ezekiel. It is fascinating because of all the separate parts that have to come together to make it a reality. As we will discover, it is indeed amazing to see all the pieces of this puzzle develop right before our very eyes!

To understand this invasion, we must first look at the overall context in the Book of Ezekiel, which sets the stage for this predicted event.

THE BACKGROUND OF THE BOOK OF EZEKIEL

Ezekiel was forcibly taken to Babylon about 606 B.C. in the first deportation by King Nebuchadnezzar of Babylon. Though he was a priest in Jerusalem, the Lord called him to be a prophet in Babylon to minister to those who had been deported with him.

During their exile, the news came that the city of Jerusalem and the Temple had been destroyed. As can be imagined, this devastated the people. Later, Ezekiel would remind those in exile that they were scattered because of their sin. He recorded the Lord saying the following to them.

> And the nations will know that the people of Israel went into exile for their sin, because they were unfaithful to me. So I hid my face from them and handed them over to their enemies, and they all fell by the sword. I dealt with them according to their uncleanness and their offenses, and I hid my face from them (Ezekiel 39:23-24 NIV).

The people in exile in Babylon had many questions. Did not God promise that their land was theirs forever? What would their future now be? Would they ever see their homeland again?

While the prophet Jeremiah predicted the return of the exiles after a seventy-year captivity, Ezekiel looked beyond the present captivity to the time of the end—the final restoration of Israel to its ancient homeland. When this restoration to their land would occur, the people would never again be removed.

In the Book of Ezekiel, from Chapter 36 verse 22 through Chapter 39, we find an emphasis upon the future restoration of the nation of Israel. We discover that Israel will *not* remain under God's judgment forever.

Indeed, the Lord had set this nation apart as His special people, and for the sake of His holy name, He will eventually fulfill all of His promises to them. These are words of restoration and hope!

A BRIEF SUMMARY OF CHAPTERS 36:22 THROUGH CHAPTER 39

Before we get to the specifics of this particular prophecy, a brief summary of Chapter 36 verse 22, through Chapter 39, is necessary.

36:22-24 In these verses the Lord emphasizes that this final return to their ancient homeland will be for His sake, not theirs. Israel has profaned His holy reputation. The Lord will right that wrong by supernaturally working with the nation at the time of the end.

36:24-37 The Lord then promises that He will eventually restore the nation spiritually. In other words, they will turn to Him in faith,

confessing their national sins. This will also lead to their material prosperity. At this time, the Messiah, whom we now know as the Lord
Jesus, will rule over His people in the Promised Land. The Lord again
emphasizes that this will be for His sake that He does this, not theirs.

37:1–8 Before this final return, and spiritual restoration, takes place,
there will be a number of events which will occur.

In the vision of verses 1 and 2, Ezekiel saw the dry bones of Israel and
Judah in a valley. He was ordered to prophesy to the bones that they
would come to life. The first time he prophesied, the sinews, flesh, and
then skin came upon the bones. In other words, the scattered bones
came together. Yet, there was no life in them.

37:9–14 The next time Ezekiel prophesied to the wind, or to the
breath. At this time, the breath came into the bodies and they lived.

The Lord then explained what this vision meant. It pictured the eventual national restoration of Israel, all twelve tribes (verses 11–14). First
there would be the restoration of the people into their land. Once
there, they would eventually become spiritually alive with all twelve
tribes restored.

37:15–23 Furthermore, Ezekiel was next commanded to take two
sticks, one representing the two tribes of Judah, and the other the ten
tribes of Israel. By holding them end to end, he joined them into one
stick. This signified that the two kingdoms, torn apart in the days of
Rehoboam, would one day be reunited. This reuniting will take place
at the time of the return of the king, the Messiah, who would rule over
them.

37:24–28 The Greater Son of David, the Lord Jesus, would be the
King of Israel. The people would obey Him. God would then make an
everlasting covenant of peace with them, and a future Temple would be
set in their midst. This Temple is outlined in chapters 40-48.

This should not be confused with the Temple we just mentioned in our previous sign. That Third Temple will be built in unbelief of Jesus. There will be a Temple built after that—a Temple in which the presence of the Lord would dwell.

38:1–16 Now we arrive at the invasion of Israel. Before the coming of the Messiah, God will lure a personage named Gog and his allies, about seven or eight nations, to gather their troops against Israel (verses 1–6). The ancient names of these nations are listed for us. This coalition will move against the land of Israel from all directions.

38:17–23 Then the forces of Gog will swarm over the land. However, once in the land they will experience the wrath of God. The Bible says that the land will be terribly shaken by a great earthquake. Gog's army will be petrified by the events that transpire. This includes pestilence, bloodshed, torrential rain, and large hailstones.

The destruction of the enemies of the people of the Lord reminds us of the His promise recorded in Isaiah 54:17: "No weapon formed against you shall prosper.... This is the heritage of the servants of the Lord." Indeed, the Lord Himself will destroy these armies!

39:1–6 The armies of this evil personage Gog will meet their utter destruction on the mountains of Israel. None of them will survive.

39:7-8 The Lord will vindicate His holy name at that time.

39:9,10 The weapons of Gog, strewn on the mountains, will provide fuel for seven years.

39:11–16 Burial of the dead bodies will take place in the Valley of Hamon Gog (Gog's multitude), east of the Dead Sea. The task will require seven months.

39:17–20 The dead bodies of the horses and riders will provide a great feast for birds and beasts of prey.

39:21–24 In that day, the Gentiles shall know that Israel's exile was not because God was unable to prevent it but because their sin demanded it.

39:25–29 These verses tell us that Israel's restoration will be complete. They will forget their shame and acknowledge the Lord, who will pour out His Spirit on the house of Israel.

This briefly sums up some of the highlights of these chapters. However, many questions arise. We will look at some of them now.

THE INVASION WILL TAKE PLACE AT THE TIME OF THE END

The first issue concerns the timing of the invasion. When will it occur? Fortunately, the context tells us when this invasion will take place.

> After many days you will be called to arms. In future years you will invade a land that has recovered from war, whose people were gathered from many nations to the mountains of Israel, which had long been desolate. They had been brought out from the nations, and now all of them live in safety (Ezekiel 38:8 NET).

It will occur in the "last days." Notice two separate statements are made as to the timing, "after many days," "in the future years."

THE TESTIMONY OF PAST BIBLE COMMENTATORS

The fact that this invasion is still future has been noted by many commentators who wrote about it before the modern state of Israel was born! First, it is understood, that this return that is mentioned in Ezekiel 37 will take place in the "last days."

In commenting on Ezekiel 37:1-10, Charles Spurgeon wrote the following.

> If there be meaning in words this must be the meaning of this chapter. I wish never to learn the art of tearing God's

meaning out of his own words. If there be anything clear and plain, the literal sense and meaning of this passage; a meaning not to be spiritual or spiritualized away; must be evident that both the two and ten tribes of Israel are to be restored to their own land (Charles Spurgeon, *The C.H. Spurgeon Collection,* Metropolitan Tabernacle Pulpit).

Spurgeon, taking the language at face value, understood these events in Ezekiel 37 to be speaking of the future.

Commenting on Ezekiel 37:15-22, Bishop W.R. Nicholson made the following observations.

Anything more conclusive than this is it not possible to put into language, or even to conceive of. Both divisions of Israel are expressly mentioned, Judah and his companions and Ephraim and his companions; they shall be taken "from among the heathen (the nations)," and be gathered "on every side" (out of all the nations); they shall be brought into their own land, the land upon the mountains of Israel," and in that land the two divisions shall be made "one nation," and never more shall they become "two nations," or be divided into "two kingdoms;" the reference being the rebellion of the ten tribes under Rehoboam, Solomon's successor, and their secession from his authority under Jeroboam. Reference to literal Israel could not be more demonstrated, nor the fact of their restoration to Palestine more positively stated . . . both houses of Israel are *yet to be* (italics his) gathered out of all the nations to their own land (Bishop W.R. Nicholson "The Gathering of Israel," in Nathaniel West, *Second Coming of Christ, Premillennial Essays of the Prophetic Conference,* Chicago, Fleming Revell, 1879, pp. 224,225).

Notice how each of these commentators made the point that, "if words mean anything," "if language means anything," then we have a prediction of the twelve tribes of Israel being restored to their ancient homeland at some time in the future.

We again remind the reader, that when these commentators wrote these things, it was eighteen centuries after the Jews had been removed from their homeland, and were scattered throughout the world. Indeed, there was no state of Israel, and no movement for the nation to return to their ancient homeland.

Yet they made it clear that the Bible predicted that the Jewish people would return to their ancient homeland. As we have seen, they have indeed!

To sum up, in the last days, the descendants of Abraham, Isaac, and Jacob will return to their ancient homeland. This is the background for the coming invasion.

WHO WILL INVADE ISRAEL?

The invaders are listed for us by name in Chapter 38. The names given were, of course, the names of the geographical areas at the time of Ezekiel. The modern names for these areas would be the following.

Ancient Name	Modern Equivalent
Rosh	Russia (or Chief)
Magog	Central Asia
Meshech and Tubal	Turkey (also southern Russia and Iran)
Persia	Iran
Cush	Northern Sudan, Ethiopia
Put	Libya

Gomer	Turkey (Armenia)
Beth-togarmah	Turkey
Many peoples	Other Islamic nations (possibly Iraq)

This is the general consensus as to what these ancient names represent in modern times—though some of the precise identifications are questionable.

CONCLUSIONS WE CAN MAKE FROM INTERPRETING THIS PROPHECY LITERALLY

There are a number of conclusions that we can make by merely looking at these three chapters of Ezekiel, 37-39, and noting what will occur. This will be highly instructive.

THE PREDICTED SITUATION IN ISRAEL BEFORE THE INVASION

According to Scripture, there are ten specific things that will be in place before this invasion can occur. They are as follows.

Prediction 1. The nation of Israel will exist in the last days.

Prediction 2. They will have been scattered throughout the world.

Prediction 3. However, at some future time, the people of Israel will return to their ancient homeland.

Prediction 4. The people will return after being away for a long time.

Prediction 5. Their returning numbers will be large, like an army.

Prediction 6. The land to which they will return, will have been decimated by war.

Prediction 7. Though they return to a desolate land, once back in the land they will create great wealth.

Prediction 8. When they return, they will form a state (some political entity).

Prediction 9. Their borders will include the mountains of Israel.

Prediction 10. They will come back in unbelief in Jesus as their Messiah.

THE FULFILLMENT OF THE TEN THINGS WHICH MUST BE IN PLACE

Let us now look at the fulfillment of these ten predictions which must be fulfilled before the invasion occurs.

FULFILLMENT 1: THE NATION OF ISRAEL DOES INDEED EXIST IN THE LAST DAYS

As we have emphasized, this would have been a rather amazing prediction when first made. Indeed, the nation had been removed from their homeland to Babylon. Humanly speaking there was no guarantee that they would ever be able to return to their own land—let alone re-form their nation in their homeland. Yet all this has happened, not once, but twice in their history.

FULFILLMENT 2: THE PEOPLE OF THE NATION HAD BEEN SCATTERED THROUGHOUT THE WORLD

This has been literally fulfilled. There is scarcely a nation that does not have, or has not had, descendants of Abraham, Isaac, and Jacob.

FULFILLMENT 3: THEY DID RETURN TO THEIR ANCIENT HOMELAND

This also has been literally fulfilled. Though scattered across the world, the people of Israel have returned.

FULFILLMENT 4: THE PEOPLE HAD BEEN AWAY FROM THEIR HOMELAND FOR A LONG TIME

Indeed, it was almost 1,900 years from the time Jerusalem and the Second Temple were destroyed, and the people were scattered throughout the world, that they returned to their homeland.

FULFILLMENT 5: THEY HAVE COME BACK IN LARGE NUMBERS

We find that the people have indeed returned to their ancient home-land, in the millions.

FULFILLMENT 6: THE LAND TO WHICH THEY RETURNED HAD BEEN DECIMATED BY WAR

The Promised Land did not look anything like a "land of milk and honey" when the people of Israel returned to it.

In fact, when he visited the Holy Land in the 19th century, American writer Mark Twain described it this way.

> A desolate country whose soil is rich enough, but is given over wholly to weeds... a silent mournful expanse.... a desolation.... we never saw a human being on the whole route.... hardly a tree or shrub anywhere. Even the olive tree and the cactus, those fast friends of a worthless soil, had almost deserted the country" (Mark Twain, *The Innocents Abroad*).

In 1867, we find that the Holy Land was a country that was desolate. Indeed, no humans, no vegetation.

Walking around the Holy City of Jerusalem, he was amazed at how small it was.

A fast walker could go outside the walls of Jerusalem and walk entirely around the city in an hour. I do not know how else to make one understand how small it is.

The Temple Mount was described in this manner.

> The mighty Mosque of Omar, and the paved court around it, occupy a fourth part of Jerusalem. They are upon Mount Moriah, where King Solomon's Temple stood. This Mosque is the holiest place the Mohammedan knows, outside of

Mecca. Up to within a year or two past, no Christian could gain admission to it or its court for love or money. But the prohibition has been removed (Mark Twain, *The Innocents Abroad*).

Another 19th century traveler, George Robinson, described Jerusalem as follows.

The Bazaar, or street of shops, is arched over, all dark and gloomy-the shops paltry, and the merchandise exposed for sale of inferior quality. This is the only part of Jerusalem where any signs of life are shown. But even here, around the heart, the pulsations of the expiring city are faint, almost imperceptible; its extremities are already cold and lifeless. In other quarters of the town, you may walk about a whole day without meeting with a human creature (George Robinson, *Travels in Palestine and Syria*, Volume 1, Palestine, London: Henry Colburn Publisher, 1837, pp. 116,117).

These descriptions of Jerusalem, as well as the rest of the Holy Land, were a literal fulfillment of the predictions of the Lord. Fortunately, the desolation was not to last forever.

FULFILLMENT 7: YET, ONCE BACK IN THE LAND THEY HAVE INDEED CREATED GREAT WEALTH

When one looks at the land of Israel at the beginning of the 20th century, and then compares it to what we see today, it is truly like "night and day." The desert has been built up, waste areas have been beautified. Modern Israel is indeed a wealthy country.

Interestingly, writing in 1840, Hugh McNeile predicted this based upon the Scripture.

The present condition of the land of Palestine is well known to be one of extreme barrenness and desolation; whereas it was a land of flocks and herds, a land flowing with milk and honey, the glory of all lands. In this way we recognize the literal fulfillment of that clause of the prophecy which predicts desolation; and from the next clause of the prophecy, we confidently anticipate a literal renovation of beauty and fertility, accompanied by a multiplication of beasts upon it, as well as men, for the consumption of its produce. In the present condition of the Jewish people, divided and dispersed, we recognize the literal fulfillment of those claims of prophecy which imply division and predict dispersion; and from similar clauses, similarly interpreted, we confidently anticipate a similar literal fulfillment of the promised restoration and reunion (Hugh McNeile, *Popular Lectures on the Prophecies relative to the Jewish nation*, London, J. Hatchard and Son, 1840, pp. 156,157).

His reasoning was simple. At his time, there was a literal fulfillment with respect to the desolation of the land. Based upon Scripture, he predicted a literal fulfillment of the predictions concerning the renovation of the land. While he did not live to see it, the predictions have come true. Israel today is indeed a wealthy country.

FULFILLMENT 8: THE MODERN STATE OF ISRAEL WAS FORMED

In Sign 3, we discussed the miraculous nature of the return of the people to their ancient homeland as well as the formation of the modern state of Israel.

FULFILLMENT 9: THEIR BORDERS NOW INCLUDE THE MOUNTAINS OF ISRAEL

This was not true in 1948 when the modern state of Israel was reborn. It was only in 1967, as a result of the Six-Day War, that this geographical area became under their control.

FULFILLMENT 10: THEY HAVE COME BACK IN UNBELIEF IN JESUS

The nation today has certainly not accepted Jesus as their Messiah. Indeed, many of the Jews are secular, having no form or religion whatsoever. In fact, according to Ezekiel 39, it will not be until the Lord supernaturally intervenes on their behalf, and destroys the invading armies, that the people will realize that the God of Israel is fighting for them.

SUMMARY OF THE FULFILLED PREDICTIONS OF EZEKIEL 37-39

As we look at Ezekiel 37-39, we find at least ten specific predictions concerning the situation of the country in the "last days" that have been literally fulfilled. These ten must be in place before this invasion can take place.

PROPHECIES THAT REMAIN TO BE FULFILLED

There are a number of predicted things which will happen in the future. These include events that will occur during the invasion, as well as after. For our purposes, we will consider those which will take place before, during, and after.

PREDICTION 1: SEVEN OR EIGHT NATIONS WILL INVADE ISRAEL.

While this part of the prophecy has not yet been fulfilled, we can certainly see it taking shape. Indeed, two of the nations mentioned, Russia and Iran are working together militarily.

In addition, Turkey, a member of NATO, a secular country for a century, has now become controlled by Islam. The former friendship they had with Israel is now a thing of the past.

Northern Sudan, Libya are also nations controlled by Islamic extremists as are the central Asian countries that were formerly part of the old Soviet Union.

PREDICTION 2: ISRAEL HAS SOMETHING THESE COUNTRIES WANT, AS WELL AS WHAT THEY NEED.

Something will exist in Israel that these nations desire, as well as need. This will be the reason for the invasion. This assumes what we already know—Israel is a wealthy country with a strategic location.

PREDICTION 3: NONE OF THESE NATIONS THAT ARE SPECIFICALLY MENTIONED BORDER ISRAEL (SYRIA, JORDAN, LEBANON, AND EGYPT).

We will have some things to say about this in our next sign.

PREDICTION 4: THE LEADER OF THIS COALITION, GOG, WILL DESIRE TO TAKE SOMETHING THAT DOES NOT BELONG TO HIM.

This has been the consistent behavior of the leaders of Russia in the past, as well as in the present.

PREDICTION 5: THEIR INVASION WILL RAISE A PROTEST FROM SHEBA AND DEDAN (MODERN SAUDI ARABIA AND THE GULF STATES).

Interestingly, like the nations bordering Israel, the Gulf States will not participate either in this invasion. They will however protest. Among other things, it shows that they are not aligned with the invading nations. We will discuss this further in our next "Sign of the End."

PREDICTION 6: THE PEOPLE OF THE LAND WILL BE LIVING IN RELATIVE PEACE.

While this is not the situation now in Israel, it certainly will be in the future (as we observed in Sign 7)

PREDICTION 7: THERE WILL BE NO SUPERPOWER WHO CAN OR WILL INTERVENE ON THEIR BEHALF.

This will be considered in more detail in Sign 11.

PREDICTION 8: WHEN THESE NATIONS ENTER THE PROMISED LAND, THEN GOD WILL SUPERNATURALLY INTERVENE AND COMPLETELY DESTROY THEIR ARMIES (EZEKIEL 39:2).

The God of the Bible has often displayed His mighty power in conquering nations. In this instance, their doom is inevitable once they enter into the Promised Land.

PREDICTION 9: THE LORD WILL ALSO DESTROY THE MAIN STRUCTURES IN THEIR COUNTRIES (EZEKIEL 39:6).

Not only will these invading armies be completely destroyed when they enter the Promised Land, many of the structures from the countries which sent them will also be destroyed. This will clearly be seen by all as the work of the Lord.

10. AT THAT TIME, THEY WILL BEGIN TO UNDERSTAND THE GOD OF ISRAEL IS WORKING ON THEIR BEHALF.

With all these supernatural events taking place, the people will know that the God of Israel is protecting them.

There are a few more things about this coming invasion that are worth mentioning. They include the following.

THE TURNABOUT OF IRAN AND TURKEY

One thing that should be noted is that these nations, that are predicted to attack Israel, are not necessarily the obvious choices that one would assume.

Take Iran for instance. Until the mid-1970's they were Israel's best friend in the Middle East. However, with the deposing of the Shah, and the rise of the Islamic Republic of Iran, we today find that Iran is Israel's worst enemy, as well as the major state sponsor of terrorism for the entire world. In fact, for years now, their constant drumbeat has been "death to Israel."

Turkey is a member of NATO. For one hundred years, it has been a secular county. However, with the rise of the leader Erdogan, they have slowly morphed into an Islamic state with him as dictator at the helm. In doing so, this former friend of Israel has become their sworn enemy.

The military alliance between Russia and Iran is also an oddity. In fact, never in the history of the world have these two geographic regions formed a military alliance. Never! That is, until today.

Hence, this invasion by these various countries is not something that could have been easily predicted. In fact, putting Iran and Turkey in the mix in the early 1970's would have seemed ludicrous. However, it is not ludicrous any longer!

WHAT WILL CAUSE THEM TO INVADE?

One of the questions that obviously arises concerns the specific motivation of these nations. The Bible does not say. It is tempting to try to speculate that the Golan Heights may have something to do with it.

THE CONFLICT OF THE GOLAN HEIGHTS

The Golan Heights is a disputed territory that is now part of Israel. Overlooking the Sea of Galilee, it has great strategic value.

From 1948-1967, this area was part of Syria. During the Six Day War, the Israelis captured the Golan. It remains in their possession to this day.

However, though they occupy this region, neither the United Nations, nor the United States, considers the Golan as Israeli territory. Syria, as can be imagined still claims it as theirs.

The Golan is not only strategic, it may contain something of inestimable value. Consider the following headline.

JEWISH PRESS OCTOBER 7, 2015: OIL DISCOVERED IN THE GOLAN HEIGHTS

Syrian rebels, the Islamic State (ISIS) and the Assad regime, and today that means Russia, now have another reason to capture the Golan Heights – oil. Drilling that began more than a year ago has exposed a huge find of billions of barrels of oil, but it is too early to know if the black gold can be extracted at a price that would make the oil commercially viable.

> Afek Oil and Gas chief geologist Dr. Yuval Bartov was quoted as saying: We are talking about a strata which is 350 meters thick, and what is important is the thickness and the porosity. On average in the world strata are 20-30 meters thick, so this is ten times as large as that, so we are talking about significant quantities. The important thing is to know the oil is in the rock and that's what we now know. The drilling is in the southern Golan Heights, far away from the northern border but several miles from the eastern border. Syria has claimed the entire Golan since it lost the strategic and water-rich area in the Six-Day War in 1967. If oil can be extracted, it will be a huge bonanza for Israel and an enormous reason for whoever rules in Syria, or for Hezbollah that is fighting with Assad's forces and is based in Lebanon, to launch a war on Israel. Israel uses approximately 270,000 barrels a day. Billions of barrels of oil would satisfy the country's need for a long time (Jewish Press, October 7, 2015).

If this turns out to be as it is claimed, it will add a whole new dimension to the Syrian fiasco. This is an American oil company which has seemingly discovered a huge oil field in the disputed Golan Heights, which both Israel and Syria claim this territory as theirs.

Syria is being defended not only by Russia, but also Iran and Hezbollah. These groups, along with the Americans, are fighting ISIS in Syria.

Will this be the reason for the invasion? Only time will tell.

ISIS, RUSSIA, IRAN, AND ISRAEL

One of the other important things that has happened recently is the rise of the Islamic State, or ISIS. While they are not in Bible prophecy, they certainly have had an impact with respect to setting the stage for the "last days."

How have they accomplished this? Simply put, by fighting in Syria and Iraq ISIS has caused other countries to join in the fight against them. Since the United States basically gave up on the Middle East during the Obama Administration, the Russians, Iranians, and well as the Turks have filled the vacuum. There are Russian and Iranian troops in Syria, which is on Israel's northern border, and they are there to stay.

Therefore, when the Ezekiel 38,39 invasion eventually occurs, neither country will have to come a great distance to send their troops to the Holy Land.

As we consider all the different facets of this upcoming invasion as predicted in Scripture, it is amazing to watch all the pieces of the puzzle come together.

SUMMING UP SIGN 9: THE PREDICTED INVASION OF ISRAEL IN THE LAST DAYS (EZEKIEL 38,39)

As we closely examine what the Bible says about the future of Israel in chapters 37-39 of Ezekiel, we can put together a scenario of what the world should look like in the last days, as well as look forward to a coming invasion that was prophesied.

What we should expect to see are a variety of nations uniting together against a common enemy, Israel. This tiny country has something these nations want, as well as something they need.

From the geographical description at the time of Ezekiel, we can determine this group of nations includes Russia, Iran, Turkey, Libya, Northern Sudan, as well as some of the republics in central Asia that used to make up part of the Soviet Union.

As we observed, when we simply read Chapters 37-39 of Ezekiel, we find that there are at least ten things that should be in place before this invasion occurs. Remarkably, we have discovered that all of them are presently in place.

There are also a number of things that will occur immediately before, during, as well as after this predicted invasion takes place. As we look at our world, we see the stage being set for this invasion to come about exactly as the Bible predicted!

All in all, it is amazing to see these things line up to fulfill another part of God's plan for the ages.

Our next sign, concerns other nations in the vicinity of Israel which will not participate in this coming invasion. In fact, there will be a number of countries that are conspicuous by their absence. As we will discover, these nations are also lining up today, just as Scripture predicted.

The Nations Missing from the Ezekiel 38, 39 Invasion

When we read the Bible, we should not only pay attention to what it says, we should also pay attention to what is missing. This is especially important when we consider the passage in Ezekiel 38 and 39.

We found that certain specific nations would invade Israel in the "last days." This list includes such modern countries as Iran, Turkey, Libya, Northern Sudan, Russia, and at least two of the central Asian countries— which were formerly part of the Soviet Union.

WHO IS MISSING?

What is fascinating about this list is not only who is involved, but also who is missing.

First, the nations which immediately surround Israel are not mentioned as being part of the invading force. That would include Syria, Lebanon, Jordan, and Egypt. The Gaza strip would also be included.

We also discover that Sheba and Dedan, the area of the modern-day Gulf States—Saudi Arabia, Qatar, Kuwait, Bahrain, Oman, and the United Arab Emirates, will protest this invasion. The Bible puts it this way.

> Sheba and Dedan and the merchants of Tarshish and all its leaders will say to you, 'Have you come to seize spoil? Have

you assembled your hosts to carry off plunder, to carry away silver and gold, to take away livestock and goods, to seize great spoil? (Ezekiel 38:13 ESV).

These nations do not participate in the invasion, neither do they come to the aid of Israel. Instead, they merely protest what is going on. The "merchants of Tarshish" are also mentioned as protesting. Their exact identity is disputed. Suggestions include southern Spain, Sardinia, and even Britain. It seems to be a country far across the sea who traded in metals with Israel.

SUMMARIZING WHAT IS PREDICTED IN SCRIPTURE

So, if we add up all the things that are predicted, then we can come to this conclusion: ten specific things must be in place to set the stage for the invasion, approximately seven modern countries will take part in invading Israel, four countries bordering Israel will not take part, and the six Gulf States, will protest this attack.

When we consider the totality of this coming invasion, there are about twenty-seven separate things that are predicted to occur before the armies enter the Promised Land.

WHAT DO WE PRESENTLY SEE?

What is fascinating about all of this is how much this lineup, on both sides, makes sense with our present world situation. In other words, we can see this sort of scenario actually taking place.

In fact, in our last sign, we saw the ten predictions already fulfilled that set the stage for the attack. In addition, we found that the major countries which are said to participate in this invasion—Iran, Russia, and Turkey, are already in some sort of coalition. Two of the other nations mentioned, Northern Sudan and Libya, are known for terrorism.

Furthermore, those who are said to "sit out" the invasion also make sense. Syria and Lebanon are divided by civil wars. Jordan is a moderate

Muslim nation and Egypt has recently teamed up with Israel to fight common foes—ISIS and the Muslim Brotherhood.

THE SITUATION WITH EGYPT

The lack of Egyptian participation in the invasion is profound. Given the fact that Egypt has been involved in every war with the modern state of Israel (1948, 1956, 1967, and 1973), it is all the more remarkable to predict that they would not be involved in this "last days" attack upon Israel.

However, as we have previously mentioned in Sign 2, Egypt, will have a godly future according to Scripture.

> In that day there will be an altar to the Lord in the midst of the land of Egypt, and a pillar to the Lord at its border. It will be a sign and a witness to the Lord of hosts in the land of Egypt. When they cry to the Lord because of oppressors, he will send them a savior and defender, and deliver them. And the Lord will make himself known to the Egyptians, and the Egyptians will know the Lord in that day and worship with sacrifice and offering, and they will make vows to the Lord and perform them. And the Lord will strike Egypt, striking and healing, and they will return to the Lord, and he will listen to their pleas for mercy and heal them (Isaiah 19:19-22 ESV).

There will be a glorious future for Egypt while these invading nations will meet their demise.

SUNNI MUSLIMS VERSUS SHIA MUSLIMS

In the Middle East, there are two countries vying for supremacy. They are Iran and Saudi Arabia. The Saudis are Sunni Muslims while the Iranians are Shia Muslims. These two groups have been fighting one another since the death of Muhammad.

Consequently, they will never unite in a coalition of nations—even to fight against a common enemy, Israel. Therefore, it makes sense that the Saudis, as well as the other Gulf States, would not be part of this coalition.

What is fascinating is that all of this has been predicted by Scripture. Ezekiel 38, 39 was written some 550 years before the time of Christ. Muhammad did not come on the scene until the seventh century A.D. Yet we are told specifically that the invading nations would not include this geographical area of the Gulf States.

SOME THOUGHT-PROVOKING QUESTIONS THAT NEED TO BE ANSWERED

So, we have to ask ourselves a couple of questions. What are the odds that someone writing some 2,500 plus years ago, in listing the invaders, as well as the non-invaders, would correctly state who would unite against Israel, and who would not participate?

Furthermore, before this invasion takes place, who could have precisely predicted these ten things that the Bible assumes would be in place?

It reminds us of what the Lord said through the prophet Isaiah.

> I am the Lord! That is my name! I will not share my glory with anyone else, or the praise due me with idols. Look, my earlier predictive oracles have come to pass; now I announce new events. Before they begin to occur, I reveal them to you (Isaiah 42:8,9 NET).

Indeed, it is the Lord, and He alone, who has revealed these events to us.

While we have looked at what nations bordering Israel are missing from this predicted invasion, there is also another nation conspicuous by its absence—the United States of America! Our next sign of the end will consider the possibilities as to why the USA is not involved in this drama.

No Superpower Will Intervene on Israel's Behalf When They Are Invaded (Ezekiel 38,39) Something Will Happen to the United States

---

Not only will there be certain nations in the geographical area around Israel that will not participate in the invasion of Ezekiel 38, 39, there is something else missing from this battle—there is no superpower who will rally to Israel's side.

We can make the following observations about the scenario the Bible gives.

THE EVIL THOUGHT OF GOG

The Bible explains the motivation of Gog—the leader of this "last days" coalition.

> Thus says the Lord God: On that day, thoughts will come into your mind, and you will devise an evil scheme and say, 'I will go up against the land of unwalled villages. I will fall upon the quiet people who dwell securely, all of them dwelling without walls, and having no bars or gates,' to seize spoil and carry off plunder, to turn your hand against the waste places that are now inhabited, and the people who were gathered from the nations, who have acquired livestock and goods, who dwell at the center of the earth (Ezekiel 38:10-12 ESV).

Interestingly, we see that an evil thought comes across the mind of the leader. When he has this thought, there is seemingly no hesitation on his part to carry through with his plan.

THE WEAK RESPONSE FROM NATIONS IN THE VICINITY OF ISRAEL

In fact, the only response we are told from any other nation comes from Sheba and Dedan—the modern Gulf States including Saudi Arabia. They are merely protesting. In other words, they are not intervening militarily on the side of Israel.

THERE WILL BE NO INTERVENTION BY OTHER NATIONS

Finally, as the invasion occurs, nothing is said about any nation coming to the aid of Israel. Nothing is said about any other nation protesting or wishing to send any help to Israel. To sum up, Israel is left on its own when this attack takes place.

SOMETHING WILL HAPPEN TO THE UNITED STATES

This scenario assumes that something will happen to the United States where it cannot, or will not, come to the aid of Israel. While we do not know exactly what will take place, there are a number of possible scenarios.

POSSIBILITY 1: THE UNITED STATES DOES NOT EXIST

While frightening to think of, it is possible that the US will no longer exist. Some type of nuclear attack, terrorist attack, plague, etc. could make the United States a wasteland.

Can it happen? Yes. Will it happen? Nobody really knows. However, we should not rule it out as being beyond the realm of possibilities. If the United States was not in the picture at all, this would explain why this leader, Gog, had no second thoughts about invading Israel.

POSSIBILITY 2: THE UNITED STATES DOES NOT HAVE THE CAPACITY TO GET INVOLVED

A more likely scenario is that the United States has reduced its military force to such a degree, or that it is so spread thin around the world, that it would not be possible for it to come to the aid of Israel in any meaningful way.

In other words, while possibly being willing to help, the USA would find itself in a position that it could not help the Israelis.

There could be other factors that would not allow the United States to become involved. Whatever, the case may be, the USA may be willing to help Israel, but for some unstated reason, they are not able.

POSSIBILITY 3: THE UNITED STATES IS NOT WILLING TO GET INVOLVED

Sadly, it is possible that the United States, while having some capacity to intervene on Israel's behalf, does not wish to. For whatever reason, America chooses to stay out of this battle. This would cause a horrific judgment by the Lord upon the USA.

A WARNING TO THE UNITED STATES

As we observed in Sign 2, the Bible made it clear that those nations which attempt to undermine Israel will be punished by God. We saw that five ancient peoples, the Amorites, Moabites, Amalekites, Philistines, and Ammonites, no longer exist because of their repeated attempts to destroy Israel.

This supernatural protection of Israel, promised by God, has never been rescinded. This will be particularly true in these last days with Israel back in the land, as the Bible predicted. According to Scripture, Israel must exist to the very end.

We can only hope and pray that this does not become the situation in the United States. If indeed it eventually does happen, then the United States will be judged by God. There is no doubt about this.

GOD WILL INTERVENE ON BEHALF OF ISRAEL

One final thing should be mentioned. Israel does indeed have someone who will intervene on their behalf during this invasion—it is God Himself. The Bible explains what will take place in this manner.

> As for you, son of man, prophesy against Gog, and say: 'This is what the sovereign Lord says: Look, I am against you, O Gog, chief prince of Meshech and Tubal . . . You will fall dead on the mountains of Israel, you and all your troops and the people who are with you. I give you as food to every kind of bird and every wild beast. You will fall dead in the open field; for I have spoken, declares the sovereign Lord. I will send fire on Magog and those who live securely in the coastlands; then they will know that I am the Lord' (Ezekiel 39:1,4-6 NET).

Scripture records the Lord completely destroying the invading armies. Hence, at the end of the day, we find that it is God Himself who will fight for Israel and defeat their enemies.

THE BIBLE IS ALL ABOUT ISRAEL, NOT AMERICA

In 1889, James Brookes offered a fitting summary of why we do not find America in Bible prophecy.

> The vast American republic is not mentioned distinctly in prophecy nor are the Power of Europe, except to announce their doom, while Israel is constantly before the mind of Jehovah through the sacred Scriptures. With Israel was inseparably bound up the fate of the mightiest empires of antiquity, as Egypt, Assyria, and Babylon, and so in the future, as the chosen hand for inflicting God's righteous judgments, it will become the center of His earthly government, and the source of earthly blessings to the nations when Jesus comes to reign (James Brookes, *Maranatha, The Lord Cometh*, Fleming H. Revell Company, 1889, pp. 398, 399).

Lest we forget, God has given us a timepiece, a clock for time and eternity— the nation of Israel.

SUMMING UP SIGN 11: THERE IS NO SUPERPOWER WHO WILL COME TO THE AID OF ISRAEL

One of the seemingly obvious truths about the Ezekiel 38,39 invasion is that the leader of the coalition, Gog, decides on his own to gather a number of nations to invade Israel. There is nothing whatsoever in the text that indicates that this future leader is afraid of any powerful nation intervening on the side of the Israelis.

This sign indicates that the United States, for whatever reason, will not become involved on the side of Israel in the Ezekiel 38,39 invasion.

Why this is so can only be a matter of speculation. There are a number of options.

First, the United States may no longer exist. While a terrifying thought, it certainly is not beyond the realm of possibility. There are weapons developed, as well as those which will be developed in the future, that could for all intents and purposes reduce the United States to a non-existent country. There may be other factors that render the United States to a non-superpower. We just do not know.

Second, for whatever reason, the United States is not willing to become involved. This would mean that America has turned its back on its number one ally in the Middle East, Israel. With the rise of Anti-Semitism in the world, it is certainly not beyond the realm of possibility that this may happen at some time in the future.

Third, it is possible that the United States is not able to become involved. This scenario would have America in such a weakened position, militarily and economically, that it would not be able to provide any help to its greatest ally in the region.

Each of these are distinct possibilities. Only time will tell which is correct. However, one thing seems to be certain with respect to the future of America—it will not remain a superpower forever.

However, as we observed, this does *not* mean Israel will be unprotected during this invasion. To the contrary, the Lord Himself will fight on their behalf and destroy the incoming armies. Israel will then learn a tremendous lesson—what they truly need is not the help of other countries, but rather the help of the Lord, the God of Israel, and Him alone.

There Will be a 10 Nation Confederation in Western Europe
(The Revival of the Ancient Roman Empire)

When it comes to what the Scripture has to say about the time of the end, there is one specific group of nations that it mentions as being a major player. In addition, we know the exact number of countries that will make up this group, ten, as well as where they come from—the old Roman Empire. They will play a significant role at the time of the end.

We know this because it was predicted some 2,500 years ago when the prophet Daniel interpreted the dream of King Nebuchadnezzar of Babylon! The evidence is as follows.

THE DREAM OF KING NEBUCHADNEZZAR

Nebuchadnezzar had this dream that troubled him. He was convinced that there was some meaning behind it. Therefore, he called all his magicians, soothsayers, and wise men of Babylon to tell him the dream, as well as its meaning. But they could not.

However, one of the Jewish captives that had been taken to Babylon, young Daniel, prayed to the Lord and asked Him to reveal the dream and its interpretation. The Lord answered Daniel's prayer and he was brought into the presence of the king. The Bible then explains what happened.

The king declared to Daniel, whose name was Belteshazzar, "Are you able to make known to me the dream that I have seen and its interpretation?" Daniel answered the king and said, "No wise men, enchanters, magicians, or astrologers can show to the king the mystery that the king has asked, but there is a God in heaven who reveals mysteries, and he has made known to King Nebuchadnezzar what will be in the latter days. Your dream and the visions of your head as you lay in bed are these (Daniel 2:26-28 ESV).

Indeed, "there is a God in heaven!" As we have already observed in our previous signs, God, through His prophets, tells us about future events which will take place.

In this instance, Daniel told the king that this dream had to do with the future—the "latter days." In fact, this dream charted the history of four Gentile kingdoms, from the time of Nebuchadnezzar until the coming of the kingdom of God to the earth! Hence, this dream still has tremendous significance in our day and age.

THE DREAM EXPLAINED BY THE PROPHET DANIEL

First, Daniel correctly explained to the king the contents of his dream.

You saw, O king, and behold, a great image. This image, mighty and of exceeding brightness, stood before you, and its appearance was frightening. The head of this image was of fine gold, its chest and arms of silver, its middle and thighs of bronze, its legs of iron, its feet partly of iron and partly of clay. As you looked, a stone was cut out by no human hand, and it struck the image on its feet of iron and clay, and broke them in pieces. Then the iron, the clay, the bronze, the silver, and the gold, all together were broken in pieces, and became like the chaff of the summer threshing floors; and the wind carried them away, so that not a trace of them could be found. But the stone that struck the image became a great mountain and filled the whole earth (Daniel 2:31-35 ESV).

THE MEANING OF THE DREAM

Daniel then explained the meaning of the dream to the king.

> You, O king, are the king of kings. The God of heaven has granted you sovereignty, power, strength, and honor. Wherever human beings, wild animals, and birds of the sky live—he has given them into your power. He has given you authority over them all. You are the head of gold. Now after you another kingdom will arise, one inferior to yours. Then a third kingdom, one of bronze, will rule in all the earth. Then there will be a fourth kingdom, one strong like iron (Daniel 2:37-40 NET).

There will be four successive empires that will rule. Each one will be, in some sense, inferior to the previous one which is represented by the metals on this great image. Indeed, starting with the head of gold, they will become increasingly inferior as we reach the feet and toes—silver, bronze, iron, iron mixed with clay.

On the other hand, while the material of each section of the statue decreases in value, it increases in strength. As we will see, this perfectly predicted the rule of each of these four kingdoms.

BABYLON

The first kingdom, Babylon, was ruling at this time. Nebuchadnezzar was the head of gold in the dream. He was an absolute ruler. Whatever he decreed was the law. In other words, he did not answer to anyone.

MEDO-PERSIA

Medo-Persia conquered Babylon. Interestingly, Daniel himself records the night Babylon fell (Daniel 5). The rule of the Medes and the Persians was inferior to that of Babylon because the Medo-Persian kings could not annul a law once it went into effect. Hence, the absolute authority of the king was restricted—as opposed to the unrestricted rule of Nebuchadnezzar.

However, the Medo-Persian kingdom covered a larger geographical area than Babylon, as well as lasting longer (539 B.C-331 B.C., 208 years).

GREECE

The next world kingdom was Greece—led by Alexander the Great. Its territory was even larger than that of Medo-Persia. Furthermore, it lasted longer (331 B.C to 31 B.C.) than either Babylonia or Medo-Persia, some 300 years.

However, it was an inferior type of rule. After the death of Alexander in 323 B.C., the empire split into four parts, where each of Alexander's four generals ruled one part.

ROME

The fourth Gentile world kingdom was Rome. In 31 B.C., Rome defeated the last remnant of the Greek Empire. The Roman Empire ruled longer than any of the previous three—until A.D. 476 in the West and until A.D. 1453 in the East.

In addition, the Roman Empire was larger than any of the three previous kingdoms. In fact, it encompassed almost all of Europe, including Spain, the British Isles, as well as India. Rome crushed all opposition with a brutality that surpassed any of the previous empires.

Yet, in terms of ruling authority, Rome was indeed inferior to the previous three kingdoms. The people, as well as the Roman senate, played significant roles in setting its policies. Consequently, they controlled the emperors—much more than had been true in these three preceding empires.

King Nebuchadnezzar was an absolute monarch. However, the rulers who followed him in the next three kingdoms, Medo-Persia, Greece, and Rome, were each increasingly less powerful personally than the previous rulers.

To sum up, Daniel's interpretation, perfectly predicted the continual inferiority of the rulers of these kingdoms, as the metals, starting with the head of gold Nebuchadnezzar, decreased in value.

On the other hand, he also correctly predicted the increasing strength of each kingdom, as the metals increased in strength. And as we observed, in the sense of geographical territory, and time ruling, each kingdom would become greater than the previous.

Again, we find another illustration of the infallibility of the Word of God when it comes to predicting the future!

THE IMPORTANCE OF THIS DREAM FOR THE LAST DAYS

The meaning of his dream charts out the history of these Gentile kingdoms, with respect to their relationship to the nation of Israel. This is why they are important.

At the time of Nebuchadnezzar's dream, the people of Israel were captives in Babylon. While there, Babylon fell to the Medes and the Persians. Two hundred years later, they were conquered by Greece, who in turn, was conquered by Rome. All four of these kingdoms had authority over Israel.

What we are most concerned about here is that there is a final phase of this fourth kingdom, Rome. In fact, it is one of the major signs of the last days.

THE KINGDOM OF GOD WILL ARRIVE IN THE DAYS OF CERTAIN KINGS

Daniel said that God's kingdom would come to earth at the time this future group of kings were ruling.

> In that the toes of the feet were partly of iron and partly of clay, the latter stages of this kingdom will be partly strong and partly fragile. And in that you saw iron mixed with wet clay, so people will be mixed with one another without adhering to one another, just as iron does not mix with clay. In the days of those kings the God of heaven will raise up an everlasting kingdom that will not be destroyed and a kingdom that will not be left to another people. It will break in pieces and bring about the demise of all these kingdoms. But it will stand forever (Daniel 2:42-44 NET).

As opposed to the other three kingdoms, Rome was not conquered. Indeed, it merely fell apart. In the last days, there will be a revival of the ancient Roman Empire. This final phase is expressed as feet which were a mixture of iron and clay, which among other things, speaks of an inferior rule than any of the previous kingdoms. Hence, this future empire will divide into ten parts but with less cohesion than the original Roman Empire.

This passage is crucial in considering the "time of the end." Observe that the Bible says, "in the days of those kings" the everlasting kingdom of heaven comes to the earth! Indeed, the total destruction of the statue, which signifies the Gentile world powers, will be replaced by the great mountain that will fill the entire earth. This is the kingdom of God—a kingdom that will last forever!

MORE INFORMATION IS GIVEN TO DANIEL (CHAPTER SEVEN)

Fortunately, we receive more information about this last phase of the Roman Empire from a vision that Daniel himself had—recorded in Chapter Seven.

19th century, writer Nathaniel West explains why certain details that were given to Daniel were not included in Nebuchadnezzar's dream and interpretation.

It is true that nothing is said or seen in chapter 2 of the Antichrist, the Son of Man, or the clouds of heaven, for the simple reason that it is Nebuchadnezzar's dream the prophet interprets and to the heathen king God made no revelation of the deliverance, but only the course and doom of the Gentile kingdoms and power. It is in the next vision where the symbols are changed in order to bring out *something further and new* (italics his) . . . Chapter 2 is the fundamental and general vision. All that follows is supplementative and more minute unveiling. Such is the law of progress in divine revelation. As the tree branches and buds, so does prophecy (Nathaniel West, *Daniel's Great Prophecy*, New York, The Hope of Israel Movement, 1898, p. 42).

DANIEL'S VISION

Rather than a great statue, these four Gentile kingdoms were shown to Daniel as four large beasts.

In the first year of King Belshazzar of Babylon, Daniel had a dream filled with visions while he was lying on his bed. Then he wrote down the dream in summary fashion. Daniel explained: "I was watching in my vision during the night as the four winds of the sky were stirring up the great sea. Then four large beasts came up from the sea; they were different from one another" (Daniel 7:1-3 NET).

THE VISION EXPLAINED

In this instance, a heavenly being explained the visions to Daniel.

As for me, Daniel, my spirit was distressed, and the visions of my mind were alarming me. I approached one of those standing nearby and asked him about the meaning of all this. So he spoke with me and revealed to me the interpretation of the vision: 'These large beasts, which are four in number, represent four kings who will arise from the earth. The holy ones of the Most High will receive the kingdom and will take possession of the kingdom forever and ever' (Daniel 7:15-18 NET).

Happily, we do not have to guess at the meaning. It concerns the same four kings, and kingdoms that were explained in Nebuchadnezzar's dream.

THE FOURTH BEAST

Interestingly, we discover that Daniel was curious about this "fourth beast."

> Then I wanted to know the meaning of the fourth beast, which was different from all the others. It was very dreadful, with two rows of iron teeth and bronze claws, and it devoured, crushed, and trampled anything that was left with its feet I also wanted to know the meaning of the ten horns on its head, and of that other horn which came up and before which three others fell. This was the horn that had eyes and a mouth speaking arrogant things, whose appearance was more formidable than the others. While I was watching, that horn began to wage war against the holy ones and was defeating them, until the Ancient of Days arrived and judgment was rendered in favor of the holy ones of the Most High. Then the time came for the holy ones to take possession of the kingdom (Daniel 7:19-22 ESV).

THE FOURTH BEAST IS THE FOURTH KINGDOM

Again, we have the explanation given to us about this "fourth beast."

> He gave me this explanation: 'The fourth beast is a fourth kingdom that will appear on earth. It will be different from all the other kingdoms and will devour the whole earth, trampling it down and crushing it. The ten horns are ten

kings who will come from this kingdom. After them another king will arise, different from the earlier ones; he will subdue three kings. He will speak against the Most High and oppress his holy people and try to change the set times and the laws. The holy people will be delivered into his hands for a time, times and half a time. But the court will sit, and his power will be taken away and completely destroyed forever. Then the sovereignty, power and greatness of all the kingdoms under heaven will be handed over to the holy people of the Most High. His kingdom will be an everlasting kingdom, and all rulers will worship and obey him.' "This is the end of the matter (Daniel 7:23-28 NIV).

From this explanation, we can observe the following points.

1. This fourth kingdom, the dreadful beast, will be different than the previous three. It will devour everything in its path.

2. The heavenly messenger interprets the ten horns as "ten kings" who will rise up from the fourth kingdom, Rome. Since the Second Coming of Christ puts an end to their rule, we know that these ten kings must reign at the end of the present age.

The ten horns are synonymous with the ten toes that were in the image of Nebuchadnezzar's dream. Nathaniel West explains.

> The fourth empire is the Roman, and the "Ten Toes" are co-existing kingdoms formed out of it. Furthermore, in prophecy terms "kings" and kingdoms" are convertible. The "kingdoms" are represented in the person of their kings, and the kings represent their kingdoms. The Four Beasts are called both "kings" and "kingdoms," Daniel 7:17. The Ten Toes are also called both "kings" and "kingdoms," in the same verse (Daniel 2:44). Kings and kingdoms are identical in 2:38,39 (Nathaniel West, *Daniel's Great Prophecy*, p. 39).

3. These kings will reign contemporaneously as one empire since all of them exist together. In fact, this is expressly stated in the Book of Revelation.

The ten horns that you saw are ten kings who have not yet received a kingdom, but will receive ruling authority as kings with the beast for one hour. These kings have a single intent, and they will give their power and authority to the beast (Revelation 17:12-13 NET).

4. We also find that one particular king, called a "little horn," will rise up from among them. This personage will subdue three of the kings.

5. At that time, this future world ruler will speak out against God, and oppress those who are His people.

6. For three and one-half years, they will be oppressed by this evil personage.

7. However, this oppression will not last. The kingdom of God will replace it—a kingdom that will last forever.

To sum up, Daniel was predicting that, at the end of the age, the old Roman Empire will revive and will be divided into ten kings, or kingdoms. It is in this last phase of the Empire that the Lord will return from heaven.

FUTILE ATTEMPTS TO REVIVE THE ROMAN EMPIRE

In the past, there have been attempts to revive the ancient Roman Empire.

All attempts have failed. However, Rome will indeed be revived in the "last days" with this ten nation confederation.

THE MOVEMENT TOWARD THE TEN AT THE TIME OF THE END

While this predicted ten nation European confederation has not yet come together, we can see that the world is moving toward it. We do know that the day will come when the ten kings, the ten toes of Daniel's image, become a reality.

With clear insight, 19th century author G.H. Pember wrote the following about these and other events recorded in the Book of Daniel.

> So then is the outline of God's dealing with the Jews, as it was revealed to Daniel. . . Messiah the Prince appeared and they rejected Him. He came unto His own and His own received Him not. Then He also rejected them, and cast them out to endure the curse uttered by Moses.
>
> Anon they will return again, and place themselves under the protection of the Fourth Gentile Empire. And when he makes a covenant with them, then may the world and Satan know that but seven short years remain for the indulgence of unbridled sin. At that time, the great body of the nation will be in unbelief, and will therefore, share in the madness of the world, and wonder after and worship the Beast. . .
>
> That they will rebuild the Temple is implied . . . in the eighth and ninth chapters of Daniel, and so it is also in the sixty-sixth of Isaiah. But the latter passage reveals to us the spirit in which the restored exiles will undertake the work, and the Lord's indignant rejection of that which is done by proud and self-willed sinners ...
>
> When the Temple has been erected by the unsuspecting Jews, all will be ready for the fearful scenes which are to close this dispensation, and which are especially foretold in the sermon on the Mount of Olives, and in some of the chapters of the Apocalypse (G.H. Pember, *The Great Prophecies of the Centuries Concerning Israel and the Gentiles*, London, Hodder and Stoughton, 1895).

In this summation of Pember, he lists a number of signs that we have already talked about.

1. Daniel 9:25-26 predicted that the Jews would reject the Messiah. In fact, it says that the Anointed One, the Messiah, will be killed.

2. After the rejection of Jesus at His "First Coming," there was a "Second Exile" of the Jews. In other words, after they rejected Him, He rejected them.

3. However, the scattered nation will not be annihilated but rather someday return to their ancient homeland.

4. At some time after they return, they will place themselves under the protection of the final phase of this fourth Gentile Empire, Rome.

5. However, the Jews will actually be placing themselves under the protection of the "man of sin," the final Antichrist (whom we will have more to say about in sign 14). He is the "little horn," the one who will be the head of the revived Roman Empire in the form of this final ten-nation confederation.

6. The Jews will rebuild their Temple, with the help of this "man of sin." This Temple, built in unbelief of Jesus the Messiah, will not be something pleasing to the Lord.

7. The Antichrist will eventually turn on the Jews and thus will begin this period of Great Tribulation.

As we have already documented in our previous signs, the Jews still exist in the last days, many have returned to their ancient homeland, as well as a number of them are now making the preparations to build the Third Temple. Of course, when Pember wrote this in 1881, none of these things were true.

THE PREDICTION WE CAN MAKE FROM SCRIPTURE: A TEN NATION EUROPEAN CONFEDERATION WILL EVENTUALLY FORM

From Scripture, we can make the following prediction as to what will take place in the future. There will be a ten-nation European confederation that will someday form. This will be a revival of the old Roman Empire. This will fulfill the prediction of Daniel the prophet when he explained to King Nebuchadnezzar the meaning of his dream—an outline of Gentile world history. We also read about these ten nations in the Book of Revelation.

Interestingly, while different confederations of European nations have come together in the past, as well as in the present, their number was *never* ten. This ten-nation group will only arise at the time of the end.

When such a group does indeed form, then Bible-believers can confidently be aware that we are indeed "at the time of the end."

THE JEWS WERE UNDER FOREIGN POWERS FOR 2,500 PLUS YEARS

In summing up, the 2,500 years that the Jews remained under foreign powers, 19th century writer James Brookes made a fitting observation about their predicted future.

> For twenty-five hundred years they have been permitted to occupy their own covenanted land only by the sufferance of their Gentile conquerors, and at the very time of the Messiah's appearing, they were compelled by the most abject humiliations to recognize the domination of a foreign and heathen power. Nothing more is needed to convince those who are willing to take God at His Word, that much remains to be accomplished of a divine and unchangeable promise to give Abraham and his seed a well-defined tract of country *forever* and for an *everlasting* possession (italics his) (James Brookes, *Maranatha, The Lord Cometh*, Fleming H. Revell Company, 1889, p. 395).

James Brookes, like these other authors we have cited in this book, wrote in faith. He believed that the unchangeable promises of God meant that someday the Jews would indeed return to their ancient homeland—never to be uprooted again. Many of the things that he said, "remains to be accomplished" have been wonderfully and miraculously fulfilled. The Jews are back in their own homeland. In 2017, the Israelis celebrated the 50th anniversary of the unification of the city of Jerusalem!

While much has indeed been accomplished, much more remains. The program of God is moving ahead, right on schedule!

SUMMARY TO SIGN 12: THE REVIVAL OF THE ANCIENT ROMAN EMPIRE

While each of our twenty-five signs of the end are important, there is an especially crucial point connected with this particular sign.

Some twenty-five hundred years ago, the prophet Daniel interpreted a dream of the Babylonian King Nebuchadnezzar. Daniel told him the subject of the dream was the "latter days."

His dream, of a huge statue made of various metals, was an outline of Gentile world history, from the time of Daniel until the time the kingdom of God comes to the earth. Four kingdoms would arise until the fifth kingdom, the kingdom of God, arrives. The kingdoms are Babylon, Medo-Persia, Greece, and then Rome.

The first three were conquered, Rome was not. In the last days, the Roman Empire will revive and it will be divided into ten kingdoms.

When Daniel interpreted the dream, he said that in the days of the fourth kingdom, a stone from heaven would strike the foot of this great image and destroy it. Then the God of heaven will raise up a kingdom that will never perish!

More information is given to us later in the Book of Daniel. Indeed, the Lord gave the young prophet a vision where he saw these four kingdoms as wild beasts. Daniel was particularly interested in the fourth beast—since it was so different than the rest. When Daniel asked the meaning of this terrifying looking beast, a supernatural being gave him the interpretation.

In the last days, ten nations will join together in a confederation of the revived Roman Empire. They will be ruled by a leader, called a "little horn." This little horn will speak words against the Lord, as well as against His people. While he will attempt to destroy Israel, he will fail. Indeed, in those days the Lord Himself shall destroy these kingdoms and then set up His own kingdom that will last forever.

Consequently, we should keep our eyes on Europe. When we see that ten- nation confederation come together, then we know that we are indeed near the time of the return of the Lord.

There Will Be a One-World Political and Economic System (Globalism)

The Bible gives us a preview of what the world will look like in the last days. One of the obvious features we find from Scripture is globalism. In other words, a central worldwide system will be created that basically controls the lives of everyone everywhere. This need for such a system will come about from a number of difficulties that humanity will face. They will include the following problems.

THERE WILL BE POVERTY AND FAMINES IN THE LAST DAYS

The Book of Revelation speaks of both poverty and famines that will exist at the time of the end. We read about this in the Book of Revelation.

> Then when the Lamb opened the third seal I heard the third living creature saying, "Come!" So I looked, and here came a black horse! The one who rode it had a balance scale in his hand. Then I heard something like a voice from among the four living creatures saying, "A quart of wheat will cost a day's pay and three quarts of barley will cost a day's pay. But do not damage the olive oil and the wine!" (Revelation 6:5,6 NET).

Jesus Himself spoke of famines occurring in the "last days."

> For nation will rise up in arms against nation, and kingdom against kingdom. And there will be famines and earthquakes in various places. (Matthew 24:7 NET).

He also said that poverty would always be around.

> For you will always have the poor with you, but you will not always have me! (Matthew 26:11 NET).

Despite the best efforts of the world, famine and poverty will not be eradicated.

This will seemingly cause the leaders of the world to attempt to take care of those who are suffering in these poverty-stricken areas—which is a commendable motive. Though their motives will be well-intended, it will set the stage for the worst time in human history—the period of the Great Tribulation.

THE WORLDWIDE ECONOMIC SYSTEM AND THE MARK OF THE BEAST

The Bible says that an economic system will be created, which is world-wide in scope.

> He also caused everyone (small and great, rich and poor, free and slave) to obtain a mark on their right hand or on their forehead. Thus no one was allowed to buy or sell things unless he bore the mark of the beast —that is, his name or his number. This calls for wisdom: Let the one who has insight calculate the beast's number, for it is man's number, and his number is 666 (Revelation 13:16,17 NET).

Because of the problems of poverty and famine in this globalist world, it seems that some type of central economic system will be created, for among other reasons, to help those who are in need.

As these verses state, this central system will be hijacked by a future world leader, one that the Bible has much to say about. We will look at this coming leader in detail in our next sign.

SUMMARY TO SIGN 13: THE COMING A ONE-WORLD GOVERNMENT (GLOBALISM)

According to the Bible, at the time of the end, there will be both famine and poverty in the world. In other words, despite the best efforts, and billions of dollars spent, there will still be areas hit with famine, as well as extreme poverty.

To help meet this need, it seems that the world will create some type of central economic system to deal with this issue. While this will not be the only reason it is created, this globalist system, which will stress "fairness," "community," and "togetherness," will attempt to solve these dual problems. However, they will fail.

This world-wide economic system will eventually be hijacked by a future world leader. While this individual will seemingly have "all the answers" to major problems of the world, he will actually be the long-awaited "man of sin," the final Antichrist. His coming will also signal the soon coming of the Lord.

The World Will Desperately
Look for a Leader

Among other reasons, with the rise of the twin problems of famine and poverty, a worldwide economic system will be created to deal with these and other problematic issues. Yet these will not be the only problems which the world will face.

THERE WILL BE NO END TO WAR

Wars will continue to be fought. Jesus said the signs of the end included the following.

> When you hear of wars and uprisings, do not be frightened. These things must happen first, but the end will not come right away (Matthew 24:9 NIV).

According to Christ, wars will continue until the time of the end.

WEAPONS OF MASS DESTRUCTION?

One of the other woes the people will experience concerns the possibility of the world destroying itself. Jesus talked about this when referring to the time of the end.

> If those days had not been cut short, no one would survive, but for the sake of the elect those days will be shortened (Matthew 24:22 ESV).

This statement seems to indicate that the Lord must intervene before humanity is destroyed. Though this is not the only possible interpretation of what He meant, it could be that He is referring to the weapons that have been created, as well as the use, or potential use, of them. As we just observed, there will be wars up until the time He returns.

Whatever the case may be, we know that the world will find itself in a desperate spot.

Ruling by consensus will not be found to work—since every geographical region, every nation, will have their own interests. Lesser leaders will fail at this monumental task of fixing these problems.

Consequently, the world will cry out for someone who can guide them during this perilous time. Scripture tells us that such a person is coming.

JESUS WARNED OF SUCH A MAN

The world has always had the desire for someone to lead them. Jesus forewarned of a coming person whom the world would accept. He stated it this way.

> I have come in my Father's name, and you do not accept me.
> If someone else comes in his own name, you will accept him
> (John 5:43 NET).

The Christ rejecting world will desire and accept this leader who will guide them into what they believe will be a time of peace and prosperity.

THE TIMES OF THE GENTILES

This coming world ruler was predicted in Daniel's vision of the four beasts (Daniel 7). He is known as the "little horn." He arrives at the end of this period known as the, "Times of the Gentiles." Adolph Saphir explains.

With the captivity in Babylon begins a period of the history of the kingdom of God which still continues, and which shall only end with the second coming of our Lord. Why is the evangelist Luke so anxious to impress upon us that the birth of Jesus Christ took place under Caesar Augustus, emperor of Rome? Why is Pontius Pilate mentioned in the creed? In order that it may be impressed upon us that the sceptre had indeed departed from Judah, and that it was under the fourth world-monarchy that Jesus the new-born King of the Jews appeared. But the times of the Gentiles appeared more clearly after the destruction of Jerusalem and the dispersion of Israel among the nations. This is the expression that our blessed Saviour Himself used, that during the times of the Gentiles Jerusalem was to be trodden under foot. And during this period we behold Israel under the displeasure of God, spiritually blind, scattered among the nations of the earth (Adolph Saphir, *The Divine Unity Of Scripture*, London, Hodder and Stoughton, 1892, pp, 104-105).

Israel has now returned to their ancient homeland, this means that we are moving closer to the end of the "times of the Gentiles." This long-awaited Antichrist of Scripture, will be the final Gentile world ruler. He is also known as "the beast."

Writing in 1848, B.W. Newton reminds us that this is no ordinary king.

The last great king that is to arise among the Gentiles—one who is called in Daniel emphatically "THE King" (11:36), and "THE Prince that shall come," is one of the chief instruments by which the judgment of the Divine hand will reach that evil people (B.W. Newton, *Aids to Prophetic Inquiry*, London: James Nisbet And Co., Berners Street, 1848, p. 52).

Scripture has informed us of his coming. Indeed, John wrote gave the following warning.

> Dear children, this is the last hour; and as you have heard that the antichrist is coming, even now many antichrists have come. This is how we know it is the last hour (1 John 2:18 NIV).

When this individual comes upon the scene, he will seemingly have all the answers to the problems of the world. In fact, he is described in this manner.

> And he was given a mouth speaking great things and blasphemies (Revelation 13:5 NKJV).

Evidently, he will have a unique ability to convince the people that he is the solution to the dire situation of the world. In doing so, he will speak against the Living God.

This confirms what was predicted about him in the Book of Daniel.

> Then the king will do as he pleases. He will exalt and magnify himself above every deity and he will utter presumptuous things against the God of gods. He will succeed until the time of wrath is completed, for what has been decreed must occur (Daniel 11:36 NET).

Once he arrives on the scene, the Bible says that this evil man will succeed—but only for a short time. The Book of Revelation echoes this thought.

> The beast was permitted to go to war against the saints and conquer them. He was given ruling authority over every tribe, people, language, and nation, and all those who live on the earth will worship the beast, everyone whose name has not been written since the foundation of the world in the

book of life belonging to the Lamb who was killed. If anyone
has an ear, he had better listen! (Revelation 13:7-9 NET).

We should pay close attention to precisely what is said about this
"beast."

First, we are told that he will go to war against those who have trusted
the Lord during this period. He is allowed to conquer them. In other
words, he will succeed for a while.

Second, ruling authority will then be given to him over everyone on
the earth.

Third, the unbelievers in the world will worship the beast. The genuine
believers in Christ will not worship this beast nor his image.

As we search the totality of Scripture, we can see the pieces of the
puzzle coming together.

As we mentioned in "Sign 12," this man of sin will rule over the predicted ten nation confederation, which comes from the revived Roman
Empire. The Book of Revelation has this to say about his rulership over
them.

> The ten horns that you saw are ten kings who have not yet
> received a kingdom, but will receive ruling authority as kings
> with the beast for one hour. These kings have a single intent,
> and they will give their power and authority to the beast.
> They will make war with the Lamb, but the Lamb will con-
> quer them, because he is Lord of lords and King of kings,
> and those accompanying the Lamb are the called, chosen,
> and faithful (Revelation 17:12-14 NET).

From this passage, we learn that these future ten kings, or kingdoms,
will rule with the beast, the Antichrist, for a short period of time.

Interestingly, they will give all their power to this evil individual.

Eventually, the Lamb, the Lord Jesus, will conquer him and his coalition. The Bible explains it in this manner.

Then I saw the beast and the kings of the earth and their armies assembled to do battle with the one who rode the horse and with his army. Now the beast was seized, and along with him the false prophet who had performed the signs on his behalf—signs by which he deceived those who had received the mark of the beast and those who worshiped his image. Both of them were thrown alive into the lake of fire burning with sulfur. The others were killed by the sword that extended from the mouth of the one who rode the horse, and all the birds gorged themselves with their flesh (Revelation 19:19-21 NET).

Such is the inglorious end of the "man of sin."

SUMMARY TO SIGN 14: THE DESPERATE SEARCH FOR A WORLD LEADER

With all the efforts of well-meaning humans, we find that in the last days poverty and famine are still with us. Wars will also continue. In other words, though desiring peace and prosperity, the world will always have conflicts and poverty. Consequently, the people of the earth will live in constant fear.

Furthermore, before the Second Coming of Jesus Christ, ten kingdoms, or nations, of unequal strength will unite to form a coalition that will rise out of the ruins of the ancient Roman Empire.

This will necessitate a strong leader who will help deliver the world from their enormous problems. One will indeed arise—the infamous Antichrist, the beast. He will be the last Gentile world ruler.

Scripture tells us that the Lord will allow him to succeed for a while. Yet he will meet his doom at the return of Christ.

The way in which this coming Antichrist will control the world is found in our next "Sign of the End."

There Will Be an Exponential Increase in Technology

One of the most amazing "Signs of the End" concerns something that seemed to be impossible until recently. As we will note, there are several passages in Scripture that seem to teach something taking place that was literally unheard of at the time the Bible was written.

In fact, these events would not have been possible until recently! However, with the rise of modern technology, these biblical explanations of what takes place are no longer impossible.

We can list the following three examples that have caused problems and concerns for past Bible commentators.

THE COMING FALSE PROPHET AND THE MARK OF THE BEAST

There is a passage in Scripture that seems to assume the times in which we live. Indeed, it speaks of a worldwide economic system where nobody can buy or sell without a particular mark—the mark of the beast.

> Then I saw another beast coming up from the earth. He had two horns like a lamb, but was speaking like a dragon. He exercised all the ruling authority of the first beast on his behalf, and made the earth and those who inhabit it worship the first beast, the one whose lethal wound had been

healed. He performed momentous signs, even making fire come down from heaven in front of people and, by the signs he was permitted to perform on behalf of the beast, he deceived those who live on the earth. He told those who live on the earth to make an image to the beast who had been wounded by the sword, but still lived. The second beast was empowered to give life to the image of the first beast so that it could speak, and could cause all those who did not worship the image of the beast to be killed. He also caused everyone (small and great, rich and poor, free and slave) to obtain a mark on their right hand or on their forehead. Thus no one was allowed to buy or sell things unless he bore the mark of the beast—that is, his name or his number. This calls for wisdom: Let the one who has insight calculate the beast's number, for it is man's number, and his number is 666 (Revelation 13:11-16 NET).

We should appreciate what the Bible predicts here. It is a worldwide system which has been put in place where nobody is allowed to buy or sell without this mark of the beast, the number 666, on their right hand or on their forehead.

This system will be managed by the "second beast," also known as the "false prophet." He will force the people of the world to worship the image of the "first beast," the Antichrist.

Those who do not personally receive the mark of the beast will not be allowed to have *any* business transactions—rather they are to be put to death!

PROBLEM 1: HOW COULD ANYONE MONITOR A WORLDWIDE ECONOMIC SYSTEM?

Can you imagine, even fifty years ago, when humans were aware as to the extent where people lived in our world, that a system could be put in place where nobody could buy or sell anywhere without a particular mark on either their right hand or their forehead? It would seem ridiculous to think that any leader could have people in all parts of the globe monitoring every business transaction. In fact, it seemed like something impossible.

PROBLEM 2: HOW COULD THE DEAD BODIES OF THE TWO WITNESSES BE VIEWED WORLDWIDE?

In the Book of Revelation, there is the account of two witnesses of Jesus Christ who testify to the people of the earth for some three and one-half years. Eventually they are killed by the final Antichrist. The Bible explains what happens in this manner.

> When they finish their testimony, the beast that ascends out of the bottomless pit will make war against them, overcome them, and kill them. And their dead bodies will lie in the street of the great city which spiritually is called Sodom and Egypt, where also our Lord was crucified. Then those from the peoples, tribes, tongues, and nations will see their dead bodies three-and-a-half days, and not allow their dead bodies to be put into graves. And those who dwell on the earth will rejoice over them, make merry, and send gifts to one another, because these two prophets tormented those who dwell on the earth (Revelation 11:7-10 NKJV).

For three and one-half days, their bodies lie in the street in the Holy City of Jerusalem. At that time, we are told that people all over the earth will see their dead bodies and then celebrate their deaths by sending gifts to one another.

As can be imagined, commentators from the past wondered how all the people of the earth could observe such a spectacle. In 1847, Horatius Bonar stated the problem for one living in the 19th century.

We read that the dead bodies of the witnesses are to lie unburied for three days and a-half (Revelation 11:8-10), that is, three and a-half literal days, if the abridged scheme be correct. And then it is added, that "they of the people and kindreds and tongues and nations, shall see their dead bodies, and shall not suffer them to be put in graves." Now, is it *possible* that within three days and a-half, people of the different nations even of the *prophetic* earth should be able to come together to the streets of the great city, and see these bodies there lying? Or is it possible, that within that short space, the intelligence of their death should be so universally diffused, that they should have time to congratulate each other and send gifts to one to the other in token of their common joy? We can hardly conceive this possible. These may perhaps appear minute pieces of criticism, but still they are real difficulties which it is right and necessary to state (Horatius Bonar, *Prophetical Landmarks*, London, James Nisbet and Co., Berners Street, 1847, pp. 184-185).

For one living in the middle of the 19th century, the problem was obvious. How could everyone on the face of the earth see their dead bodies for three and one-half days? Even if this only referred to people living in the same geographical area, this would still be impossible.

PROBLEM 3: HOW COULD EVERYONE SEE THE ABOMINATION OF DESOLATION?

A third example has to do with a warning that Jesus gave to people living in the "last days." The Lord said the following.

So when you see the abomination of desolation—spoken about by Daniel the prophet—standing in the holy place (let the reader understand), then those in Judea must flee to the mountains. The one on the roof must not come down to take anything out of his house, and the one in the field must not turn back to get his cloak (Matthew 24:15-18 NET).

The abomination of desolation takes place in the Holy Place, the area of the Temple that is off limits to everyone except the Great High Priest. Even then, he is only allowed into the Holy of Holies once a year.

From Scripture, we know that when this future event takes place, this final Antichrist will then turn on the Jewish people in an attempt to annihilate them. Those in the immediate vicinity will be the first to suffer the consequences.

How then are those in the area of Judea to know about it? Those in the field, how are they to get the news? In what sense are they going to "see" this happen?

In the 19th century, B.W. Newton explained it the best way that he could.

> It is true, indeed, that this commandment to quit Jerusalem and Judea can be addressed only to a few, because howsoever many of the servants of Christ may be in Judea then, they will be necessarily few in comparison with the multitude of their Christian brethren who will be scattered up and down throughout the earth (B.W. Newton, *The Prophecy of Jesus as Contained in Matthew XXIV. & XXV. Considered*, Third Edition, London: Houlston and Sons, 1879, p. 15).

HOW THESE PROBLEMS WERE DEALT WITH IN THE PAST

In the past, Bible commentators dealt with these problems in different ways. Some ignored them. Many assumed that the language was not meant to be understood literally but rather symbolically.

Those who did address them, like the example we gave, admitted that they could not conceive how these events could be literally possible. In other words, they were baffled at the idea of understanding these events to occur just as the Bible stated.

The proper view, of how to interpret these difficulties, was stated by A.H. McNeile in 1840.

> It is one thing to anticipate the facts predicted, according to the literal meaning of the same words, when used in other books, or in other places of the same books, acknowledging our ignorance as to the *mode* (italics his) of accomplishment, because that mode is not revealed; and it is quite another thing, to put a different meaning on the same words, in different places of the same sentence, in order to make the mode of accomplishment more intelligible.

> I had rather avov my inability to answer the question *"How* (italics his) can that be?"*—*in a thousand instances, that to put an evasive interpretation upon a single verse of the word of God (Hugh McNeile, *Prospects of the Jews, or a Series of Popular Lectures on the Prophecies Relative to the Jewish Nation*, Orrin Rodgers, Philadelphia, 1840, p. ii).

How could these things be literal? How indeed could the whole world see the bodies of the two witnesses lying dead in the streets of Jerusalem, or the people actually witnessing the abomination of desolation.

Furthermore, how would it be possible to monitor a worldwide system of buying and selling in every corner of the globe?

Again, we should pay attention to McNeile's answer. He was unable to explain *how*, but that did not stop him from interpreting these events in a literal manner. He did not believe that the Bible allowed such a non-literal interpretation—even though nobody had the slightest idea as to how these predicted events could be literally fulfilled.

Of course, this was something which was impossible to conceive of in 1840! McNeile admitted that he did not know the *mode* of how this would take place but he was not going to twist the words of Scripture to make them mean something different than what they clearly mean.

NOBODY WONDERS ANY LONGER HOW IT COULD BE DONE

Well, of course, there is no question in our day and age about these predictions coming to a literal fulfillment. The technology is here to monitor buying and selling worldwide, as well as all the people in the world to view these dead bodies in the city of Jerusalem in a three and one-half day period.

In addition, "seeing" the abomination of desolation take place is not out of the realm of possibility for the people of the earth. In fact, in "Sign 8," when we spoke of the preparations to build a Third Temple, we cited a promotion of the Temple Institute that referred to their architectural plans of the coming Temple.

Recall that one of the items this new Temple will have is, "full computerization." This would allow people in all parts of the globe to view what is going on in the Temple in "real time."

Yet it is only in recent times that these things could be considered a possibility. Hence, if we interpret these predictions literally, we can now see how they can indeed literally come to pass!

THE RATE OF TECHNOLOGICAL INCREASE AND THE MARK OF THE BEAST

It is often asked about the specific technology which will be used to number each person living in the world. In other words, what exactly is the "mark of the beast."

At the rate technology is increasing, it is likely something that none of us could ever even imagine. Predictions in the past, of what the mark will be, now seem naïve compared to what is available now. We can only imagine what is to come. The point is that it is coming and that it will include everyone on the globe. Hence, these predictions made long ago in Scripture are now possible to be literally fulfilled.

SUMMARY TO SIGN 15: THE EXPONENTIAL INCREASE IN TECHNOLOGY

When we say the exponential increase in technology is one of the signs of the end, we are referring to certain future events predicted in Scripture that would have been physically impossible to be fulfilled in biblical times. In fact, the possibility of literal fulfillment could only have been in our modern day and age. Three events seemingly confirm this.

The fact that the entire world will see the bodies of the two witnesses lying in the city of Jerusalem for three and one-half days.

Scripture predicts that this final Gentile world leader, the Antichrist, will have a worldwide economic system in place. His cohort, the false prophet, will cause everyone everywhere on the earth to take the number of this man, 666, on their right hand or on their forehead. Nobody will be able to buy or sell without it. This assumes some type of global monitoring system.

Jesus warned the inhabitants of Jerusalem to flee when they "saw" the abomination that causes desolation. How in the world could people "see" this event take place when it is confined to the Holy of Holies in the Temple of Jerusalem—a place where only the Great High Priest can go, and even then, only once a year?

With modern technology, we now know that each of these three predictions can be literally fulfilled.

In sum, it seems that the Scriptures do indeed anticipate the technology that all of us are so accustomed to—the ability to view and control events on a worldwide scale.

Plagues and Pestilence
Will Trouble the World

History testifies that plagues and pestilence have been part of the human experience—sometimes on a global scale.

THE BIBLICAL PLAGUES

Most people are familiar with the ten plagues which were recorded in the Book of Exodus. Scripture gives other accounts where the Lord Himself sent plagues and pestilence on the sinning people.

PLAGUES AND PESTILENCE WILL CONTINUE IN THE LAST DAYS

We also find that these types of scourges will continue until the time of the end. Indeed, Jesus spoke of the last days as a time of plagues and pestilence.

> For nation will rise against nation, and kingdom against kingdom. And there will be famines, pestilences, and earthquakes in various places. All these are the beginning of sorrows (Matthew 24:7,8 NKJV).

Famine and pestilence will continue until the time of the end.

The Book of Revelation also has much to say about this.

> Then when the Lamb opened the fourth seal I heard the voice of the fourth living creature saying, "Come!" So I looked and here came a pale green horse! The name of the one who rode it was Death, and Hades followed right behind. They were given authority over a fourth of the earth, to kill its population with the sword, famine, and disease, and by the wild animals of the earth (Revelation 6:7,8 NET).

In this instance, this future plague, as with the other judgments in the Book of Revelation, will be the result of the wrath of God.

WARNING: WE SHOULD BE CAREFUL ABOUT DRAWING CONCLUSIONS FROM CURRENT EVENTS

A word of warning is in order. When we see famines, pestilence and disasters on a large scale we should not conclude that this is the fulfillment of what was predicted at the "time of the end." Nineteenth century writer, G.H. Pember, offered some wise counsel on this subject.

> Famines too have occurred in divers places—in different parts of India, in Persia, in China, in Morocco, and in several other countries; while various kinds of sickness and disease seem to be more than usually prevalent.
>
> Now all these things, and many others which might be mentioned, do indeed forebode disasters and widespread distress, but not necessarily the last tribulation, the final throes of the world. For the earth has had her times of convulsion, suffering, and change, in former days. God's sore plagues, war, famine, pestilence, and the beasts of the earth have often desolated her lands in past years, and yet the end has not followed. Nay, were we to feel the solid ground trembling beneath us, and behold the mountains lifted up and cast into the sea, even such a sight would not itself prove that the great Day of the Lord had come.

Men have often forgotten this, and when appealing to Scripture, have too frequently drawn inferences from an exaggeration of one or more detached texts, instead of carefully considering all that the prophets have spoken. Hence there have been many false alarms and panics (G.H. Pember, *The Great Prophecies Concerning the Jews, the Gentiles, and the Church of God*, 1881, p. 16).

These words, written in 1881, could have been written yesterday. Indeed, too often we find that when a horrific famine, a plague, or some type of pestilence takes place, there are people who immediately claim that it is the specific fulfillment of Bible prophecy. In doing so, it has caused widespread panic, as well as unsubstantiated claims that "the end is at hand."

However, when major disasters strike the earth, we should not assume that the end has come. Indeed, these types of events will characterize the age in which we are living. When the time of the end does come, the famine, plagues, pestilence, etc., not only will be unprecedented, it will be accompanied with other predicted signs which the Bible gives to us.

Pember offered some wise words about these false claims.

Now these alarms, and many others, sprang from crude and baseless arguments which do not for a moment endure the test of intelligent investigation. And their result was something worse than the mere delusion of those who were affected by them: for they caused a general discredit of, and distaste for, the prophetic scriptures; since men are ever ready to cast upon the Word of God the blame of failure which is solely due to their foolish and shortsighted interpretation (G.H. Pember, *The Great Prophecies Concerning the Jews, the Gentiles, and the Church of God*, 1881, p. 16).

This cannot be emphasized enough! Well-meaning people will come upon the scene and make predictions based upon their understanding of the Word of God. When the predictions do not turn out to be true, then it is usually the Bible that is ridiculed—rather than the misinterpretation of it by someone.

We discuss this issue in Appendix 1 as we look at objections people make with respect to predictive prophecy. We will also cite illustrations that Pember gives that highlights the problem.

THE ORIGIN OF THESE NATURAL PLAGUES

Plagues and pestilence are a result of the fallen world in which we live. Once sin entered into our world, the natural order, which was perfect, became unbalanced.

THE WARNING TO ADAM

In fact, we can trace the origin of disease, pestilence, and plagues to the very beginning of life on earth. The Lord warned Adam, the first man, what would happen if he sinned.

> The Lord God took the man and placed him in the orchard in Eden to care for it and to maintain it. Then the Lord God commanded the man, "You may freely eat fruit from every tree of the orchard, but you must not eat from the tree of the knowledge of good and evil, for when you eat from it you will surely die" (Genesis 2:17-19 NET).

The Lord warned Adam that the moment he sinned, he would begin to die. His body would break down, be susceptible to disease and death.

In fact, everything on the earth would eventually die. Furthermore, nature would no longer be friendly. In fact, the ground would begin to produce things that were not beneficial to humankind.

As we know, Adam did indeed sin and the judgment was pronounced against him.

But to Adam he said, Because you obeyed your wife and ate from the tree about which I commanded you, 'You must not eat from it,' cursed is the ground thanks to you; in painful toil you will eat of it all the days of your life. It will produce thorns and thistles for you, but you will eat the grain of the field. By the sweat of your brow you will eat food until you return to the ground, for out of it you were taken; for you are dust, and to dust you will return (Genesis 3:17-19 NET).

Nature, which at one time was perfect, would now become a problem for humans. It would produce things which could cause both disease and death. This would be the future for all humans until the Lord returns and creates a new world.

In other words, medical science will never get to the place where diseases and pestilences are eradicated.

The following headline says it all!

THERE ARE MORE THAN 1 MILLION VIRUSES THAT WE KNOW ABSOLUTELY NOTHING ABOUT (THE WEEK 12-27-16)

Consequently, science agrees that viruses, plagues, and pestilence, will always be with us.

HUMAN-MADE PLAGUES (BIO-TERRORISM, CHEMICAL WARFARE)

Unfortunately, there is another type of plague that is not a result of the original fall of humankind, but rather is purposely created. This type of disease or plague is known by a number of names including chemical warfare, or bio-terrorism. Basically, it consists of compounds created in a laboratory with the express purpose to use as a weapon—to cause sickness, disease and death.

THE WORLD HAS SEEN EXAMPLES OF CHEMICAL WARFARE, BIO-TERRORISM

Our world has already seen a number of examples of these types of weaponized chemicals. While chemical warfare is not something new to our age, the advance in the sophistication by which these deadly weapons are created, certainly adds to the nervousness of the people of the earth.

In sum, until the return of Christ, the world will see plagues and pestilence resulting from the fallen world in which we live. Unfortunately, our world will also continue to experience specially created biological compounds which will be used as terrorist weapons.

In addition, the Lord Himself, will send plagues upon the Christ-rejecting world during the period of the Great Tribulation.

Therefore, among the things which will cause fear for human beings is the continuing concern of plagues and pestilence. This scourge will not go away until the Lord returns.

Eventually, all things will be made new! The Bible says.

> And the one seated on the throne said: "Look! I am making all things new!" Then he said to me, "Write it down, because these words are reliable and true" (Revelation 21:5,6 NET)

What a wonderful day that will be!

The World Will Be Characterized by Lawlessness

Another feature of the last days, concerns the attitude and behavior of the people of the earth. It will be one of lawlessness.

THE DAYS OF NOAH AND THE DAYS OF LOT

Jesus emphasized that the last days will be similar to the days of Noah, as well as in the days of Lot. The Lord put it this way.

> Just as it was in the days of Noah, so too it will be in the days of the Son of Man. People were eating, they were drinking, they were marrying, they were being given in marriage— right up to the day Noah entered the ark. Then the flood came and destroyed them all. Likewise, just as it was in the days of Lot, people were eating, drinking, buying, selling, planting, building; but on the day Lot went out from Sodom, fire and sulfur rained down from heaven and destroyed them all. It will be the same on the day the Son of Man is revealed (Luke 17:26-30 NET).

During those times, life continued to go on as usual, but life was anything but good.

In fact, we find that at the time of Noah, there was wickedness constantly upon the earth.

> But the Lord saw that the wickedness of humankind had become great on the earth. Every inclination of the thoughts of their minds was only evil all the time (Genesis 6:5 NET).

Scripture says that the people, at the time of the Flood, were continually thinking about doing evil.

LAWLESSNESS AT THE TIME OF LOT

Lot, the nephew of Abraham, was rescued from the evil cities of Sodom and Gomorrah. Scripture tells us of the depths of evil to which these cities found themselves.

> He [the Lord] rescued Lot, a righteous man, who was distressed by the depraved conduct of the lawless (for that righteous man, living among them day after day, was tormented in his righteous soul by the lawless deeds he saw and heard) (2 Peter 2:7-9 NIV).

Day and night, Lot saw the total depravity of these cities. In fact, there could not be found ten righteous people dwelling in either Sodom or Gomorrah. The Lord said to Abraham.

> For the sake of ten, I will not destroy it (Genesis 18:32 NIV).

Sadly, even ten righteous people could not be found. Hence, these evil cities were destroyed.

LAWLESSNESS WILL CONTINUE TO INCREASE

This wickedness, this lawlessness, as in Noah's day, as well as at the time of Lot, will increase in the last days. Jesus said the following.

> And because lawlessness will increase so much, the love of many will grow cold (Matthew 24:12 NET).

While lawlessness has always been with us, there will be an increase at the time of the end.

THE LOVE OF PEOPLE FOR ONE ANOTHER WILL GROW COLD

Interestingly, Jesus spoke of the love of people growing cold toward one another. This is in contrast as to what the Lord said would be the "mark" of the Christian.

> A new command I give you: Love one another. As I have loved you, so you must love one another. By this everyone will know that you are my disciples, if you love one another (John 13:34,35 NIV).

Christians are to be known by their love for one another. At the time of the Lord's return, it seems the love of many people will grow cold.

THERE WILL BE DIFFICULT TIMES AHEAD

Paul wrote about the difficult time the world will face at the time of the end.

> But understand this, that in the last days difficult times will come. For people will be lovers of themselves, lovers of money, boastful, arrogant, blasphemers, disobedient to parents, ungrateful, unholy, unloving, irreconcilable, slanderers, without self-control, savage, opposed to what is good, treacherous, reckless, conceited, loving pleasure rather than loving God. They will maintain the outward appearance of religion but will have repudiated its power (2 Timothy 3:1-5 NET).

At the time of the end, we will see a world that will become increasingly hostile to the laws of God and humans. It reminds us of how the Lord summed up the 350 year-period of the rule of the Judges.

> In those days there was no king in Israel. Everyone did what was right in his own eyes (Judges 21:25 ESV).

Therefore, according to Scripture, lawlessness will continue until the return of Christ. In other words, there will never be a world which will evolve to some kind of paradise with universal peace and love with everyone everywhere.

To the contrary, people will act wickedly toward one another, like at the time of Noah, like the evil cities of Sodom and Gomorrah.

THE COMING OF THE "LAWLESS ONE"

Interestingly, the final Antichrist is described in Scripture as the "lawless one." Note how his coming is described.

> For the hidden power of lawlessness is already at work. However, the one who holds him back will do so until he is taken out of the way, and then the lawless one will be revealed, whom the Lord will destroy by the breath of his mouth and wipe out by the manifestation of his arrival. The arrival of the lawless one will be by Satan's working with all kinds of miracles and signs and false wonders, and with every kind of evil deception directed against those who are perishing, because they found no place in their hearts for the truth so as to be saved (2 Thessalonians 2:7-10 NET).

This passage is highly instructive. While lawlessness is already at work in our present age, it is being restrained, or held back by some thing or someone. The best answer to the identity of the "Restrainer" is the Holy Spirit of God who is living in believers.

Therefore, at the time of the end, when He who is restraining lawlessness shall be removed from the world, then the "lawless one," the Antichrist, will be revealed. When this "man of sin" does come upon the scene, he will perform every kind of evil deception to lead the people of the earth astray. We are told that the people will follow this "lawless one" because there is no place in their hearts for the truth of God.

In the 19th century, G.H. Pember made an astute observation concerning the true nature of the lawlessness and evil which is all around each and every one of us.

Men are ever ready to break out into the appalling wickedness of the end: we live over a [land]mine that might be sprung at any moment; but hitherto there has been a restraining power. The Spirit, Who descended at Pentecost, is still with the church who mightily convinces even the world of sin, righteousness, and of judgment, that men dare not do their worst. Nevertheless, defiant rebellion is in their hearts; and as soon as the Spirit leaves the earth with those believers who are to be gathered to their Lord, then the Powers of Darkness and their earthly subjects will manifest their real character.

Accordingly, that character is revealed to us beforehand, that we may know the true nature of lawlessness around us (G.H. Pember, *The Great Prophecies Concerning the Jews, the Gentiles, and the Church of God*, 1881, p. 11).

This is a profound truth—the Lord wishes us to know the true nature of the lawlessness which is all around us.

Presently, the Spirit of God is restraining evil from becoming worse than it truly is. However, there will come a day when He is removed and the evilness of the human heart will know no bounds.

Thankfully, that will stop when the Lord Himself returns. Until then, we should expect to see lawlessness on the increase.

Our next sign will be the logical result when the world is characterized by lawlessness.

SIGN 18

The World Will Be Characterized by Violence

We have discovered that lawlessness will increase at the time of the end. In fact, the Bible says that the world will be like it was in the days of Noah, and at the time of the destruction of the wicked cities of Sodom and Gomorrah—wicked all the time.

This lawlessness will naturally lead to our next "Sign of End"—violence.

While the people of the world will believe that they are evolving into some type of perfected humanity, the situation on our planet will not reflect this. In fact, it will be just the opposite.

THE TIME OF THE END WILL BE LIKE THE DAYS OF NOAH

As we just mentioned, the Lord said the time of the end would be like the "days of Noah."

> Just as it was in the days of Noah, so too it will be in the days of the Son of Man (Luke 17:26 NET).

In the Book of Genesis, we read about this time period. We discover that it was characterized by violence.

> The earth was ruined in the sight of God; the earth was filled with violence (Genesis 6:11 NET).

One of the reasons that the Lord destroyed the population of the earth, except for Noah and his family, was because of the violence of humankind. In fact, Scripture says the earth was "ruined" because of it.

VIOLENCE WILL BE ON THE INCREASE

Jesus warned of the violence that would characterize the world at the time of the end. The violence would mainly be directed at two groups—those who have believed in Him, the Christians, and the Jewish race.

The Lord said the following to believers.

> Then they will hand you over to be persecuted and will kill you. You will be hated by all the nations because of my name (Matthew 24:9 NET).

Hatred for Christians will be worldwide. Much of the violence in the world will be directed at believers in Christ.

19th century author B.W. Newton commented on the course of this age.

> Such is the picture of our Dispensation. Violence and wasting among the nations; destructive judgments inflicted from time to time by the hand of God: hatred and persecution of the Church . . . Such, I repeat, is our Lord's own description of the Dispensation in which we live. Has any description ever been more fully verified by the facts than this? (B.W. Newton, *The Prophecy of Jesus as Contained in Matthew XXIV. Considered*, Third Edition, London, Houlston and Sons, 1879, p, 10).

In fact, this has been a "perfect" description of the age in which we live.

THE FUTURE WAR CAMPAIGNS PREDICTED BY SCRIPTURE

The idea that violence will characterize the earth can also be seen by the various predictions of Scripture as to the wars that will occur at the time of the end. We can make the following observations.

THE EZEKIEL 38,39 INVASION OF ISRAEL

As we documented in "Sign Nine of the End," there will be an invasion of Israel in the last days by a number of surrounding nations. Every member of the invading army will be destroyed by the Lord Himself.

> On the mountains of Israel you will fall, you and all your troops and the nations with you. I will give you as food to all kinds of carrion birds and to the wild animals. You will fall in the open field, for I have spoken, declares the Sovereign Lord (Ezekiel 39:4,5 NIV).

THE CAMPAIGN OF ARMAGEDDON

In fact, Scripture says that humans will be fighting to the very end. We discover this from the Book of Revelation.

> The sixth angel poured out his bowl on the great river Euphrates, and its water was dried up to prepare the way for the kings from the East. Then I saw three impure spirits that looked like frogs; they came out of the mouth of the dragon, out of the mouth of the beast and out of the mouth of the false prophet. They are demonic spirits that perform signs, and they go out to the kings of the whole world, to gather them for the battle on the great day of God Almighty. "Look, I come like a thief! Blessed is the one who stays awake and remains clothed, so as not to go naked and be shamefully exposed." Then they gathered the kings together to the place that in Hebrew is called Armageddon (Revelation 16:12-16 NIV).

There will be one final attempt to destroy all the Jews which are still living in the world. This will take place at the Battle, or Campaign, of Armageddon. Hence, violence will be a way of life until the Lord returns.

A NEW KIND OF VIOLENCE: TERRORISM

There is one more thing which we must mention. While the world has always been a violent place, we discover that in our time a different type of violence has come upon the scene—terrorism. Terrorists use violence, not only to kill and maim, but to strike fear in the hearts of the people.

Jesus also warned us that the time of the end would be a fearful time for those living upon the earth.

There will be terrifying sights (Luke 21:11 NET).

When we put these signs together, we discover that humankind, instead of evolving into a more peaceful, co-existing specie, will actually become more violent, more wicked, more intolerant as we get closer to the time of the coming of the Lord. The confused world will become a fearful world—a world looking for peace, looking for answers, looking for hope.

Unfortunately, as we saw in a previous sign, they will accept a person who will give them a false hope and a false peace. This acceptance of the final Antichrist will lead the world into the most lawless and violent time in the history of our planet.

While the antidote for lawlessness and violence is found in the message of Jesus Christ, we discover that another "Sign of the End" will attempt to thwart the clear gospel message. Incredibly, it will come from those who claim to be followers of Christ!

The Organized Church
Will Turn Away from the Faith (Apostasy)

While the world at the time of the end will be characterized by law-lessness and violence, it seems that those who should have been the solution to this problem, the church, will actually turn its back on the Lord.

This brings us to our next "Sign of the End"—the visible church will turn away from the truth of the Christian faith.

THEY WILL ABANDON THE FAITH, BETRAY AND HATE ONE ANOTHER

Scripture predicts that many people, who belong to the organized, or visible, church, will actually turn away from the faith in the last days. Jesus gave the following warning.

> At that time many will turn away from the faith and will betray and hate each other (Matthew 24:10 NIV)

Interestingly, we have three specific things that Jesus warned about from those who were seemingly believers in Him.

STEP ONE: PEOPLE WILL TURN AWAY FROM THE FAITH

Jude made it clear that the "faith" had been "one-and-for-all delivered to the saints."

> Beloved, while I was very diligent to write to you concerning our common salvation, I found it necessary to write to you exhorting you to contend earnestly for the faith which was once for all delivered to the saints (Jude 3 NKJV).

The fact that many will turn away from the faith in the "last days" is indeed something that the New Testament wrote about.

Peter wrote about false teachers that would turn people away from the faith.

> But there were also false prophets among the people, even as there will be false teachers among you, who will secretly bring in destructive heresies, even denying the Lord who bought them, and bring on themselves swift destruction (2 Peter 2:1 NKJV).

THE WARNING FROM THE APOSTLE PAUL

The Apostle Paul also warned about false teachers coming into the congregations.

> Be on guard for yourselves and for all the flock of which the Holy Spirit has appointed you as overseers, to shepherd the church of God, which he purchased with his own blood. I know that after my departure savage wolves will come in among you, not sparing the flock. Men will rise up even from your own number and distort the truth to lure the disciples into following them (Acts 20:28-30 CSB).

While there have always been those who will sneak their way into Christian congregations to pervert the truth of Christ, we discover that the time of the end, there will be a large uptick in this.

STEP TWO: PROFESSING CHRISTIANS WILL BETRAY EACH OTHER

It is not merely that those who once professed Christ will turn away from the faith, to the contrary, we find that they will betray one another.

It seems that once someone abandons their profession of faith in Jesus Christ, they do not merely leave Christians alone, they will actually try to persecute them.

STEP THREE: THEY WILL HATE EACH OTHER

The betrayal leads to genuine hate. Interestingly, Jesus said the world would know who His true disciples are by the love they have for each other. Here we find that those who once professed Christ were never genuine believers. They demonstrate it by turning on the true believers.

So, what we have here is not merely people leaving what they once seemingly believed, it is much more than that. They have a hatred for what they previously stood for. Hatred to the point that they will desire to destroy those who still believe.

Jesus warned of the hatred believers would, in fact, face.

> If the world hates you, keep in mind that it hated me first. If you belonged to the world, it would love you as its own. As it is, you do not belong to the world, but I have chosen you out of the world. That is why the world hates you. Remember what I told you: 'A servant is not greater than his master.' If they persecuted me, they will persecute you also (John 15:18-20 NIV).

Though this was originally spoken to His inner circle of disciples, the truth of the Lord's prediction has been evident for two thousand years.

While the Lord Himself was betrayed by one of His own disciples, we find that those who were seemingly part of us, will actually turn away, betray, and hate.

John put it this way.

> They went out from us, but they did not really belong to us. For if they had belonged to us, they would have remained

with us; but their going showed that none of them belonged to us (1 John 2:19 NIV)

Hence, we are warned ahead of time, as hurtful and surprising as it will be, that we should expect this sort of behavior from those whom we had once trusted.

Turning away from the truth of the Christian faith will naturally lead to our next "Sign of End"—the rise of false teachers, false prophets, and false Messiahs.

There Will Be a Rise in False Prophets, False Teachers, and False Christs

Not only will many people turn away from the faith at the time of the end, Jesus also warned us about false prophets, false teachers, and also false Christs, or Messiahs. He put it this way.

> For many will come in my name, claiming, 'I am the Messiah,' and will deceive many. . . and many false prophets will appear and deceive many people (Matthew 24:5,11 NIV).

In Luke's gospel, we read this warning of Jesus.

> He said, "Watch out that you are not misled. For many will come in my name, saying, 'I am he,' and, 'The time is near.' Do not follow them! (Luke 21:8 NET).

From these predictions of Jesus, we can make the following assumptions about the Christian faith in the "last days."

ASSUMPTION 1: CHRISTIANITY WILL STILL EXIST

This first point is one that is often missed—but it certainly should not be! For these predictions to be fulfilled, Christianity must exist at the time of the end.

However, this prediction, from a human perspective, was far from certain to become a reality. Indeed, countless religions have sprung up, have had their followers, but now they cease to exist. Christianity, on the other hand, remains the most populous religion in world.

ASSUMPTION 2: THE MESSAGE ABOUT CHRIST WILL STILL BE PREACHED

Not only does the Christian faith exist in these last days, it is assumed that the message of Jesus Christ will still be widely proclaimed. In fact, the whole point of Jesus' warnings assume that people are talking about Him and His return.

Again, we emphasize, at the time Jesus made this statement, from a human standpoint, it did not seem that there was much chance for it to be fulfilled. Yet the message of Christ continues to be proclaimed worldwide.

ASSUMPTION 3: PEOPLE WILL BE CLAIMING FALSE THINGS ABOUT HIS RETURN

As the message is being proclaimed, there will be those so-called prophets who will lead the people of God astray. This is in context of Jesus' return to the earth.

THERE HAS BEEN MANY FALSE PREDICTIONS CONCERNING THE RETURN OF CHRIST

We could fill up an entire book with the false predictions made about the return of Jesus Christ. In fact, from the time the Lord ascended into heaven, until the present, there have been those who have claimed to know the precise time of the Lord's return.

As is obvious, all of these predictions have miserably failed. However, this will not stop others in the future from making the same sort of false predictions.

The problem with these predictions is that Jesus Himself specifically said that *nobody* knows the time of His return!

But as for that day and hour no one knows it—not even the angels in heaven—except the Father alone (Matthew 24:36 NET).

If the Lord Jesus says that nobody knows, then nobody knows!

ASSUMPTION 4:   MANY FALSE MESSIAHS WILL APPEAR

Jesus also warned that there will be false Christs which will appear.

In fact, there have been at least forty people in the history of Israel who have appeared on the scene and have claimed to be the Messiah. David Baron writes.

> More than forty false Messiahs appeared in the history of the Jewish nation, all of whom were followed by multitudes, and a few of them were in turn proclaimed to be the true Messiah by some of the greatest Rabbis, the only recommendation of their claims being promises of revenge and flatteries which gratified the national vanity; but at the present day, except to a few students of history, the remembrance of their names has perished from off the earth, while Jesus of Nazareth, Who was despised by His own nation and crucified, is worshipped by hundreds of millions, some of whom have in the past, and would now, count it the greatest honour to endure the rack or the stake for His Name's sake; and the religion He has founded is admittedly the only one suited for all . . . classes, and is destined ere long to cover the earth as the waters cover the sea (David Baron, *Rays of Messiah's Glory*, 1886, p. 30).

At the time of the end, these false Christs will continue to appear.

ASSUMPTION 5: PEOPLE WILL FOLLOW THOSE WHO CLAIM TO BE THE CHRIST

Jesus told believers, "Do not follow them!" This certainly tells us that others are following after them. Hence, the warning.

In sum, false messiahs have come and gone for the last two thousand years. They will continue to come on the scene and attract many followers. However, the one thing all of them will have in common is that they will lead the people astray—away from the truth of the true and living God.

Finally, as we have noted in a previous sign, there is a false Messiah who is coming, whom the entire world will receive. He will be the final Gentile ruler. Instead of being "the Christ," this personage will be the "anti-Christ." His coming will bring the darkest time in the history of our planet.

SUMMARY TO SIGN 20: FALSE PROPHETS, FALSE TEACHERS, AND FALSE CHRISTS WILL CONTINUE TO APPEAR

With respect to the time of the end, Jesus gave stern warnings about the false prophets, false teachers, as well as false Christs that would come upon the scene.

From the warnings the Lord gave, we can make the following observations.

At the time of the end Christianity will still exist. We must remember when this prediction was made there were a number of religions in the Roman Empire—all vying for converts. In other words, it was not a given that Christianity would even survive a generation, much less two thousand years. Of course, as we know, it has.

Furthermore, people will still be preaching about His return. This is another prediction which seemed unlikely at the time. Yet, it too has come to pass.

We are also told that false prophets will arise and lead people astray. In fact, the history of the church has been filled with people who have led Christians astray by claiming to know the exact time of the return of the Lord.

Others will appear who claim to be the Christ. As author David Baron documented, over forty people in Jewish history have claimed to be the long-awaited Messiah.

Because we have been forewarned, none of this should surprise us. Jesus, as God the Son, has correctly predicted all these things.

We also know that a false Christ is coming whom the world will receive. His appearance will bring the world into the worst time of trouble that they have ever experienced—the Great Tribulation.

The message of the false prophets and false Messiah's will include the hatred for God's chosen people—the Jew. Our next sign will examine this phenomenon.

There Will Be a
Rise in Anti-Semitism

We have mentioned a number of signs of the last days that pertain to the modern state of Israel. Unhappily, this next sign is seen too often in our world today—anti-Semitism.

THE WHOLE WORLD WILL BE AGAINST THEM

We have already observed what the Scripture says—the entire world will be against Israel at the time of the end.

> On that day, when all the nations of the earth are gathered against her, I will make Jerusalem an immovable rock for all the nations. All who try to move it will injure themselves (Zechariah 12:3 NIV).

We also saw in a previous sign that Israel would be in the spotlight in the last days. Specifically, the Bible mentions the nations in their region, as well as all the nations of the earth. Not only will they constantly be aware of Israel, the whole world will be against them!

In other words, they will be hated by a large majority of the people of the earth. Sadly, this includes many people in the organized church.

BDS

This refers to the idea of boycotting, divesting from, and sanctioning any company that has dealings with Israel—specifically companies that deal with them in the disputed territories.

It has not only caught on in the secular world. In fact, the largest Presbyterian denomination in the United States, PCUSA, has joined the boycott. Other "Christian" institutions have also joined in with the BDS movement.

UNESCO

This organization, United Nations Educational Scientific and Cultural Organization has been infamous for its anti-Semitism. Indeed, they have made rulings that Jerusalem has never belonged to the Jews, that the Temple Mount was not the site of the previous Temples, and that the entire Temple Mount is exclusively a Muslim holy site.

Daily, we see stories that confirm this prediction of Scripture—the Jews are hated by the world. The hatred will become more and more obvious as we get closer to the time of the end.

THIS IS NOTHING NEW

Anti-Semitism has always been with us. In fact, historically, the Jews have been singled out as problematic in most, if not all, of the countries where they have migrated. We will consider this in more detail in Appendix 3.

THIS HAS BEEN PREDICTED BY THE LORD

As is true with all of our other signs, the hatred of the descendants of Abraham, Isaac, and Jacob, has been predicted by Scripture.

> You will become a thing of horror, a byword and an object of ridicule among all the peoples where the Lord will drive you (Deuteronomy 28:37 NIV).

This has certainly been the experience of the Jews as they have wandered across the earth.

As is true with some of our other signs, such as lawlessness and violence, anti-Semitism, while it has always been with us, will see an increase at the time of the end. To confirm this, all one has to do is look at the news of the day. It seems that Israel is blamed for about every woe that the world experiences.

The good news is that this will all someday come to an end when the people of Israel recognize Jesus as the Messiah, and He comes again to establish His kingdom—while ruling from Jerusalem.

However, until that happens, we should expect the hatred of the Jews to become more and more visible in this Christ rejecting world.

As we previously mentioned, it will not only be the Jews who will be hated and persecuted at the time of the end. The violent persecution of Christians will continue—as we will observe in our next sign.

Christians Will
Continue to be Persecuted

While the world considers itself to be more and more enlightened and tolerant, as they believe they are continually "evolving," there is one area where it seems they are going backwards—they still are still persecuting certain groups. In our previous sign, we noted the anti-Semitism that continues, the persecution of Jews.

However, there is another group in our present-world that continues to be hated, ridiculed, and in many cases, killed—Christians

JESUS WARNED BELIEVERS ABOUT CONTINUAL PERSECUTION

Again, this should not take us by surprise.

> Then you will be handed over to be persecuted and put to death, and you will be hated by all nations because of me (Matthew 24:9 NIV).

From the warnings of Jesus, we can conclude the following things.

CHRISTIANS WILL EXIST AT THE TIME OF THE END

There will still be believers in Jesus Christ in the last days. From a human point of view, this was anything but certain at the time the Lord made the statement.

Yet, His church, His true believers will continue to exist—just as the Lord predicted.

> On this rock I will build my church, and the gates of Hades will not overcome it (Matthew 16:18 NIV).

Nothing can stop this from happening. Nothing.

THE HATRED FOR CHRISTIANS WILL BE WORLDWIDE

Not only will believers in Christ exist, they will be found everywhere. Furthermore, wherever they do reside, there will be hatred because of the name of Christ.

BELIEVERS IN JESUS CHRIST WILL BE PERSECUTED BECAUSE OF HIM

We discover that Christians will also be persecuted for their beliefs. Jesus said.

> But before all this, they will seize you and persecute you. They will hand you over to synagogues and put you in prison, and you will be brought before kings and governors, and all on account of my name (Luke 21:12,13 NIV).

The Apostle Paul echoed this truth.

> In fact, everyone who wants to live a godly life in Christ Jesus will be persecuted (2 Timothy 3:12 NIV).

This has certainly been the experience of Christians throughout the ages.

CHRISTIANS WILL BE PUT TO DEATH FOR THEIR BELIEFS

In many cases, persecutions will lead to death. History tells us that more Christians were martyred for their belief in Jesus Christ in the 20th century than in the previous nineteen centuries combined! This will only increase as we get closer to the end.

This sad reality is seen every day in our world. Indeed, hardly a day goes by where there is not some story of Christians being persecuted, kidnapped, or murdered, merely because they are followers of Jesus Christ. As the Lord warned us, this will continue until the time of His return.

Though persecuted, Christians will continue to preach the message of Jesus Christ—that He has died for the sins of the world, and then came back from the dead to demonstrate that He is the One whom He claimed to be. Our next sign looks at a particular segment of Jesus' message that is ridiculed—the predictions that He is coming again!

Unbelievers Will Scoff at the Idea Of Christ's Return

For the last two thousand years, Christians have claimed that Jesus Christ will return to the earth. Indeed, this is the hope that we all have.

On the night of His betrayal, Jesus gave these comforting words to His disciples:

> Do not let your hearts be distressed. You believe in God; believe also in me. There are many dwelling places in my Father's house. Otherwise, I would have told you, because I am going away to make ready a place for you. And if I go and make ready a place for you, I will come again and take you to be with me, so that where I am you may be too (John 14:1-3 NET).

The Lord has promised to "come again." We should note that He *always* keeps His promises!

In fact, the New Testament closes with this hope:

> I, Jesus, have sent my angel to testify to you about these things for the churches. I am the root and the descendant of David, the bright morning star! And the Spirit and the bride say, "Come!" And let the one who hears say: "Come!" . . . The one who testifies to these things

says, "Yes, I am coming soon!" Amen! Come, Lord Jesus! (Revelation 22:16,20 NET).

MANY CONTINUE TO SCOFF AT THE IDEA OF THE RETURN OF THE LORD

As is obvious, there are many people who reject this idea. Indeed, they scoff and ridicule the prediction that a man who lived and died two thousand years ago will return to the earth as King of Kings and Lord of Lords.

In fact, the lack of interest from Christians about the Second Coming of Christ led to a conference in New York City from concerned Bible teachers. The "Call for the Conference," began with the following words.

> Dear Brethren in Christ: When from any cause some vital doctrine of God's Word has fallen into neglect or suffered contradiction and reproach, it becomes the serious duty of those who hold it, not only strongly and constantly to re-affirm it, but to seek by all means in their power to bring back the Lord's people to its apprehension and acceptance. The precious doctrine of Christ's second personal appearance has, we are constrained to believe, long lain under such neglect and misapprehension.
>
> In the Word of God we find it holding a most conspicuous place. It is there strongly and constantly emphasized as a personal and imminent event, the great object of the Church's hope, the powerful motive to holy living and watchful service, the inspiring ground of confidence amid the sorrows and sins of the present evil world, and the event that is to end the reign of Death, cast down Satan from his throne, and establish the kingdom of God on earth. So vital, indeed, is this truth represented to be that the denial of it is pointed out as one of the conspicuous signs of the last days (Nathaniel

West, *Second Coming of Christ, Premillennial Essays of the Prophetic Conference*, Chicago, F.H. Revell, 1879, p. 11),

This was written for a conference that took place on October 30,31, and November 1ˢᵗ in 1878!

RIDICULING THE TEACHINGS OF CHRIST IS NOT SOMETHING NEW

Interestingly, as soon as believers in Jesus Christ started talking about His return, the scoffers began rejecting their claims. The Apostle Paul, in preaching to a group of inquirers in Athens, said the following concerning the God of the Bible:

> Therefore since we are God's offspring, we should not think that the divine being is like gold or silver or stone—an image made by human design and skill. In the past God overlooked such ignorance, but now he commands all people everywhere to repent. For he has set a day when he will judge the world with justice by the man he has appointed. He has given proof of this to everyone by raising him from the dead." When they heard about the resurrection of the dead, some of them sneered, but others said, "We want to hear you again on this subject." At that, Paul left the Council (Acts 17:29-34 NIV).

We discover that when they heard about Jesus' resurrection from the dead, and that He would be the One who would one day judge the world, many of the crowd sneered. As we noted, this type of ridicule has continued to this day.

PETER WARNED OF LAST DAYS SCOFFERS

In fact, Peter wrote that there would still be scoffers in the "last days."

> Above all, you must understand that in the last days scoffers will come, scoffing and following their own evil desires. They will say, "Where is this 'coming' he promised? Ever since our

ancestors died, everything goes on as it has since the beginning of creation" (2 Peter 3:3-4 NIV).

They taunt Christians with the fact that it has been two thousand years since Christ lived.

JUDE

We also find that Jude said the same thing:

> But, dear friends, remember what the apostles of our Lord Jesus Christ foretold. They said to you, "In the last times there will be scoffers who will follow their own ungodly desires." These are the people who divide you, who follow mere natural instincts and do not have the Spirit (Jude 17-19 NIV).

Sound familiar? Yes, today the world is filled with scoffers. Indeed, we could fill an entire book with the claims of present-day scoffers who ridicule the idea that Jesus Christ will return to the earth.

In fact, this is a point that everyone, Christians and non-Christians, can agree upon—there are many scoffers today.

Hence, there is really no reason to fill page after page of the accusations, denials, rebuffs, and ridicules of non-believers. We all know that, for whatever reason, countless people reject the claims of Christ's return.

Peter then reminded his readers of this when he wrote the following.

> Dear friends, don't overlook this one fact: With the Lord one day is like a thousand years, and a thousand years like one day. The Lord does not delay his promise, as some understand delay, but is patient with you, not wanting any to perish but all to come to repentance (2 Peter 3:8-9)

Well, one hundred years ago, it may have looked like the scoffers were right. But, as we have documented in this book, *not* any longer!

THESE PASSAGES ASSUMES CERTAIN THINGS ABOUT THE LAST DAYS

While it is probably rarely thought of, these passages predict certain things which will be true in the "last days." Indeed, like all of the other signs that we have considered, there are assumptions that these writers make. They include the following.

ASSUMPTION 1: CHRISTIANITY WILL BE AROUND IN THE LAST DAYS

The assumption of these passages is that there will be Christians existing at the time of the end. We can only imagine how inconceivable these predictions would have been at the time when they were written.

ASSUMPTION 2: CHRISTIANS WILL STILL BE PREACHING THE RETURN OF CHRIST

Furthermore, those who believe in Jesus will still be proclaiming the coming of the Lord at the time of the end.

ASSUMPTION 3: PEOPLE HAVE BEEN PREDICTING THE COMING OF THE LORD FOR A LONG TIME

In the last days, scoffers will object by saying that Christians have been predicting for a long time that Christ will return. This assumes that these claims, about Christ's return, have been being made for a lengthy period of time—and are continuing to be made.

THEY WILL DENY GOD'S MIRACULOUS INTERVENTION

Peter says they willingly forget, that is, they deny God's past intervention in the world. This is certainly true in the example which he gives—most people in the world would ridicule the idea that the Lord sent a flood to destroy the earth in Noah's day. He wrote:

> For they deliberately suppress this fact, that by the word of
> God heavens existed long ago and an earth was formed out
> of water and by means of water. Through these things the

world existing at that time was destroyed when it was deluged with water. But by the same word the present heavens and earth have been reserved for fire, by being kept for the day of judgment and destruction of the ungodly (2 Peter 3:5-7 NET).

We should carefully observe what Peter states in this passage. The unbelievers are "deliberately suppressing the fact" of God's past intervention into the world. In particular, the Flood that the Lord sent in the days of Noah that destroyed the world. Consequently, the ungodly are not expecting any future judgment by the Lord.

In sum, we find that these three assumptions, and the denial of God's miraculous intervention, are true in our day.

THE EXAMPLES OF THOSE WHO HAVE FAITHFULLY BELIEVED GOD'S WORD IN PAST GENERATIONS

Before we go on to our next sign, we should say a word about the people, whom we have quoted in this book, who have lived and died, during the time these "Signs of the End" were not taking place.

As we have documented, there were a number of people who, despite the scoffers, believed that the predictions in the Bible would someday be fulfilled. Of course, they were ridiculed, and as we have mentioned in the case of Henry Finch, publicly disgraced.

In 1789, Elhanan Winchester wrote of the ridicule he received for believing that these future prophecies would be literally fulfilled:

> I am not at all ashamed, boldly and openly, to be bear my testimony to the truth and reality of the literal sense of prophecy, however I may be laughed at, and ridiculed, by men of this dissolute age. I do not doubt but Noah was ridiculed, when he told the old world, that God would destroy all living from the face of the earth, by a flood of waters . . .

Doubtless, they judged the waters could not possibly overwhelm the dry land, and therefore treated the old patriarch with the greatest contempt. But the long-threatened, long derided period came at last . . . Therefore, since the apostle Peter tells us that 'The heavens and the earth, which are now by the same word, are kept in store, and reserved unto fire against the day of judgment and perdition of ungodly men;' I cannot see any reason at all, why we should not believe, that God's threatening of the general conflagration, and fiery lake, will be as fully and exactly, yea, and as literally accomplished; as those he denounced against the old world were fulfilled, when the unexpected flood of water came upon ungodly inhabitants, who had long laughed at the idea (Elhanan Winchester, *A Course Of Lectures on Prophecies That Remain To Be Fulfilled*, Volume 1, London, 1789, p. 18).

It seems that these brave individuals should be placed in the same category of people whom the writer to the Hebrews spoke when he wrote the following:

Others experienced mockings and scourgings, as well as bonds and imprisonment. . . The world was not worthy of them (Hebrews 11: 36,38 CSB).

Against all odds, these Bible teachers chose to literally believe what the Lord had promised would take place in the future. Although, they never lived to see it, they have been vindicated.

Indeed, with the Bible and the Bible alone, they predicted that the Jews would still exist at the time of the end, return to their ancient homeland, and form a modern state with a united city of Jerusalem as their capital.

They also recognized that this newly formed country would search for peace, as they would be in the spotlight of the world, with everyone against them. In addition, they would then build a Temple, and offer animal sacrifices—because they have returned to their homeland in unbelief of Jesus.

All of these things have literally come to pass with the exception of the building of the Temple—which as we have noted, the preparations are now being made.

Consequently, the Bible teachers which we have quoted in this book are the complete opposite of the scoffers, false prophets, and false teachers who lead people astray.

In fact, they are examples, to each and every one of us, to believe what the Lord has promised in His Word. Indeed, the Lord means what He says, and says what He means!

A WISE WORD FOR SCOFFERS FROM A PAST BIBLE COMMENTATOR

J.C. Ryle, in the 19th century, offered a fitting conclusion for those who would scoff at the prophecies in Scripture:

"Ah!" I can imagine some reader saying, "This is all foolishness, raving, and nonsense! This writer is beside himself. This is all extravagant fanaticism. Where is the likelihood, where is the probability of all this? The world is going on as it always did. The world will last for my time. Do not say so. Do not drive away the subject by such language as this.

> This is the way that men talked in the days of Noah and Lot—but what happened? They found to their cost that Noah and Lot were right. The Apostle Peter foretold, eighteen hundred years ago, that men would talk this way. "There shall come in the last days scoffers, he tells us, "saying, Where is the promise of His coming? For since the fathers fell asleep, all things continue as they were from the beginning of the creation (2 Peter 3:3,4). Oh, do not fulfill this prophecy by your unbelief! (J.C. Ryle, *Coming Events and Present Duties*,

Second Edition, London, William Hunt and Company, 1879, pp, 36, 37).

Indeed, we trust that those reading this book will not fulfill Peter's prophecy by scoffing at the evidence that is so readily available to all.

SUMMING UP SIGN 23: PEOPLE WILL CONTINUE TO RIDICULE THE IDEA OF THE RETURN OF JESUS CHRIST TO THE EARTH

At the time of the end, there will still be those people who scoff at the idea that Christ is coming back. In fact, it seems that the ridicule will only intensify.

Fortunately, the Lord has warned us about this ahead of time. While the doubters have always been around, this will increase in the last days.

In contrast, we have examples of godly Bible commentators who believed the day would come when the prophecies would find their literal fulfillment. While ridiculed during their lifetime, they have indeed been vindicated by the recent events in the world.

Therefore, though it has indeed been two thousand years since Jesus was here upon the earth, this is not a problem as far as God is concerned. He is certainly in no hurry to fulfill the predictions that Scripture has made. We know that He will fulfill all that has been predicted—in His time!

The Wicked Will Not
Understand the Signs of the Times

The Bible not only tells us the basic outline of what to expect in the future, as well as many specific details, it also tells us that those who are wicked will *never* understand what is taking place—try as they might.

THE WICKED WILL SEARCH FOR ANSWERS BUT WILL NOT FIND THEM

In Daniel 12, we are told about the situation that humanity will find itself in the last days. It is highly instructive.

People will be looking for answers as to what is happening in the world. In fact, the Bible says that they will search here and there. In other words, they will try to find out the meaning, but they will not be able to. Daniel was told the following.

> But you, Daniel, roll up and seal the words of the scroll until the time of the end. Many will go here and there to increase knowledge (Daniel 12:4 NIV).

The knowledge these people will seek is knowledge of the Book of Daniel, knowledge about Bible prophecy. Though they seek it, they will not understand what it means.

The prophet Amos also spoke of such a day.

People will stagger from sea to sea and wander from north to east, searching for the word of the Lord, but they will not find it (Amos 8:12 NIV).

THE WICKED WILL NOT UNDERSTAND WHAT IS HAPPENING

In fact, later in this chapter, we are specifically told that the wicked will *not* understand what is taking place.

> He replied, "Go your way, Daniel, because the words are rolled up and sealed until the time of the end. Many will be purified, made spotless and refined, but the wicked will continue to be wicked. None of the wicked will understand (Daniel 12:10 NIV).

This could not be clearer. At the time of the end, the wicked will continue to be wicked. Though they will seek to know what is going on in the world, they will never understand the plan and purposes of God.

In the 18th century, John Gill wrote the following concerning the phrase, "and none of the wicked shall understand."

> Neither the doctrines of the Gospel spiritually and experimentally; nor the providences of God, and what he is doing in the world; and particularly not the prophecy of this book, and especially what has been just delivered (John Gill, "Daniel," *Exposition of the Old Testament*, 6 Volumes, 1748-1763).

LIFE WILL GET WORSE NEAR THE TIME OF THE END

In speaking of the "last days" the Apostle Paul wrote about how things would actually get worse.

> But evil people and charlatans will go from bad to worse, deceiving others and being deceived themselves (2 Timothy 3:13 NET).

Not only will it go from bad to worse, as we saw in a previous sign, false prophets will arise who will deceive the people, as well as deceiving themselves!

THE REASON WHY THE WICKED WILL NOT UNDERSTAND

The Lord Jesus gave the reason as to why these people will never understand God's truth.

> This is the verdict: Light has come into the world, but people loved darkness instead of light because their deeds were evil (John 3:19 NIV).

Simply put, they do not want to understand. People love the darkness rather than the light.

The Apostle Paul wrote something similar.

> As it is written: "There is no one righteous, not even one; there is no one who understands; there is no one who seeks God" (Romans 3:10 NIV).

In sum, God is *not* hiding from us. In fact, the Bible says the problem is with the human race. Indeed, we are running from Him.

The situation is similar to those in Israel during the time of the prophet Isaiah.

Our courts oppose the righteous, and justice is nowhere to be found.

> Truth stumbles in the streets, and honesty has been outlawed. Yes, truth is gone, and anyone who renounces evil is attacked (Isaiah 59:14-15 NLT).

Truth is indeed gone with those who turn their back on the Lord.

JESUS SPOKE OF THE FEARFUL TIMES THAT ARE COMING

Since humans will not be able to make sense out of the catastrophic events which will be happening in the world, fear will grip them. Jesus spoke of this when asked about the state of the world in the last days.

> Men's hearts failing them from fear and the expectation of those things which are coming on the earth (Luke 21:26 NKJV).

This will be a fearful time for those living upon the earth.

Paul wrote to the Thessalonians about how these events of the end times will take the wicked by surprise.

> Now, brothers and sisters, about times and dates we do not need to write to you, for you know very well that the day of the Lord will come like a thief in the night. While people are saying, "Peace and safety," destruction will come on them suddenly, as labor pains on a pregnant woman, and they will not escape (1 Thessalonians 5:1-3 NIV).

It will indeed be a horrific ordeal for those living on the earth who reject the message of Christ. Terrible things will be happening, but they will not have any idea as to *why* these events are taking place.

THE LEADERS FORGET THAT GOD IS IN CONTROL

In a chapter titled, "God Again Takes Control" in his 1939 book, *Prophecies I Have Seen Fulfilled In My Lifetime*, Swiss author Paul Perret, wrote these insightful words.

> In spite of the grandiloquent and thundering speeches of men who considers themselves masters of this hour, it becomes increasingly evident that, before the insolvency of world politics, God is resuming the direction of the nations. This is most striking show in a recent event that dominates contemporary history.

I refer to the proclamation of Lord Balfour, dated November 2nd, 1917, opening up Palestine to Jews throughout the world who might wish to return to their home land. This proclamation was solemnly confirmed by the League of Nations—the most notable piece of work, perhaps, accomplished by that august assembly.

Diplomatic centers are plunged in the deepest ignorance as to what the future holds in store for the world. What is to become of France, Germany, Great Britain, Italy, America? Complete mystery—question without an answer. One thing only is certain to intelligent minds, that is, the Jews will return to Palestine and that it will belong to them, in spite of all the obstacles that might be raised.

The policy of the entire world is still dominated by the promise given to Abraham: "This land will I give to you and to your seed forever." And there is another saying that soars still higher above the world. "Heaven and earth shall pass away, but My words shall not pass away" (Paul Perret, *Prophecies I Have Seen Fulfilled*, London, Marshall, Morgan & Scott LTD., 1939, p. 86).

While these profound words were written in 1939, as the Second World War was taking shape, they sound like something we would read in a present-day editorial.

Indeed, the leaders of the world believe that they are controlling their own destiny, when right in front of their very eyes the eternal Word of God is being fulfilled. However, they cannot see the truth, nor hear it, because they do not wish to.

And, as Perret predicted, the Balfour Declaration in 1917 set the stage for the Jews to return to their ancient homeland; even though in the intervening years from the time he wrote, 1939 and the fulfillment, 1948, the Nazi Holocaust claimed six million Jewish lives.

THE RESPONSIBILITY THAT HUMANS HAVE

Almost 200 years ago, Alexander Keith explained the situation in which humans find themselves.

> If the prophecies of Scripture can be proved to be genuine—if they be of such nature as no foresight of man could possibly have predicted—if the events foretold in them were described hundreds or even thousands of years before those events became parts of the history of man—and if the history itself correspond with the prediction, then the evidence which the prophecies impart is a sign and a wonder to every age: no clearer testimony or greater assurance of the truth can be given (Alexander Keith, *Evidence of the Truth of the Christian Religion*, New York, Harper and Brothers, 1839, pp, 18,19).

Clearly, the evidence is there for all to see. Yet, for the most part, the unbelieving world will not look at this evidence which the Lord has given to them. Therefore, they will *never* understand what is taking place.

In fact, Paul wrote that unbelievers are actively suppressing the truth of God.

> But God shows his anger from heaven against all sinful, wicked people who suppress the truth by their wickedness (Romans 1:18 NLT).

The picture of unbelieving humanity is not of a person actively looking for truth. To the contrary, they are actively and willingly suppressing the truth which the Lord is revealing to them. In other words, God is speaking to them but they are covering their ears! They purposely do *not* want to hear His truth. This is why they are in darkness.

James Brookes made this insightful comment about the truth the Lord has revealed.

> To the Jew . . . may be applied with the fine language . . . "For his sakes empires had risen and flourished, and decayed;" . . . Edom, Assyria, Babylon, Persia, Rome, the mightiest powers of earth have sought to crush them, and have perished for the attempt. Well might Fredrick the Great say, "Meddle not with the Jews; no man has ever touched them and prospered;" and of the celebrated Hegel his biographer states that having often and long thought upon Hebrew history, and often changed his thoughts, "all his life long, it tormented him as a dark enigma." It is a dark enigma indeed unless studied in the light of God's prophetic word (James Brookes, *Maranatha, The Lord Cometh*, Fleming H. Revell Company, 1889, p. 444).

The meaning of history is indeed a dark enigma without the light of God's Word. However, when one examines the promises and predictions of the Bible, and then honestly checks them out with the facts of history, Scripture will be found to be miraculously accurate in all that it states.

Over two hundred years ago, Bible commentator Elhanan Winchester stated this important truth.

> Among all the evidences of Divine revelation that have ever appeared to mankind, the fulfilling of prophecies is one that deserves our most regard . . . To foretell future events with exactness, that have no dependence upon natural causes, can only be done by Jehovah himself, or those whom he inspires (Elhanan Winchester *A Course Of Lectures on Prophecies That Remain To Be Fulfilled*, Volume 1, London, 1789, p. 26).

This is indeed true! Only the Lord Himself could do something like we have documented in this book—accurately foretell the future.

Long ago, the Lord put it this way to those who are willing to examine the evidence.

You have heard; now look at all the evidence! Will you not admit that what I say is true? (Isaiah 48:6 NET).

SUMMARY TO SIGN 24: THE WICKED WILL NOT UNDERSTAND WHAT IS HAPPENING IN THE WORLD IN THE LAST DAYS

Those who have rejected the idea that God has spoken to us through the Bible, as well as through the Person of Jesus Christ, have cut themselves off from any possibility of knowing the truth of the basic questions of life. Who am I? Why am I here? What will happen to me when I die?

Bible prophecy has been given by God, to the world, so that everyone who wishes to know, can know, that He does indeed exist, that He knows the future, and that He is in control of the future.

Along this line, the Lord has provided an objective witness to the world in the nation of Israel. Therefore, if anyone truly wants to know the truth-of -the-matter, all they have to do is examine God's dealings in history with the descendants of Abraham, Isaac, and Jacob.

In other words, if anyone truly wants to know the truth, they can know.

However, as Daniel 12 tells us, the wicked will go on searching, but they will never understand.

Jesus provided the reason as to why this is so—people loved the darkness rather than the light because their deeds are evil. Therefore, they remain "in the dark" with respect as to the meaning of what is taking place in the world.

It is only when a person humbly turns to the living God that they can know the answers to the most important questions of life.

Bible-Believers Will Understand What is Taking Place

We now come to our last "Sign of the End," which basically sums up all that we have been saying in this book. Simply put, we *can* understand what is taking place in the world today because the Lord has told us these things ahead of time! We can make the following observations.

WE ARE COMMANDED TO EXAMINE THE EVIDENCE

To begin with, Scripture encourages people to think—to examine the evidence. Paul wrote.

> But test everything that is said. Hold on to what is good (1 Thessalonians 5:21 NLT).

Testing involves using our minds—weighing the evidence.

Another New Testament writer, John, put it this way.

> Beloved, do not believe every spirit, but test the spirits, whether they are of God; because many false prophets have gone out into the world (1 John 4:1 NKJV).

We "test" the spirits by thinking, by using our "minds."

The Apostle Paul encouraged the church at Corinth to judge, as sensible people, the things that he said. He wrote.

> You are reasonable people. Decide for yourselves if what I am about to say is true (1 Corinthians 10:15 NLT).

To sum up, we have the famous words of Jesus.

> You shall love the Lord your God with all your heart, and with all your soul, and with all your mind (Matthew 22:37 NRSV).

We are to love the Lord with "all of our mind." The Bible, therefore, encourages thinking, investigating the facts, and then weighing and evaluating the evidence.

SCRIPTURES SAYS WE CAN KNOW THE TRUTH OF BIBLE PROPHECY

Along this line of investigating the evidence, we find that in the last chapter of the Book of Daniel, there is a conversation between Daniel and a supernatural being. One of the things that the prophet learns is that our knowledge, about these "events of the last days," will increase as we get closer to the time of the end.

> But you, Daniel, close up these words and seal the book until the time of the end. Many will dash about, and knowledge will increase (Daniel 12:4 NET).

This is a specific prediction about the time of the end and the understanding of Bible prophecy. Indeed, as we get closer to the coming of the Lord, the knowledge and understanding of certain aspects of Bible prophecy will become clearer and clearer.

This is precisely what we have discovered in our study. Certain things, that did not seem to make sense to commentators in the past, have now become clear to us. This will continue to be true as we approach the time when these predicted events will take place.

Furthermore, in this same passage, the prophet Daniel, though he himself did not understand what these things meant, was explicitly told that, at the "time of the end," the wise will indeed understand what is taking place.

> I heard, but I did not understand. So I said, "Sir, what will happen after these things?" He said, "Go, Daniel. For these matters are closed and sealed until the time of the end. Many will be purified, made clean, and refined, but the wicked will go on being wicked. None of the wicked will understand, though the wise will understand (Daniel 12:8-10 NET).

We should not miss this promise of Scripture—the wise will understand! Who are the wise? They are those who take the Word of God, and the subject of Bible prophecy, seriously.

Bible commentator John Gill, writing in the 1700's, made the following astute observations about this passage in Daniel.

> That is, towards the end of the time appointed, many persons will be stirred up to inquire into these things delivered in this book, and will spare no pains or cost to get knowledge of them; will read and study the Scriptures, and meditate on them; compare one passage with another; spiritual things with spiritual, in order to obtain the mind of Christ; will peruse carefully the writings of such who have gone before them, who have attempted anything of this kind; and will go far and near to converse with persons that have any understanding of such things: and by such means, with the blessing of God upon them, the knowledge of this book of prophecy will be increased; and things will appear plainer the nearer the accomplishment of them is; and especially when accomplished, when prophecy and facts can be compared together: and not only this kind of knowledge, but knowledge of all spiritual things, of all evangelic truths and doctrines, will be abundantly enlarged at this time; and the earth will be filled and covered with it, as the sea with its

waters (John Gill, Daniel, *Exposition of the Old Testament*, 6 Volumes, 1748-1763).

This could not have been said any better in our present day!

About one hundred years before John Gill, Increase Mather, wrote something similar.

> The angel Gabriel, commanded Daniel to "shut up the words, and seal the Book, even to the time of the end," Dan. 12.4, which shows that this Prophesie, though it be obscure before, yet when the time for the accomplishment of it approacheth, many shall be stirred up to inquire with all diligence into the meaning . . . and the promise of their encouragement so to do, that knowledge shall be increased, that is, by the assistance and blessing of the Lion of the Tribe of Judah, the root of David, who alone is worthy to open the sealed Book, Rev. 5,5,9 (Increase Mather, *The Mystery of Israel's Salvation Explained and Applied*, 1669, p. A 3).

John Gill wrote over 250 years ago, Increase Mather wrote over 350 years ago. Amazingly, based upon this Scripture, each predicted the same thing—as humanity gets closer to the "time of the end," Bible prophecy will become more understandable for those who diligently search the Scriptures with the assistance and blessing of the Lord.

WE CAN KNOW THE TRUTH!

We also find that Jesus made a similar promise about His own teachings. John records Him saying the following.

> If anyone wants to do God's will, he will know about my teaching, whether it is from God or whether I speak from my own authority (John 7:17 NET).

This is a promise of God! Indeed, the Lord said that anybody who wants to know, can know whether or not He speaks for God.

Consequently, we can know the truth. The Lord Jesus elsewhere said.

Then you will know the truth, and the truth will set you free (John 8:32 NIV).

This is another promise of God!

In sum, the Bible makes it plain that those who want to know the truth will indeed know it! Specifically, when it comes to the understanding of Bible prophecy in the "last days," we *can* know the truth!

BACK TO THE KEY TO BIBLE PROPHECY: THE JEW

As we have seen in our previous "24 Signs of the End," if we wish to know God's plan for the world for time and eternity, it is absolute imperative that we look at the Jews. This includes Jesus, the Messiah of the Jews, as well as the history of the Jewish people.

In the early part of the 19th century, A.H. McNeile explained it well.

Of this universally pervading, but hitherto invisible kingdom of God, an outward and visible index has been given to the world in the history of the Jewish nation. From the page of that history, as from a bright reflector, we learn the great principles of God's management in the history of the Jewish nation . . . first, the person character, and ministry of Jesus Christ, "the faithful witness," who himself was a Jew; and secondly, the history of the Jewish nation, to who Jehovah says, "Ye are my witnesses."

In turning our attention to the Jews, then we are not merely gratifying an historical, prophetical, or intellectual curiosity; but if we look aright, we are putting into operation upon our souls God's own manifested witness for Himself, unto our knowledge of Him, which is life eternal (A.H. McNeile, *Prospects of the Jews*, preface, pp vii, viii, 1838).

Eternal life is indeed found in the Person of Jesus Christ. Therefore, we must always look to Him for the answers to the meaning of life.

Furthermore, the Lord has continually provided a living objective witness to the truthfulness of His Word—the Jew. In sum, God wants us to know the truth about Himself!

CHRISTIANITY HAS REPLACED GOD'S PREVIOUS REVELATION

This point is crucial. While the religion revealed in the Old Testament was, in fact, God's Word to the human race, it has been superseded by the coming of the Messiah, Jesus Christ. This is essential to understand. Again, we cite 19th century Bible scholar A.H. McNeile.

> This was the true religion, as then revealed in the wisdom of the living God, and the enjoyment of it issued in true salvation. But all this has long since ceased. That which was then future and foreordained, has since been actually performed. The substance of all this is Christ. The miraculous rending of the veil in the temple, when Jesus expired on the cross, was God's own sentence of abrogation upon ancient Judaism as such. The destruction of the temple itself, and the holy city, completed the manifestation of Jehovah's purpose regarding ancient Judaism. He took away the type, that he might establish the antetype. He took away the sign, that he might establish the thing signified. He took away a dispensation consisting of significant promises, superseding it by a dispensation based upon actual performances. Sacrifice, and offering, and burnt-offering for sin he would have no longer, but the all sufficient sacrifice of the death of Jesus Christ *once offered*. Ancient Judaism, therefore, which was the truth of God *then*, merged into Christianity, which has been, and is, the truth of God forever (A.H. McNeile, *Prospects of the Jews*, Preface, 1838, p. ix.).

Since the Lord Jesus, in His coming, has fulfilled what the Old Testament was pointing to, the Temple, the sacrifices, and the rituals are no longer necessary. Indeed, only Jesus Christ is necessary.

WHAT WILL YOU DO WITH JESUS?

In reality, the ultimate question, that every human being must answer, comes down to when Jesus came "the first time." The Bible says that He lived a perfect life, died for our sins on the cross of Calvary, rose from the dead, and then ascended into heaven. Today, He is our "High Priest"—the One who intercedes to God the Father on behalf of believers.

At some time in the future, known only to the Lord, He will come for those who have believed in Him. This has been the hope of Christians for the last two thousand years.

Eventually, every human being will stand before Him. Those who have believed in Jesus will experience eternal life in His presence, while those who have rejected Him will spend eternity apart from Him.

The good news is that we have been told that we can "know" that we have eternal life. John explained it this way.

> The one who has the Son has this eternal life; the one who does not have the Son of God does not have this eternal life. I have written these things to you who believe in the name of the Son of God so that you may know that you have eternal life (1 John 5:12,13 NIV).

This is the "good news!" If one believes in Jesus Christ they can *know* that they have eternal life!

So, we conclude our "Signs of the End" by asking the reader this question, "Do you know that you have eternal life in Jesus Christ?"

Summing Up the 25 Signs of the End

In this book, we have looked at 25 distinct signs that the Bible gives about what the world will be like in the "last days"—the time before the return of the Lord.

We have cited Scripture, the testimonies of many past commentators, as well as current events that support the predictions of the Bible. As we said in our introduction, there will be more and more stories in the future which will give further evidence that what Scripture says is true.

There will be many more stories, that will make the headlines, which could call for an update of this book. However, what will never be updated is the teaching of the Bible itself on this subject. Indeed, Jude wrote.

> Dear friends, although I have been eager to write to you about our common salvation, I now feel compelled instead to write to encourage you to contend earnestly for the faith that was once for all entrusted to the saints (Jude 3 NET).

The faith has been once-and-for-all delivered, or entrusted, to believers. In other words, the Bible, as completed some two thousand years ago, is a sufficient source for human beings to know who God is, who we are, as well as what He wants from us.

SUMMING UP THE SIGNS

Let's now review these 25 signs that we have just considered. As we do so, ask yourself this question, "What are the odds that all of this could have happened by chance?"

SIGN 1: THE MIRACLE OF ISRAEL'S SURVIVAL

As we have noted in this book, the nation of Israel is the key in understanding Bible prophecy. Indeed, they have been central to God's timetable throughout history as a "living witness" to the truthfulness of His Word.

They will also be center-stage at the time of the end. Simply put, without understanding the role of Israel, one will not understand Bible prophecy.

We continued by documenting certain promises that the Lord made in the past to Abraham, Isaac, and Jacob. We discovered that each of these promises were literally and miraculously fulfilled.

Since the Bible already has a history of predictions that have been fulfilled, we should not be surprised that what it predicts about future events will also be fulfilled.

The fact that Israel is "the key," to Bible prophecy means that the nation will still exist in the "last days," just as it exists today. Therefore, not surprisingly, we find in Scripture that the Lord has specifically promised Israel that they would always exist. Indeed, God said as long as the sun and moon are in the sky, there would be the nation of Israel.

Furthermore, in many passages, in both testaments, Israel is explicitly mentioned in Scripture as existing at the time of the end.

Given their history of rejection, persecution, suffering, as well as two complete removals from their ancient homeland, this is a remarkable prediction. Yet, it has come to pass just like the Bible said.

Moreover, the fact that the nation still does exist is all the more amazing when we consider their recent history—such as the Holocaust of World War II which was instituted by the Third Reich to rid the world once-and-for-all of the Jewish race. While six million human beings were murdered by this regime, the nation continued to exist. God would not allow them to be annihilated.

Since the Jewish people are at the center of "last days" events, the miraculous existence of the nation of Israel is our first "Sign of the End."

SIGN 2: AS THEIR ENEMIES HAVE DONE TO ISRAEL, SO GOD HAS DONE TO THEM

While the Bible speaks of the existence of the nation of Israel in the "last days," it also predicts the demise of some of Israel's ancient enemies. In fact, when God called Abraham, the father of the nation, some four thousand years ago, the Lord said that He would bless those who blessed the descendants of Abraham and curse those who cursed them. History records that this promise has been literally fulfilled.

In fact, there were a number of nations living in the Old Testament period that the Lord cursed. Their demise was certain and the predictions about their destruction were literally fulfilled. Indeed, there are no more Ammonites, Amalekites, Edomites, Moabites, or Philistines.

On the other hand, one of Israel's mortal enemies, Egypt, is said to experience a national conversion at the time of the end. And as Scripture predicted, Egypt does still exist to the present day while these other nations do not.

There is something else which we must consider. The promise of punishment upon those nations and individuals which persecute Israel holds true to this very day. Consequently, it could possibly explain why we do not find the United States as a major player in the last days (see Sign 11). Indeed, if the USA completely turns its back on Israel, then judgment will indeed be coming.

To sum up these first two signs, Israel and Egypt are specifically said to exist in the "last days" —seeing that, from Scripture, they are "players" in the Biblical end-time scenario. Other nations which existed alongside Israel have had their demise predicted and they no longer exist.

Therefore, we are told of two specific nations that will exist at the time of the end, as well as five others that will not. The Bible has proved correct in these seven predictions.

SIGN 3: ISRAEL WILL MIRACULOUSLY RETURN TO ITS ANCIENT HOMELAND IN THE LAST DAYS

Not only does Israel exist in the last days; but against all odds of history, they have returned to their ancient homeland and have been recognized as a modern country. This, too, fulfills that which the Bible has promised.

What is also so amazing is that no other nation in the history of the world has ever been entirely removed from their homeland and then returned, and it has happened to Israel, not once, but twice— the first time it was for 70 years, the last time for almost 1,900 years! Furthermore, each time their exile, as well as their return, was predicted in Scripture.

Another remarkable thing is that the second exile of Israel was predicted before they even entered into a first exile!

We should also remember that the rebirth of the modern state of Israel took place just three short years after the Holocaust of World War II. The miraculous worldwide return of Israel to their ancient homeland in these last days is something unheard of in all of history. It is indeed a major sign that we are nearing the time of the end.

SIGN 4: THE NATION WILL RETURN IN TWO STAGES

The Bible also gives further predictions regarding Israel and their return to the Promised Land. Interestingly, we find that it will be in two phases.

First, they will return physically but the people will be in unbelief of Jesus as their Messiah. Then, after an unprecedented time of great distress or tribulation, they will look to Him whom they put to death. At that time, there will be a national conversion. After that, the Lord will return from heaven and then gather the remaining Jews from around the world.

The first prediction has come to pass. Since 1948, Israel has been accepted as a modern country; and, as the Bible predicted, their return has been in unbelief in Jesus as their Messiah.

There is also something else to re-emphasize—not only do the Scriptures predict the Jews return to their land in unbelief of Jesus, as we have documented, a number of past Bible commentators have also recognized this truth. Hence, this is how they were able to predict the return of the nation in unbelief. These commentators did this before there was any hint of the future state of Israel that would one day exist.

How were they able to do this? Especially when some of the predictions were made some 1,800 years after Israel had been removed from their homeland and were still scattered across the face of the earth? Simply put, they believed what the Bible predicted would happen. Even though these people of faith never lived to experience it, their predictions, based upon the Bible have come to pass.

SIGN 5: JERUSALEM WILL BE UNITED UNDER ISRAELI RULE

In 1948, when the modern state of Israel was reborn, the city of Jerusalem was divided between two countries—Israel and Transjordan. While the Israeli's were in control of west Jerusalem, east Jerusalem was in the hands of Transjordan.

With this in mind, careful Bible students went on to predict that another war must take place. Why? The reason was the Scripture assumes that Jerusalem will be united under Israeli rule in the "last days." Indeed, the Word of God predicts certain events will take place involving Israel and east Jerusalem at the time of the end. Hence, it is these passages from Scripture, that assume Israeli control over all of Jerusalem, that explain why Bible students have foretold of another war

As expected, in June of 1967, the city of Jerusalem was united under Israeli rule. This was the first time this has happened in 2,600 years! The Six Day War saw the Israeli's capture the entire city and it remains under their control to this day. In fact, in 2017, the people celebrated the 50th anniversary of the reunification of Jerusalem.

Again, the predictions of Scripture prove to be correct. The unification of Jerusalem further sets the stage for the fulfillment of end-time events. In fact, it is a major sign that we are near the time of the end.

SIGN 6: ISRAEL WILL BE IN THE WORLD'S SPOTLIGHT

While all of these previous predictions have been literally fulfilled, another notable one considers Israel's place in the world at the time of the end. Not only will Israel remarkably become a modern state, or country, and the city of Jerusalem will be unified in the last days, this tiny nation will also be in the world's spotlight.

We know this because the Bible speaks of the entire world being against Israel at the time of the end. This could only take place if the various nations were aware of Israel, as well as the current political climate with them and their neighbors.

Now, it is one thing to predict the return of the people, it is quite another thing to predict that the headlines of the world will continually feature this small nation. Yet, this is precisely what we find. Indeed, it seems that hardly a day goes by without Israel being mentioned somewhere in the headlines.

SIGN 7: THERE WILL BE A CONTINUAL SEARCH FOR PEACE IN ISRAEL

Our world has not accepted the idea of a unified Jerusalem under Israeli rule. In fact, a great part of the world has not accepted the idea of a Jewish state at all! This fits with what the Scriptures predict—that Israel at the time of the end will have the whole world against them.

Consequently, there has been a continuous call for some sort of peace agreement that would give away much of Israeli land, as well as divide Jerusalem again. This has been advocated from the moment the city was unified.

This idea of a "peace treaty" is an important concept in the "last days" scenario of Scripture. In fact, it assumes that there are major problems between Israel and its neighbors and that they cannot seem to find a solution.

When a peace treaty is eventually made by a certain individual who comes on the scene; known, among other names as the Antichrist, it will start the clock ticking for the last seven-year period of our present history. It will culminate with the return of Jesus Christ to the earth. Hence, the uproar around the state of Israel—the right for it to exist, and the extent of its borders—will continue until the time of the end.

Furthermore, for this prophecy to be fulfilled, about a search for peace at the time of the end, we should consider how many things must be in place. Israel must exist, must be in their land, must have unified the city of Jerusalem, must be in the spotlight of the world, and must be despised by the great majority of the nations. Again, all of this has been literally fulfilled—just as the Bible has predicted.

SIGN 8: PREPARATIONS WILL BE MADE TO BUILD THE THIRD TEMPLE

We now come to one of the most amazing prophecies of the last days—the predictions of a Third Temple that will be built in Jerusalem. As we have mentioned, the return of the nation to their ancient homeland will be in two stages. First, the physical return in unbelief, then the spiritual awakening. The Bible predicts that a Third Temple will be built before the Second Coming of the Lord. This construction of the Temple demonstrates that the nation has not yet recognized Jesus as their promised Messiah.

We say this because the New Testament is clear that the Temple is no longer necessary in the plan of God. Jesus Christ took the penalty of the sins of the world upon Himself on the cross of Calvary. He rose from the dead, ascended into heaven, and then sat down at the right hand of God the Father. This demonstrated that the work of God, with respect to sacrifices for sin, has been finished. Hence, sacrifices for sin are no longer necessary. The fact that the returning Jews will build a Temple shows that they are still in unbelief of Jesus.

The importance of this Third Temple, which will be built in unbelief is this: certain events will take place at that Temple which will signal that the coming of the Lord is only three and one-half years away! This is why we have emphasized that Israel is God's clock—the nation being the hour hand, Jerusalem the minute hand, and the Temple Mount the second hand.

The fact that we see stories, almost daily, of those in Jerusalem who are preparing to build the Third Temple, as well as restore the sacrificial system, is another amazing fulfillment of what Scripture predicted long ago.

As was learned in many of our other signs, past commentators of the Bible have not only predicted the return of the Jews to their ancient homeland, but the construction of a Third Temple as well.

When we examined the Scriptures, we found that at least nine things must be in place in order to fulfill what the Bible says about this "last days" temple. Five of them are already in place, and preparations are now being made to fulfill the other four.

This is truly a remarkable sign that shows that we are indeed near the time of the end.

SIGN 9: IN THE LAST DAYS, CERTAIN SPECIFIED NATIONS WILL INVADE ISRAEL (EZEKIEL 38,39)

The Bible speaks of an "end-time" invasion of Israel from eight nations. The identity of these nations is given to us in Scripture with the listing of their ancient names at the time of Ezekiel. When we look at a modern map, we can determine precisely which modern nations will become involved.

Presently, we are seeing the lining up of these specific nations which sets the stage for the future invasion—including Russia, Iran, Turkey, Northern Sudan and Libya.

This invasion will culminate in the Lord destroying their armies, as well as supernaturally destroying many of the structures in the countries that sent them. At that time, Israel will begin to recognize that it was the Lord Himself who caused this obliteration of their enemies.

What is all the more fascinating is how the Bible sets the stage for this invasion. Indeed, it says that Israel will return to its ancient homeland after having been away for a long time. As we mentioned in "Sign Four," Ezekiel, in Chapter 37, also predicts the return will be in two stages—first unbelief, then eventually belief in the Lord.

Furthermore, the Bible says that they will return to a land that has been devastated by wars. The Bible also predicts that these nations will invade Israel because this tiny nation has turned this desolate land into a place of great wealth.

Remarkably, this is exactly the situation we see today! Everything the Scriptures have predicted is now in place for this future invasion.

In fact, we discovered some ten separate predictions that are given to us in Ezekiel that have to do with what the world will be like *before* this invasion occurs. Amazingly, we found that each of these ten predictions have been literally fulfilled!

This particular sign provides further evidence that the God of the Bible exists, that He knows the future, and that He correctly tells us certain things that will happen in the future.

SIGN 10: THE NATIONS MISSING FROM THE EZEKIEL 38,39 INVASION

While the Scripture specifies the different countries that will invade Israel, it also mentions certain others that will protest the attack. Remarkably, we see these countries, which are not mentioned as being part of the invasion recorded in the Ezekiel 38,39, presently not being involved in any coalition with these attacking nations. This includes the gulf states such as Saudi Arabia, Kuwait, the United Arab Emirates, Bahrain and Oman.

Furthermore, other countries that are not mentioned in this invasion include Lebanon, Syria, and Jordan. However, each of them border Israel and have participated in wars against her in the past. Today, Jordan and Israel are at peace, while Syria and Lebanon have internal wars taking place which would not allow them to participate.

Another nation conspicuous by its absence is Egypt. It has participated in every modern war with Israel (1948, 1956, 1967, 1973) since the founding of the state in 1948. Yet, remarkably, today Egypt is on much better terms with Israel.

When all is said and done, it is mind-boggling that all the nations mentioned in the invasion of Ezekiel 38, 39, are presently working together, while the other surrounding nations, including those bordering Israel, as well as the Gulf States, are not part of this group. Again, the lineup is precisely what the Bible predicted.

SIGN 11: NO SUPERPOWER WILL INTERVENE ON ISRAEL'S BEHALF WHEN THEY ARE INVADED (EZEKIEL 38,39) SOMETHING WILL HAPPEN TO THE UNITED STATES

When Israel is invaded, it will be on its own as far as the world is concerned. No nation can, or will, come to its aid. Furthermore, there does not seem to be any concern, on the part of the invaders, that a greater human power will intervene on behalf of Israel. In other words, there is no superpower who can or will come to help Israel.

This, of course, brings up the obvious question, "What will happen to the United States?" As of the time of the writing of this book, the United States remains a superpower in the world. Furthermore, it strongly supports Israel.

This was not true of previous administrations, and it will not be true at some time in the future. This means that something must happen to the United States to keep it from intervening on behalf of Israel. The USA may lose its superpower status, or they may choose not to support Israel. In other words, they may not be willing, or not be able, to come to the aid of Israel. We just do not know what will happen. What we do know is that the United States will not be a major player at the time of the end.

We must always remember that the only reason any country is mentioned in Scripture is because of their direct relationship with God's chosen people—Israel. In other words, unless there is something they are doing, either good or bad, with reference to Israel, they are not mentioned in the Bible.

SIGN 12: THERE WILL BE A 10 NATION CONFEDERATION IN WESTERN EUROPE (THE REVIVAL OF THE ANCIENT ROMAN EMPIRE)

Some 2,500 years ago, God gave a pagan King named Nebuchadnezzar a supernatural dream—the meaning of which charted the history of the Gentile kingdoms from that time, until the time that God's kingdom would come to the earth. As we noted, these predictions have been minutely fulfilled in the four kingdoms of Babylon, Medo-Persia, Greece, and then Rome.

Based upon the prophet Daniel's supernatural interpretation of the dream, Scripture speaks of a revival of the ancient Roman Empire in the "last days." Indeed, there will be ten nations that unite at the time of the end which will constitute an economic powerhouse. While Europe, in the past, has had various coalitions, as it has today, it has *never* had a ten-nation confederation.

From these ten, there will come a powerful leader who will eventually rule the world. He is the predicted "Antichrist" of Scripture.

Furthermore, we are specifically told that in the days of those ten kings the Lord will return from heaven, destroy these kingdoms, and the Antichrist, and then set up His everlasting kingdom. This is why the coming together of this ten nation European confederation is such a huge "Sign of the End," as far as the Bible is concerned.

SIGN 13: THERE WILL BE A ONE-WORLD POLITICAL AND ECONOMIC SYSTEM (GLOBALISM)

At the time of the end, there will be a centralized economic system put in place. Indeed, the Bible predicts that nobody will be able to buy or sell without a particular mark on their right hand or forehead. The emphasis will not be so much upon nationalism, as it will be on globalism.

We have seen the rise of globalism in our time. Indeed, "globalism," "diversity", and "no borders," seem to be the catch-words of our day. This is setting the stage for what the Bible says will take place.

Seemingly, one of the motivations for the globalist society will be to rid the world of hunger and poverty. However, this economic system, instead of ridding the world of its problems, will allow this final world leader, the Antichrist, to become a global dictator and to take control all business transactions throughout the world. Therefore, all the talk about the world being a "community" or a "global village," fits right into the "last days" scenario as predicted in Scripture.

SIGN 14: THE WORLD WILL DESPERATELY LOOK FOR A LEADER

With all the problems that arise from the circumstances the world finds itself in, there will be the deep desire for a leader to properly guide this new globalist world. It seems that many individual nations will give up their sovereignty to be ruled by this one-world system with this one strong leader. The Bible predicts that such a leader will arise.

When he does come onto the scene, this predicted final Antichrist will charm the world into believing that he is the one who will lead them into better days. And for a while, this is exactly what will happen.

However, eventually he will lead them into a time of unprecedented horror—the Great Tribulation. In fact, it will only be the Second Coming of Jesus Christ that will prevent the world from being destroyed.

What we see today, is the world, with all its issues, readying itself for this coming world leader.

SIGN 15: THERE WILL BE AN EXPONENTIAL INCREASE IN TECHNOLOGY

Many of the biblical predictions, concerning what the world will be like in the last days, assume technological advances that were unknown in ancient times. In fact, a few of these specific predictions were confusing to those living in the recent past!

How, they ask, could a world-wide system of buying and selling, with a specific mark on the right hand or forehead, be monitored? It did not seem conceivable to have any possible way to monitor financial transactions in all parts of the world. Yet, the Bible predicts that such a system will be in place at the time of the end.

Scripture also predicts that for three and one-half days, the entire world will be able to view the bodies of two individuals, the two witnesses to Jesus Christ, who are killed in the streets of Jerusalem. For these three and one-half days, the people of earth will celebrate their deaths by sending gifts to one another. How could it be possible that their dead bodies are viewed worldwide during this short period of time?

Jesus also warned the people of Jerusalem to flee when they "saw" the abomination of desolation—which occurs in the "Holy Place," of the Temple. Since the Holy of Holies is only entered once a year, and by only one person, the great high priest, how could the world possibly see something like that take place?

Of course, we do not wonder about this any longer. Modern technology has solved that issue. However, until recent times, this system of monitoring our financial transactions did not seem to be a possibility. The fact that this technology is now in place is a huge sign that shows us that we are at the time of the end.

Viewing global events in real time is the norm today. Therefore, it is certainly possible for everyone to view bodies lying in the streets of Jerusalem, as well as to "see" what will take place in a future Temple in the city of Jerusalem.

Hence, this exponential increase in technology will not only allow this final Antichrist to be in control of all financial transactions, it will also allow some of the major predicted events of Scripture to be viewed worldwide.

SIGN 16: PLAGUES AND PESTILENCE WILL TROUBLE THE WORLD

Jesus spoke about the time of the end as being characterized by plagues and pestilence. Interestingly, with all the advances of modern science, the world is still beset by all sorts of deadly viruses.

As we documented, there are presently some one million viruses that we no absolutely nothing about!

We can add to these human-made plagues—bio-terrorism, chemical warfare. These are created to kill, maim, and terrorize. Unfortunately, this type of savagery will only increase in the future.

These facts make it clear that this prediction of Jesus will remain fulfilled—that plagues, famine, and pestilence will continue until the time of the end. Plagues and pestilence, whether natural or human-made, are here to stay.

SIGN 17: THE WORLD WILL BE CHARACTERIZED BY LAWLESSNESS

Another problem with the world at the time of the end will be lawlessness. In the past, there was at least an acknowledgement of right and wrong, good and bad.

However, as it was in the days of Noah, the distinction between right and wrong has become blurred, or even non-existent. Today, evil is called good and good is called evil. The laws of God and humans are being ignored. People are openly doing whatever they wish to do, with no regard for the law and no shame in what they are doing.

Unhappily, all of us are painfully aware how this taking place before our very eyes. The sad truth is that it will get only worse. The Utopia that people have hoped for will never come about. A law-abiding world is a thing of the past.

In fact, the coming Antichrist is called "the lawless one." During the short time that he will rule the world, the earth will experience lawlessness like never before. Fortunately, this will all come to an end when the Lord Jesus returns to the earth and rules the world through righteousness.

SIGN 18: THE WORLD WILL BE CHARACTERIZED BY VIOLENCE

Lawlessness leads to our next sign, violence. As we noted, the Lord compared the time of the end to the days of Noah. In the Book of Genesis, we are told that the world before the flood was characterized by violence.

While there has always been violence in our world, today we are seeing terrorism—the likes of which the world has never experienced. Simply put, the world will become a less safe place as we get closer to the coming of the Lord.

What this tells us is that all the world's efforts for a global peace will miserably fail. While the desire may be noble, the fallen condition of the human heart will not allow this to happen.

Therefore, the idea that we will "evolve" into a peaceful world is only a dream. It is only at the return of the Lord that we will finally experience peace. Until that time, violence will increase.

SIGN 19: THE ORGANIZED CHURCH WILL TURN AWAY FROM THE FAITH (APOSTASY)

The last days will be a time when the visible church will abandon many of its central beliefs. Indeed, Jesus asked the question, "Will He find faith in the world when He returns?" (Luke 18:8). The fact that He even asked the question speaks volumes.

Sadly, this is exactly what we see today. Historic Christianity is being rejected by much of the leadership in the visible church in favor of uniting it with the beliefs and practices of other religions. Tolerance seems to be the main idea of the day.

Indeed, in too many churches, the original message of Jesus and the New Testament is ridiculed as being out-of-date. It has been replaced by the whims of those who believe they know better.

Consequently, there is no clear message about who God is, who we as humans are, why there is evil in the world, the solution to the problem of evil, how we can be saved from our sins, and how we can know our identity as humans, our purpose, and our destiny. Since the Bible has been rejected, they have no place to go for answers.

Fortunately, there are still churches who believe the Bible, preach the gospel, and are not ashamed to call themselves Bible-believing Christians.

SIGN 20 THERE WILL BE A RISE IN FALSE PROPHETS, FALSE TEACHERS, AND FALSE CHRISTS

This next sign always follows the previous one. Indeed, when the truth of the Christian message is rejected something has to replace it.

Jesus warned about false prophets, false teachers and false Christs that would arise during this age, and especially at the time of the end. He predicted that they will deceive many people.

In fact, the 19ᵗʰ century writer David Baron documented some 40 people who had come to Israel, at different times, and claimed to be the Messiah, the Christ.

While these false Christs and false prophets have always existed, today we see a huge increase of people falsely predicting what will take place in the future.

The one thing they all have in common is that their predictions contradict what is clearly stated in Scripture. Hence, these false prophets confuse people, hold the gospel up to ridicule, and cause the unbelievers to reject any idea that the Bible accurately predicts the future.

This includes false teaching with respect to the events of the Second Coming. Either the Second Coming is denied, or is said to have already taken place.

On the other hand, there are the sensationalists—the date-setters. They claim to know either the day, or the year, in which Christ will return. Of course, every prediction has been wrong. The result? People do not think they can trust the Bible as an accurate guide for the future.

Whatever the case may be, there will continue to be false prophets, false teachers, and false Messiahs who will lead the people astray. The fact that they are still around, and increasing in number, is truly a sign of the end of the age.

SIGN 21: THERE WILL BE A RISE IN ANTI-SEMITISM

This sign can also be connected to the previous two, as well as with all of the other signs regarding Israel. With the rejection of any future for Israel which is taught by the mainline church, and with false prophets teaching a different message with respect to Christ's coming, we should also expect a rise of anti-Semitism at the time of the end.

In fact, this is precisely what the Scripture teaches. Not only would Israel exist, return to their ancient homeland, and be in the world's spotlight at the time of the end, we are told that the whole world would be against them. In fact, at the time of the end they will basically be on their own.

In "Sign Nine," we observed that there will a number of nations who will invade Israel in the last days (Ezekiel 38,39). We also discovered that nobody will come to Israel's defense at that time. In other words, they will be without human help. However, although abandoned by other nations, Israel would not be forgotten by them. To the contrary, they will be hated and vilified by the entire world.

Again, this is exactly what we see in our world today. Israel is despised by a great part of humanity. Furthermore, that hatred will only grow worse as we approach the time of the end.

SIGN 22: CHRISTIANS WILL CONTINUE TO BE PERSECUTED

While the Jews will be vilified and persecuted at the time of the end, the Bible says they will not be alone in this experience. Indeed, Christians will also be singled out for persecution.

While humankind likes to boast how civilized and advanced they have become, we find that does not include their treatment of Christians. Jesus predicted that the persecution of His followers would continue to the very end. In other words, the unbelieving world will never tolerate the message of Christ.

History records that more Christians have been killed for the cause of Christ in the 20th Century than in the first nineteen centuries combined. The 21st Century is actually ahead of last century with the number of believers being martyred for their faith.

Sadly, we read daily of some type of persecution of believers somewhere in the world. Whether it be the terrorist bombing of churches, the imprisonment of Christians, or the disappearance of believers, the persecution continues. However, as Jesus promised, He will build His church and the Gates of Hades will not stop it. Indeed, nothing can.

SIGN 23: UNBELIEVERS WILL SCOFF AT THE IDEA OF CHRIST'S RETURN

Not only will unbelievers refuse to embrace the fact of the Lord's return, they will also ridicule it. This was predicted long ago in Scripture. Indeed, both Peter and Jude warned us about the scoffing that would take place in the last days—when believers would continue to look for the coming of the Lord.

Interestingly, scoffers for centuries ridiculed the prophecies predicting that Israel would somehow return to the Promise Land, form a modern state, and unify Jerusalem. In fact, many kings and tyrants tried to stop it from happening. Yet, as we have noted, these ridiculed predictions of Scripture have indeed literally come to pass.

However, it does not seem to matter to those who refuse to believe. Ridiculing the Bible and its predictions has become more and more the norm as we head into the time of the end.

Jesus Christ is coming again! Indeed, as we have documented in this book, the evidence clearly says so!

SIGN 24: THE WICKED WILL NOT UNDERSTAND THE SIGNS OF THE TIMES

While unbelievers will scoff at the idea that Jesus Christ is returning to the earth, the Bible makes it clear that they will desire to know if there is any meaning to the events that transpire in our world. However, Scripture tells us that they will never understand. Though they search here and there, they will never discover the answer.

The sad thing is that the solution is right in front of them, in the Bible. Yet they refuse to consider the answers the Scriptures give. This is why they will find themselves constantly searching but never coming up with any answers.

Jesus explained the reason as to why they will never come to a knowledge of the truth. He said, "the light has come into the world and people loved the darkness rather than the light, because their deeds were evil" (John 3:19). In other words, they are not really interested in the truth.

Someday, they will know the truth—but it will be too late. The Bible says that every knee will one day bow to Jesus Christ, and every tongue will confess that He is Lord of all.

Yet, the wicked will do it when they are in a place that is forever separated from God and His goodness. Hopefully, there is no one reading this right now that will be in that dreaded place.

SIGN 25: BIBLE-BELIEVERS WILL UNDERSTAND WHAT IS TAKING PLACE

Finally, in light of everything that Scripture says, we discover that there will be those who do understand exactly what is happening in the world. In fact, the Book of Daniel says that "the wise" will understand what is taking place at the time of the end (Daniel 12:10).

Who are they? They are the ones who take the Bible seriously, as well as the predictions which it makes about the future.

As we have documented, for those who take the predictions of Scripture at face value, and construct from the Bible an end-times scenario, they can clearly see and understand what is presently taking place.

This book has laid out some of that evidence; but, as we have mentioned, there is so much more that we could say. Yet, what we have documented is sufficient to demonstrate that God has indeed spoken to us in the Bible, as well as providing for us "Signs of the End."

Answering
Some Objections

Is Bible Prophecy Really That Important to Study? Isn't the Subject Too Difficult to Understand?

What About All the False Predictions That Have Been Made By Bible Interpreters? How Then, Can Anyone Know What Is True?

Should These Biblical Predictions Regarding Israel And The "Last Days" Be Understood Literally? Have They Already Been Fulfilled Symbolically by The Church?

Were These Prophecies Fulfilled at The Return from Babylon?

Has The "Time of Jacob's Trouble" Already Occurred At The Destruction Of Jerusalem?

While we have documented many of the marvelous fulfillment of the predictions made in Scripture, with respect to the "last days," there have been objections to doing this. They include the following:

To begin with, there is the objection that Bible prophecy is not a subject to which we should give our attention. For one thing, it is thought that it is really not that important for us as we live our daily lives. In addition, it is also thought of to be too difficult for the average person to understand.

The second objection has to do with commentators, based upon their understanding of the Bible, making predictions that have not come true. How then, can anyone know what they should believe about these passages that remain to be fulfilled—if teachers of the Bible get them wrong?

A third objection says that we are not to understand these "last days" passages about the nation of Israel literally, but rather spiritually. In fact, many people say that these passages, originally about Israel, are now to be fulfilled in the church. Therefore, it is thought that we should not look for any literal fulfillment of the promises to the descendants of Abraham, Isaac, and Jacob.

Another objection says that these predictions about Israel coming back to their land have already been fulfilled at the Babylonian captivity. In other words, Bible passages that have yet to be fulfilled are mistakenly looked at as passages that have already been fulfilled long ago.

A fifth objection says that the predicted "Time of Jacob's Trouble," has already been fulfilled at the destruction of Jerusalem in A.D. 70.

What, then, shall we say to these things?

We will let the past commentators answer these five objections for us— seeing they have done an excellent job.

ANSWER TO THE FIRST OBJECTION: BIBLE PROPHECY IS AN IMPORTANT SUBJECT AND IT IS NOT TOO DIFFICULT TO UNDERSTAND

This objection comes in two forms. First, it is contended that we should not spend our time on the subject of Bible prophecy because it is not that important. Furthermore, it is too difficult for the average person to understand.

IT IS A VERY IMPORTANT SUBJECT FOR PEOPLE TO STUDY

This first objection was answered long ago by Elhanan Winchester, back in 1789. He put it this way.

Thus, seeing that the eternal Jehovah hath spoken to us, in his word, those great and important things, that intimately concern each and every one of us, if we attend not to him, we are guilty in his sight of pouring contempt upon his word, upon his authority, upon His Spirit. Since God is the speaker, since God is the great inditer [composer] of these sacred prophecies, it becomes us to read them with attention, and diligently to search into the meaning, that we may know the great things of God, that we may be acquainted with those matters of fact that will soon be realized. Hence to encourage us to the greatest diligence and industry in this matter, God hath been pleased to pronounce, in a remarkable manner, a blessing upon readers and hearers of the prophecy contained in this book. *Blessed is he that readeth, and they that hear the words of this prophecy, and keep those things which are written therein: for the time is at hand.* Let us therefore, in the first place, consider, what tempers, or disposition of mind, are necessary, in order that we may be entitled to the blessing here promised (Elhanan Winchester, *A Course of Lectures on Prophecies That Remain To Be Fulfilled*, Volume 1, London, 1789, p. 6).

It would be difficult to say it any better than this! Indeed, since God has spoken to us in His Word, and Bible prophecy is a subject that covers a large part of Holy Scripture, it is vital that we pay attention to what it says. Furthermore, there is a special blessing pronounced for those who study and obey what is written in the Book of Revelation. Hence, it is our duty to spend time studying these passages that deal with Bible prophecy.

James Brookes made similar comments that are worth considering.

We are at least certain that however unimportant the study of prophecy may be in the judgment of men, it is of very great importance in the judgment of the Holy Spirit, for it is written, "We have also a more sure word of prophecy; whereunto ye do well that ye take heed, as unto a light that shineth in a dark place, until the day dawn, and the day star arise in your hearts" (2 Pet. 1:19). Prophecy here is obviously to be taken in the ordinary sense as meaning the prediction of future events, and in the language of Wordsworth, "the Apostle compares Prophecy to a *lamp* which guides the footsteps of the wayfaring man in a gloomy, desolate place, where he is not likely to meet any one to direct him on his way; and serve as his guide in the night and the twilight, till the dawn appears, and he no longer needs the lamp." The inspired writer does not say, as so many seem to think, that prophecy is a dark place which we should do well to avoid, but it is a *light that shineth in a dark place*, whereunto we do well to take heed. If then, we do well to take heed unto the sure word of prophecy, certainly we can not do well if we refuse to take heed unto it, and dismiss it from our minds with the flippant remark that it is of no importance (James Brookes, *Maranatha, The Lord Cometh*, Fleming H. Revell Company, 1889, pp. 31-32).

Under the title, "The Call to Prophetic Study," Horatius Bonar wrote the following wise words.

> Man's thoughts about the future and the unseen are of little worth. They are at best but dreams; no more than blind guesses of fancy. They approach no nearer to the truth than do a child's conjectures regarding the history of some distant star, or as to the peopling of space beyond the outskirts of the visible creation.
>
> But the thoughts of God respecting the future are precious above measure. They are truth and certainty, whether they touch upon the far off or the near, the likely or the unlikely. They are disfigured with no miscalculations, for they are the

thoughts of the great Designer regarding his own handiwork. Of however little moment it may be for us to know what *man* thinks about the future, it is of vast moment for us to know what God thinks of it. However few these revealed thoughts of God may be, yet they ought to be estimated by us as above all price. They are the thoughts of the infinite mind; and they are the thoughts of that mind on a subject utterly inaccessible to us, yet entirely familiar to Him who sees the end from the beginning, and whose wisdom has pre-arranged the whole.

These thoughts of God about the future are what we call prophecy; and in studying prophecy we are studying the thoughts of God, the purposes of his heart (Horatius Bonar, *Prophetical Landmarks*, London, James Nisbet And Co., Berners Street, 1847pp. 1,2).

Therefore, the importance of the study of Bible prophecy cannot be overestimated. Indeed, it provides us with knowledge we could not otherwise gain.

IT IS POSSIBLE TO UNDERSTAND THE SUBJECT OF BIBLE PROPHECY

Furthermore, since the Lord has revealed these prophetic truths to us in His Word, they should be understandable to the masses. In fact, as we mentioned in Sign 25, we find that in Daniel 12:10, Scripture predicts that "the wise" will understand Bible prophecy at the time of the end.

G.H. Pember comments about the logical system that the Lord has given to us.

We are well aware that many object to the very mention of a system of prophecy: but surely it does not require much reflection to discover that such a sentiment is simply irra-tional. If the prophecies are all utterances of one and the

> selfsame Spirit, they must be capable of reduction to an
> orderly scheme, and certainly cannot be comprehended in
> any other way. And unless we find out what this scheme is,
> woe to us; for if, as nearly all Christians seem to agree, we
> are now on the borders of the last times, the knowledge of
> it will soon become the distinguishing mark of those whom
> God has chosen. For at the time of the end, "none of the
> wicked will shall understand but the wise shall understand"
> (G.H. Pember, *The Great Prophecies Concerning the Jews, the
> Gentiles, and the Church of God*, 1881, p. 3).

Therefore, Bible prophecy has been given to us so that we can understand what is happening in our world today, as well as what will happen in the future. Since God has made it understandable for us, we
have no excuse for neglecting this subject.

William Blackstone stated the matter perfectly.

> Peter says, "We have a more sure word of prophecy, whereunto
> you do well that you take heed (as unto a light that shineth
> in a dark place, until the day dawn and the day star arise) in
> your hearts." He exhorts us to be mindful of these words [2
> Peter 3:1-2]. Therefore, *we are not speculating* (italics his) when
> we prayerfully study prophecy (William Blackstone, *Jesus Is
> Coming*, Fleming H. Revell Company, 1878, p. 19).

Indeed, we are not speculating when we study what the Lord has said
about the future!

To sum up, the study of Bible prophecy is important, understandable,
and absolutely necessary.

ANSWERING OBJECTION NUMBER TWO: FALSE PREDICTIONS BY BIBLE INTERPRETERS SHOULD NOT KEEP US FROM STUDYING THE SUBJECT

We now come to our second objection—which is sometimes built
upon the previous one. It is common for people to say that the idea of

the Lord coming again, as well as other future events that have been predicted in Scripture, have been misinterpreted by certain students of the Bible. According to these individuals, this invalidates the study of Bible prophecy.

Ford Ottman states the problem.

> Conflicting interpretations have confused and discouraged prophetic study. This is peculiarly unfortunate because it has led some to the conviction that the study of the prophets is fruitless and leads only to perplexity (Ford C. Ottman, *The Coming Day*, Philadelphia, The Sunday School Times Company, 1905, p. 11).

We will let some of the commentators from the past answer this particular objection. J.C. Ryle wrote.

> It proves nothing against the doctrine of Christ's second coming and kingdom, that it has sometimes been fearfully abused. I would like to know what doctrine of the Gospel has not been abused. Salvation by grace, has been made a pretext for licentiousness; election, has been made an excuse for all manner of unclean living . . . we are not therefore obliged to throw aside good principles. We do not give up the gospel because of . . . outrageous conduct (J.C Ryle, *Coming Events and Present Duties*, *Coming Events and Present Duties*, Second Edition, London, William Hunt and Company, 1879, p. 27).

This is an excellent point which shows the logical fallacy of such of an argument. In fact, in the history of the church, every major doctrine of the Christian faith has been abused at one time or another! Yet, we do not give up on our study of these subjects because some have abused the topic.

There is a valuable lesson to learn in all of this. We will illustrate this point, as to the abuse of Bible prophecy, with the following examples.

TWO PAST EXAMPLES OF WRONG CLAIMS OF FULFILLMENT OF BIBLICAL PROPHECIES

In one of our previous "Signs of the End," Sign 16, we documented the Bible saying that famine, plagues and pestilence are signs of the "last days."

We also cited the warning from 19th century author G.H. Pember concerning finding fulfillment in these predictions with past events. He listed a couple of illustrations as to how past interpreters got it wrong in applying these sorts of plagues, famines, and earthquakes in their day to what the Bible predicted for the time of the end. The following are his highly instructive examples of what "not to do!" Pember wrote.

> A remarkable instance occurred at the close of the sixth century. At that time men had become so accustomed to the domination of Rome that they believed her power could only perish with the world itself. And so, when they saw her apparently in the pangs of dissolution, with her lands wasted by war, famine, and disease, to such a degree that many once populous places had become pestilential through neglect; when they beheld her supplies cut off, and not a few of her buildings destroyed by storms and inundations, they imagined that the world also had run its course, and that the last dread judgment was near at hand.
>
> Gregory the Great was strongly imbued with this idea, and, in a letter to King Ethelbert, he thus expresses it:—"We know from the word of Almighty God that the end of the present world is now at hand, and that the reign of the saints, which can never be terminated, is about to commence. And now that the end of the world is approaching, many things will take place which have not happened before. For there will be atmospheric changes, terrors from heaven, deranged seasons, wars, famines, pestilence, and earthquakes in divers places" (Bede, *Ecclesiastical History*, 1:32).

And since there was an Antichrist required for the last days, Gregory was sure he had detected him in the Patriarch of Constantinople, John the Faster, who had just irritated the See of Rome by proclaiming himself Universal Bishop (G.H. Pember, *The Great Prophecies Concerning the Jews, the Gentiles, and the Church of God*, 1881, p. 16).

Interestingly, these events made it seemingly certain, to everyone living at that time, that the end was near! However, the end was not yet.

Pember then lists another illustration of believers making this same mistake again.

Again, in the tenth century, there was a still more general panic. It was imagined that Satan had been bound from the time of our Lord's first appearing, and that, since the thousand years were almost accomplished, he was about to be loosed as a preparation for the last judgment. As the supposed time of this event drew nearer the terror of men became piteous. Some handed over their property to the monkish foundations, and set out on a pilgrimage to Palestine, whither they expected Christ to descend. Many bound themselves by solemn oath to be serfs to churches or monasteries, in hope that, if they were found acting as servants to the servants of Christ, they would be more gently dealt with at the judgment. Buildings were allowed to fall into decay, since it was supposed that there would be but little further use for them. And if there happened to be an eclipse of the sun or moon, affrighted crowds would fly to the caverns of the rocks, or to any other places which they thought might shelter them from the glory of the dreaded appearing. But the year One Thousand passed by; nothing happened, and presently the excitement subsided (Pember, *The Great Prophecies Concerning the Jews, the Gentiles, and the Church of God*, 1881, pp. 16-17).

There is a valuable lesson in this for all of us. While certain contemporary events may *seem to be* a fulfillment of Biblical prophecy, we must understand precisely what the Lord predicted as to the timing of these events. When people mistakenly claim, as in the above examples, that certain things they are experiencing are "the fulfillment" of Scripture, they are misinterpreting what the Bible predicts.

In short, the mistake is not with the predictions of Scripture—they will indeed be fulfilled "in their time." Instead, the mistake is with the overzealous interpreter who makes unfounded claims as to fulfillment in their particular day and age.

Therefore, the fact that some people have made wrong conclusions about certain predictions that we find in Scripture has nothing whatsoever to do with the truth of these prophecies and the reality that they will be fulfilled.

In fact, as we have documented, many "last days" Biblical predictions have already been fulfilled, while the stage is now set for the others too. The key is to understand precisely what is predicted, as well as when, in God's timeline, we should expect to see the fulfillment.

Horatius Bonar said it well.

> It is certainly to be deplored that error and fanaticism have been so often mingled with prophetic studies. God has been thereby dishonored, and his word profaned. The lips of scoffers have been opened in taunt and derision, while timid believers have kept silence, as if unable to reply.
>
> We need not keep silence. Let us admit the fact on which the mockery was founded, and there let it rest. It will humble us; it will inspire caution; it will teach us wisdom, but it will do more. It will not deter us from such studies nor will it lead us to impeach the Word of God for consequences in which man alone is delinquent. It will not lead us to join the fears of the

over-prudent respecting the perilous nature of these investigations, nor to relinquish the field as either impractical, barren, or injurious (Horatius Bonar, *Prophetical Landmarks*, London, James Nisbet And Co., Berners Street, 1847, p. 6).

Indeed, the mistakes of certain Bible interpreters will not stop us from obeying God and His Word! We will search the entirety of Scripture—since everything in it is profitable for study. This especially includes the subject of Bible prophecy.

OBJECTION THREE ANSWERED: THESE BIBLICAL PREDICTIONS ABOUT ISRAEL SHOULD BE UNDERSTOOD IN A LITERAL MANNER. THEY ARE NOT FULFILLED SYMBOLICALLY IN THE CHURCH

There are those who have assumed that some of the predictions in Scripture, when speaking of the "last days," were never meant to be understood literally. In other words, that it is a mistake to try to find a literal fulfillment of these predictions; which they say were never meant to be understood in this manner.

Others argue that the predictions that were originally given to Israel are now being symbolically fulfilled in this age by those who believe in Jesus—the church. In other words, since Israel rejected Jesus as their Messiah, the descendants of Abraham, Isaac, and Jacob have now been replaced in God's timetable by the New Testament church.

J.C. Ryle wrote the following wise words in answering this claim.

We got into a wicked habit of taking all the promises spiritually—and all the denunciations land threats literally. The denunciations against Babylon and Nineveh, and Edom and Tyre, and Egypt and the rebellious Jews, we have been content to take literally ... The blessings and promises to Zion, Jerusalem, Jacob and Israel—we have taken spiritually, and comfortably applied to ourselves . . .

Now I believe that this has been an unfair system of interpreting Scripture. I hold the first and primary sense of every Old Testament promise as well as threat, is the literal one—and that Jacob means Jacob, Jerusalem means Jerusalem, Zion means Zion, and Israel means Israel—as much as Egypt means Egypt and Babylon means Babylon. The primary sense, I believe, we have sadly lost sight of. We have adapted and accommodated to the Church—the promises that were spoken by God to Israel and Zion. . . I do mean to say that the primary sense of every prophecy and promise of Old Testament prophecy—was intended to have a literal fulfillment, and this literal fulfillment has been far too much pushed aside and thrust into a corner (J.C Ryle, *Coming Events and Present Duties*, Second Edition, London, William Hunt and Company, 1879, p. 23).

He then went on to say the following about Biblical predictions that are yet to be fulfilled:

All are yet without their accomplishment—and all shall be literally and exactly fulfilled. I say literally and exactly fulfilled, and I say so advisedly. From the first day that I began to read the Bible with my heart, I have never been able to see these texts, and hundreds like them, in any other light. It always seemed to me that as we take literally the texts foretelling the walls of Babylon shall be cast down—so we ought to take literally the texts foretelling that the walls of Zion shall be built up; that as according to prophecy the Jews were literally scattered—so according to prophecy the Jews will be literally gathered; and that as the least and minutest predictions were made good on the subject of our Lord's coming to suffer—so the minutest predictions shall be made good which describe the Lord's coming to reign (J.C Ryle, *Coming Events and Present Duties*, Second Edition, London, William Hunt and Company, 1879, p. 27).

Therefore, in 1879, J.C. Ryle claimed that these Biblical prophecies concerning the "last days" will someday be literally fulfilled by the literal descendants of Abraham, Isaac, and Jacob. As we have documented in this book, he was absolutely correct! Some have already been literally fulfilled, while other predictions are in the process of being literally fulfilled.

Hugh McNeile responded to those who claim that these prophecies, that are literally meant to be fulfilled by the Jews, have already been fulfilled, either in the past, or symbolically:

> Only admit this idea of yet unfulfilled, and a thousand difficulties vanish. And why should this idea not be admitted? We have seen that so long as we have the history of the Jews to compare with the prophecies concerning them—that is, up to this time; a certain mode of interpreting those prophecies is rendered indispensable: then why not simply continue that same mode of interpretation, when we have prophecy alone not yet illustrated by history? If prophecies concerning the Jews, delivered two or three thousand years ago, be proved, by the history of the interim up to our own days to be fulfilled in a literal sense, and therefore to demand literal interpretation; upon what principle can it be alleged that other prophecies delivered in similar language by the same prophets, are not to be similarly interpreted after our days? Must God have done before our days, all the literal things which he ever intended to do upon the earth? Is there, indeed, anything magical in our age of the world we live in, that it should change the nature of the prophecy or its fulfillment? Or is it that unbelief, though forced to yield to the testimony of history; yet refuses to be effectually taught, even by that plain lesson, and will not take God at his word, or trust him for a moment? (Hugh McNeile, *Popular Lectures on the Prophecies Relative to the Jewish Nation*, London: James Hatchard and Son, 1840, p. 155).

His logic is impeccable. For the last two thousand years, the world has been able to view the literal fulfillment of the history of the Jewish people as given in Scripture. Why then, should we expect anything but a literal fulfillment of the rest of the predictions about the Jews from the same Biblical authors?

We should expect a literal fulfillment of the unfulfilled predictions! And, as we have noted in this book, this is precisely what we see happening in front of our very eyes.

JESUS MEANT WHAT HE SAID!

In a similar argument, William Blackstone, in 1878, put a number of questions to his readers.

> Perhaps you ask, "Shouldn't these prophecies be interpreted spiritually? And doesn't this 'coming' mean our acceptance of Him at conversion, and the witness of the spirit? Or doesn't it refer to His reign over the church?" etc.

> No! Not at all. Think for a moment. Do you condemn the Jews for rejecting Christ, when He came in such a literal fulfillment of prophecy, and yet you reject the same literalness about His second coming? . . .

> What is the purpose of language, if not to convey definite ideas? Surely the Holy Spirit could have chosen words to convey His thoughts correctly. Indeed, it is summed up in the question of a little child, "If Jesus didn't mean what He said, why didn't He say what He meant? But we believe that He did mean what He said and that His words will "not pass away" (Matthew 24:35) William Blackstone, *Jesus Is Coming*, Fleming H. Revell Company, 1878, pp. 21, 23-24).

Excellent questions!

The Jewish/Christian writer of the 19th century, David Baron, explained that that predictions in Scripture, concerning the last days and a literal nation of Israel, should be understood at face value. This includes Israel's literal return to their ancient homeland.

Baron also asked these questions to those commentators who do not interpret the prophecies about Israel literally but instead applies them symbolically to the church.

If Israel be the Church, who is Judah? If Judah be the Church, who is Israel? What is the "captivity" the Church has endured? And where is "the land" from which the church has been driven out, and to which it will return? At the end of the prophecy we read:

> Behold, the days come, saith the Lord, that the city shall be built to the Lord from the tower of Hananeel unto the gate of the corner. And the measuring line shall yet go forth over against it upon the hill Gareb, and shall compass about to Goath. And the whole valley of the dead bodies, and of the ashes, and all the fields unto the brook of Kidron, unto the corner of the horse gate toward the east, shall be holy unto the Lord; it shall not be plucked up, nor thrown down any more for ever (Jeremiah 31:38-40 KJV).

> In what particular locality in heaven are the tower of Hananeel and the corner gate? And what will our allegorical interpretations make of the hill Gareb, and Goath, and the brook Kedron: All these are known to me in the environs of literal Jerusalem in Canaan; but I confess some difficulty in locating them in heavenly places. If Israel does not mean Israel, and "the land gave to the fathers" does mean Palestine, then I do not know what is meant (David Baron, *The Jewish Problem, Its Solution, or Israel's Present and Future*, 1890, pp. 13).

Baron then went on to make this observation:

> The announcement is "He that scattereth Israel will gather him." Now when it comes to scattering; of course, this is allowed to refer to literal Israel, to the Jews, "scattered and peeled;" but when in the same sentence, a gathering is mentioned; oh, this is the gathering of spiritual Israel. What consistently or honesty, I pray, is there in such interpretations! (Baron, *The Jewish Problem*, p. 14).

Very good question! What consistently is there in interpreting the Bible in this manner?

J.C. Ryle also wrote.

> To what may we attribute the loose system of interpreting the language of the Psalms and the prophets, and the extravagant expectations of the universal conversion of the world by the preaching of the gospel, which may be observed in many Christian writers?

> To nothing so much, I believe, as to the habit of inaccurately interpreting the word 'Israel,' and the consequent application of the promises to the Gentile churches with which they have nothing to do . . . What I protest against is, the habit of allegorizing plain sayings of the Word of God concerning the future history of the *nation* Israel, and explaining away the fullness of their contents in order to accommodate them to the Gentile Church. I believe the habit to be unwarranted by anything in Scripture, and to draw after it a long train of evil consequences (J.C. Ryle, "Scattered and Gathered").

Among other things, the evil consequences of replacing Israel with the church misses the marvelous fulfillment of these predictions in our day and age.

Commenting on the 37th chapter of Ezekiel, William Kelly wrote the following words:

> To a mind simple and subject to scripture there can be no hesitation here. To whatever use or application we may turn the vision, its direct and express meaning is God's revival of His ancient people Israel . . . His own faithful grace will undertake to do what is manifestly beyond the power of man. He declares that he will not only disinter them from the graves wherein they now lie buried as a nation, but will bring them to the land of Israel ... restoration to their land is the simple and necessary complement of the national resuscitation of Israel. And so all of the Old Testament testifies (William Kelly, *Notes on Ezekiel*, George Morrish, Paternoster Row, 1876, p. 184).

His point is well-taken. The passage could not be clearer. God will literally restore the nation of Israel to their ancient homeland at the time of the end. As we have seen, this process has already begun in 1948.

Horatius Bonar put it this way:

> In all cases, then we are bound to adhere to the literal until we can show *reasons* for departing from it. These reasons ought to be well weighed and found sufficient before we venture to disturb the plain meaning of God's own words (Horatius Bonar, *Prophetical Landmarks*, London, James Nisbet And Co., Berners Street, 1847 p. 276).

As someone once wisely said, "If the literal sense makes good sense, then seek no other sense, lest you come up with nonsense!"

David Baron gave his own personal testimony as to the importance of interpreting the Bible, as well as the future promises to Israel, literally:

Like thousands more, the writer has in the infinite grace of God been brought out of the darkness of Rabbinical Judaism into the marvelous light and liberty of the glorious gospel of Christ. He accepted Jesus of Nazareth as the Messiah of Israel and Saviour of the world on the ground of a literal interpretation of the prophecies concerning Him; and he cannot consistently, without doing outrage to his convictions, accept one principle of interpretation for one set of prophecies which have already been fulfilled, and another principle of interpretation for another set of prophecies not yet fulfilled. Rather he honestly believes that the manner of fulfillment of those prophecies which are now history, supplies the only sound basis for the interpretation of those prophecies with regard to Israel and the kingdom which await their fulfillment ... "He that scattereth Israel:" From whence? From the Church or gospel blessings? No, no; but from Palestine. "Will gather him:" Where to? Why surely to the land which He gave to their fathers, from which Israel on account of disobedience, was banished and scattered (David Baron, *The Jewish Problem, Its Solution, or Israel's Present and Future*, 1890, pp. 15-17).

This testimony is highly instructive. Here was a man who came to faith in Jesus as his Messiah from a Jewish background, after, among other things, it was seeing prophecies about Jesus be literally fulfilled in the past. As he said, they are now history. Logically, the remaining passages should be interpreted the same way.

David Baron did not live to see the day, when these Biblical prophecies about Israel's restoration to their ancient homeland became a literal reality. Rather, by faith, like so many others, he believed that they would someday come to pass; and, indeed, they did.

These commentators have a testimony that we should never forget. Indeed, if the Lord predicts something will literally take place, sooner or later, it will. This should be our attitude with respect to all unfulfilled prophecy.

Ford Ottman summed it up perfectly.

> The literal fulfillment of prophecies already accomplished should confirm our faith in the literal fulfillment of other predictions given by the same prophets concerning events that are related to the coming of the Lord and the consummation of the age (Ford C. Ottman, *The Coming Day*, Philadelphia, The Sunday School Times Company, 1905, p. 11).

THE FOURTH OBJECTION ANSWERED: THESE PREDICTIONS WERE NOT FULFILLED AT THE RETURN FROM BABYLON

Another objection to understanding these prophecies as referring to a future restoration of Israel to their homeland, is to see them as having a past fulfillment—when the people returned from Babylon in 536 B.C.

A.C. Gaebelein states the simple answer to this claim:

> He will gather them from among the nations and all countries and bring them back to their own land. Only a superficial expositor can speak of a fulfillment when they returned from Babylon ... the verses which follow have never been fulfilled in the past (A.C. Gaebelein, *The Prophet Ezekiel*, New York, Our Hope, 1918, p. 241).

Indeed, when one considers the specific predictions, then looks at what happened in the return from Babylon, there can be no question that many predictions about Israel's future remain unfulfilled.

In commenting upon the 37th chapter of Ezekiel, William Kelly made this wise observation:

> It is in vain to wrest such language to the remnant of Jews that returned from Babylon, as it is to the church at

Pentecost. There is not even analogy. It is a union of the two long-divided houses of Israel, and nothing else. Not even a shadow of its accomplishment has appeared yet. Words cannot be conceived more explicit. Every sense but the future ingathering and union of all Israel as a single nation under one king is excluded. As the Jew cannot say that this has yet been, so it is absurd for any Gentile to say it for them . . . A remnant of Jews returned from Babylon to be defiled not merely with transgressions, but with a more detestable thing than their old idolatry, even the rejection and crucifying of their Messiah: was this a fulfillment of Ezekiel's glowing words? (William Kelly, *Notes on Ezekiel*, George Morrish, Paternoster Row, 1876, p. 188).

His comment, "Words cannot be conceived more explicit" says it all! The passage is clearly speaking of a yet future gathering of the descendants of Abraham, Isaac, and Jacob—something that had not taken place at the time Kelly wrote in 1876.

David Baron answers this objection in detail.

But perhaps the most plausible way of explaining such predictions is to represent them as having had their fulfillment at the restoration from Babylon, since they were given before the Babylonish captivity. To this I reply that this and other predictions are in terms of which we vainly seek an adequate fulfillment at that period. It may be well to give here a few reasons in justification of the position that there is a future Restoration of the literal Israel to the land which by unconditional promise and covenant was given to them as an everlasting possession (Genesis 15:7-21; 17:7,8, 19, 21).

I. The Restoration promised here is a *complete* one (italics his): I will bring again the captivity of My people Israel and Judah (Jeremiah 31:8). And the number who will return shall be "a great company," so that even the whole of the promised land will not be large enough for them (Zechariah 10:10; Isaiah 49,19,20). The same appears in that remarkable prophecy of Isaiah 11, which on whatever system of interpretation we adopt, is admittedly future in its application, where "the outcasts of Israel" and "the dispersed of Judah" are to be gathered together. The same appears in Ezekiel 37, where the future is announced for the whole twelve tribes reunited into one kingdom. Many more passages might be cited which speak of a complete Restoration of the entire nation in terms most unequivocal and minute; which certainly could not be said to have received their fulfillment in the—comparatively speaking—mere handful who returned from Babylon.

II. After the Restoration predicted in this and other prophecies, Israel is to enjoy at least national independence, if not supremacy.

> For it shall come to pass in that day, saith the Lord of hosts, that I will break his yoke from off thy neck, and will burst thy bonds, and strangers shall no more serve themselves of him (Jeremiah 30:8 KJV).

Backsliding Israel, because he served not Jehovah with joyfulness and with gladness of heart for the abundance of all things, was to be taught a lesson by comparison; and was given over by God to be in servitude for a time to the Gentiles.

But this iron yoke of Gentile oppression was not to last forever. This is clear from the solemn words of the Lord Jesus, when announcing the fact that Israel "shall fall by the edge of the sword, and shall be led away captive into all nations" (Luke 21:24). He suspends in the midst of the darkness of threatened judgment the bright star of hope which ultimately shall banish the darkness, and cause judgment to be forgotten in the abundance of mercy; inasmuch as He announces a limit to the time of Israel's servitude to Gentile oppression.

"Jerusalem shall be trodden down of the Gentiles until the times of the Gentiles be fulfilled."

And when they be fulfilled, the yoke will be broken, and Israel will once more not only be free and independent, but nationally *supreme* among the nations.

But has this ever yet taken place? Let those who point to the restoration of Babylon as an exhaustive fulfillment of these prophecies compare for instance, such a passage as Isaiah 14:1-3, where we read after.

> For the Lord will have mercy on Jacob, and will yet choose Israel, and set them in their own land: and the strangers shall be joined with them, and they shall cleave to the house of Jacob. And the people shall take them, and bring them to their place: and the house of Israel shall possess them in the land of the Lord for servants and handmaids: and they shall take them captives, whose captives they were; and they shall rule over their oppressors (Isaiah 14:1-3 KJV).

III. According to the express declaration of the prophet Isaiah, there is to be a second Restoration, which is to be universal in its character.

> And it shall come to pass in that day, that the Lord shall set his hand again the second time to recover the remnant of his people, which shall be left, from Assyria, and from Egypt, and from Pathros, and from Cush, and from Elam, and from Shinar, and from Hamath, and from the islands of the sea. And he shall set up an ensign for the nations, and shall assemble the outcasts of Israel, and gather together the dispersed of Judah from the four corners of the earth (Isaiah 11:11,12 KJV).

IV. Israel has never yet in its fullness possessed the land which God has promised them; and Palestine may still be said to be "the land of promise." Its boundaries are given in Genesis 15:18, Ezekiel 42:13 and 48:1.

V. ... Leaving out for the moment the . . . ordeal and baptism of suffering which awaits Israel . . . on their return to their land . . . the Restoration announced in this and other prophecies is to be followed by a *National Conversion* (Jeremiah 30:8-10). Israel nationally is then to enter into the blessing of the New Covenant announced in this very prophecy (Jeremiah 31:31-34), which the election of individuals from all nations now enjoy, as it were, by anticipation. . .

VI. There is to be a gathering of Israel to the land of their fathers, which is to be *final* (italics his). This is announced in this very prophecy, where at the end of chapter 31, after describing with the greatest minuteness and geographical exactness the rebuilding of the Holy City, it closes with the declaration "it shall not be plucked up nor thrown down any more forever" (David Baron, *The Jewish Problem, Its Solution, or Israel's Present and Future*, 1890, pp. 17-25).

It is clear that the predictions of Israel's future return to the land did not happen in 536 B.C. with the return from Babylon. Indeed, as these past commentators have so eloquently stated, these predictions will be fulfilled in "the last days."

ANSWER TO THE FIFTH OBJECTION: THE TIME OF JACOB'S TROUBLE DID NOT OCCUR AT THE DESTRUCTION OF JERUSALEM

What about the possibility that this time of horror for Israel, the time of Jacob's trouble, has already occurred? Is it possible that it took place at the destruction of Jerusalem in A.D. 70? There are several reasons as to why this is not possible. David Baron writes:

> But may not this "time of Jacob's trouble" refer to the awful calamity that befell the nation at the destruction of Jerusalem by Titus, which was repeated with perhaps greater severity about sixty-five years later in the time of Bar Cochba and Hadrian? NO! The ordeal announced here through which Israel is to pass is terribly sharp, but brief in its duration .

. . and ends in their salvation; while the sufferings at the destruction of Jerusalem by Titus only inaugurated a long series of dispersions, massacres, spoilations, and oppressions, which has already continued for more than eighteen centuries. Of course, it is not denied that these long-enduring sufferings were predicted in the Word of God, and have their place and relation to Israel's apostasy and future glory . . .but it is clear that there is a time of purging by fiery judgment awaiting Israel *after they return to their land* (italics his), which will . . . precede their national conversion and the revelation to them of the Messiah, whom, as a nation, they have so long rejected (David Baron, *The Jewish Problem, Its Solution, Or Israel's Present And Future*, 1890, pp. 27,28).

We can add to this something that David Baron, and other past commentators never could foresee—the Holocaust of World War II. While the number of Jews who perished was greater than what took place at the destruction of Jerusalem, this did not fulfill that which the Bible has predicted. Indeed, the people had not yet returned to their ancient homeland when this took place. Hence, a greater "time of trouble" is still in the future.

There are several lessons we learn from this:

First, this was written in the 19th century when there was no modern state of Israel. Indeed, the nation had been wandering for some 1,800 years.

Second, though there was no indication that the writer would have ever viewed the fulfillment in his lifetime, nevertheless, he believed that the nation would return to its ancient homeland, as the Bible promised.

Third, the key for him was a literal understanding of Scripture. As he so brilliantly pointed out in his answer to the first of these five objections, to understand these predictions in any other manner makes no sense whatsoever.

SUMMING UP THE FIVE OBJECTIONS

As we have seen from the learned arguments of these past commentators, these five objections against Biblical prophecy being understood as literal, future predictions, carry no weight whatsoever.

Indeed, these predictions, made by the Lord through His prophets, were written to be understood. In addition, they were meant to be interpreted literally.

Furthermore, they dealt with "the latter days, "the time of the end." They were not fulfilled at the return from Babylon, nor at the later destruction of Jerusalem in A.D. 70, and they certainly are not symbolically fulfilled today, in "the church."

As we have observed, against all odds, many of them have been literally fulfilled in our day and age while the stage is being set for the literal fulfillment of the remaining predictions.

In sum, predictive prophecy demonstrates the God of the Bible does exist, that He knows the future, and that He is in control of the future. We, again, refer to the Lord's own words on the subject:

You have heard; now look at all the evidence! Will you not admit that what I say is true? (Isaiah 48:6 NET).

Some Predictions by Past Bible Commentators That Have Now Been Literally Fulfilled

In this book, we have included a number of predictions by past Bible commentators as to what will happen in the future. Each of these predictions was based upon a literal understanding of the Bible taught would eventually happen at the "time of the end."

Space did not allow us to add many similar comments by these, as well as other Bible teachers. Consequently, this appendix is dedicated to documenting some of the various predictions that were made with respect to the future by these scholars of yesteryear.

THE SPECIFIC PREDICTIONS WE WILL DOCUMENT

Specifically, we will look at predictions of the importance of Bible prophecy, predictions of Israel's return to their ancient homeland, predictions that they will return in unbelief, and predictions that they will eventually build a Temple and offer sacrifices.

Remember, that when the things were written, circumstances made it seem impossible that the predictions would ever be literally fulfilled. Nevertheless, they did indeed take place—just as the Bible has said!

COMMENTATORS ON THE IMPORTANCE OF THE SUBJECT OF BIBLE PROPHECY

We have already noted the words of a few past commentators on the importance of studying what the Bible has to say about the future. In fact, almost every commentator from the past emphasized the importance of this study. Consequently, we will add a few more quotations from these authors to again emphasize the necessity of examining the Scripture with respect to future events.

G.H. Pember wrote.

> The supreme God has deigned to give revelations whereby He seeks to communicate his purpose to men, and thus, by a gentle process, to bend their minds to His mighty and irresistible will. Nevertheless, myriads of professing Christians are content to reach the end of life in total ignorance of these gracious disclosures, while accredited ministers of Christ are too frequently unable to expound them.

> But since God has thought fit to set them before us, are we not deliberately charging Him with folly while we neglect them? And is not the significance of our conduct much the same if we persist in perverting them from their proper meaning and use? (G.H. Pember, p. *The Great Prophecies Concerning the Gentiles, the Jews, and the Church of God*, 1881, p. 1).

Excellent questions! What are we saying about God and His Word if we neglect to study a large portion of Scripture—the portions containing Bible prophecy?

A.C. Gaebelein, like many other writers, emphasized, "the lamp of Bible prophecy" which the Lord has given to us throughout the Scripture. Commenting upon 2 Peter 1:19-21, he wrote the following.

> In the above passage we also read the comparison which is made between the prophetic Word and a lamp, and we are exhorted to take heed to it. This God-given lamp shone out from the beginning. Its light was kindled by Jehovah in the garden, its first ray fell upon the guilty pair and brought them hope and cheer, as well as guidance through the dark

night of Eden. It continued its blessed shining; new oil was constantly added to it. By its light generation after generation by *taking heed to it* [italics his] found joy and comfort as faith looked on towards the future. And this lamp, the prophetic Word, is still shining, and we are, like all believers before us, to take heed to it. The "dark place" is the present age, still an evil age (Arno C. Gaebelein, *The Harmony of the Prophetic Word*, New York, Fleming H. Revell Company, 1907, p. 18).

These are wise words! From the very beginning of the human race, God has provided the lamp of Bible prophecy to light the path for believers, to give us hope for the future. We need to pay attention to that shining lamp for guidance through the darkness.

B.W. Newton wrote about certain practical advantages that result from a study of Bible prophecy.

If it be asked, what practical advantage is derived from attention to the prophetic Scriptures? It would be sufficient to reply that they are the revealed instruction of God; be we will farther say, that those who have neglected them will be found to have fallen, not only into loose and vague interpretations (as well as false applications) of Scripture, but there will also be found in them an impression of the relation in which the Church and the world stand towards each other, and towards God; a total blindness of the coming judgments, which are the great subjects of Scripture warning; and an indifference with respect to the coming of the Lord, which is the *one* [italics his] prescribed object of hope (B.W. Newton, *Prospects of Ten Kingdoms of the Roman Empire*, London, Houston and Son, 1873, p. 176).

Blindness, to the future plan of God, will indeed result from neglecting the prophetic Scriptures.

To sum up, these past commentators whom we have quoted made it clear that the study of Bible prophecy was crucial for the believer.

COMMENTATORS PREDICTING THE FUTURE RESTORATION OF ISRAEL

Scores of past commentators, based on a literal understanding of the Bible, have predicted a future restoration of the nation of Israel in their own land. We will give merely a small sample of their predictions.

In 1890, David Baron, under a chapter heading "Is there a yet Future Restoration?" wrote the following.

> Until all the writings of the prophet were compiled in one book as we now have it, Jeremiah 30 and 31 formed a distinct prophecy, and was doubtless in circulation amongst the people in a separate prophetic book; and in verse 2 we read that it is a "book" dictated by God Himself. The subject, then, with which it deals must be one concerning which He is especially anxious to reveal His thoughts. Whatever man may think of it, He considers this matter of immense importance, so that every word must be preserved. . . .

This book, dictated by God Himself, is a very remarkable one; for though it concerns Israel, it is addressed chiefly to the Gentile nations.

Baron the cites Jeremiah 31:7-10

> This is what the Lord says: "Sing with joy for Jacob; shout for the foremost of the nations. Make your praises heard, and say, 'Lord, save your people, the remnant of Israel.' See, I will bring them from the land of the north and gather them from the ends of the earth.
>
> Among them will be the blind and the lame, expectant mothers and women in labor; a great throng will return. They will come with weeping; they will pray as I bring them

back. I will lead them beside streams of water on a level path where they will not stumble, because I am Israel's father, and Ephraim is my firstborn son. "Hear the word of the Lord, you nations; proclaim it in distant coastlands: 'He who scattered Israel will gather them and will watch over his flock like a shepherd.'

It is a testimony, then, not so much to Israel as to the Gentile nations about Israel. Just as, in the epistle to the Romans, we find as it were an epistle within an epistle; three chapters, 9,10,11 for the purpose of enlightening Gentile Christians with regard to God's purposes in Israel. The apostle is most impressed with the importance of the Church having the correct views on this subject; and feels that he cannot leave them ignorant . . . lest, through the erroneous notion that God hath cast away His people Israel which He foreknew and the special promises and privileges reserved for Israel nationally in the Word of God have been transferred to the church ...

So here, through the prophet Jeremiah, there is a definite message, a proclamation, a warning to the chief of the Gentile nations, and to the isles afar off, to the same purport, viz. that God is not done with Israel; that "He that scattereth Israel will gather him and keep him as a shepherd does his flock" (David Baron, *The Jewish Problem, Its Solution, Or Israel's Present And Future*, 1890, pp. 9-11).

Elsewhere he wrote.

Apart from God's revelation, the Jew is an enigma, a problem beyond the vain attempts of man to solve; and attempts of the kind, if not based upon the Word of God, are futile and impious. The future of Israel is one of those subjects concerning which the great God has deigned to speak; and however difficult or improbable to man that future may appear, it behoves us to believe and receive, and not to speculate and rebel (Baron, *The Jewish Problem,* p. 11).

Indeed, instead of speculating, or denying what the Bible literally says, we should humbly wait for the fulfillments of these predictions in the proper time. The nation of Israel will indeed return to the Land of Promise!

In the 17th century, John Gill wrote the following concerning the Jews and the "last days."

> The land of Canaan, given to Abraham, etc. shall be again possessed by the Jews their posterity; for without supposing that the Jews upon their call and conversion to their own land, in a literal sense, I see not how we can understand this, and many other prophecies (John Gill: *"An Exposition of the Old and New Testament,"* Exposition of the Old Testament, 6 Volumes, 1748-1763, p. 133).

Gill also wrote.

> It is certain that the prophecy refers to what should be in "latter years", and in the "latter days," Ezekiel 38:8 Ezekiel 38:16, phrases which respect the times of the Messiah, the Gospel dispensation, and oftentimes the latter part of that; and even those times when the Jews shall return to their own land, and continue in it for ever, as the preceding prophecy, with which this is connected, shows; and so the Jews always understand it of an enemy of theirs yet to come (John Gill, Commentary on Ezekiel, *An Exposition of the Old and New Testament, Exposition of the Old Testament,* 6 Volumes, 1748-1763).

When Gill wrote, over 250 years ago, there was nothing taking place in the world that would indicate these predictions would be soon fulfilled. Like all the others we cite, he believed the promises of God "by faith."

In 1889, Nathaniel West explained the necessity of understanding a future for Israel in a literal manner.

> The postmillennarian assumption, that Israel is nationally cast away forever, that God has no national future for Israel restored, and that Israel is now the 'Church,' is the one fundamental and false postulate that blinds so many to the true interpretation (Nathaniel West, *The Thousand Years*, 1889, p. 105).

Indeed, it "blinds" people to the marvelous fulfillment that we have now seen in our day and age.

A.C. Gaebelein, his commentary on Ezekiel, wrote about the fulfillment that was yet future.

> When the Lord keeps His promise and brings them back, their sorrows will be at an end. What are the sorrows and sufferings of the Babylonians captivity in comparison with the sufferings that befell them in the year 70 and throughout this dispensation! And the last page of Israel's sorrow is yet to be written. All is preparing now for the great tribulation, and then there will be the intervention from above, and the coming Lord will wipe away all their tears. Four times the prophet uses the words "any more" (verses 14-15), "Neither shalt thou bear the reproach of the peoples any more, neither shalt thou cause thy nation to stumble any more saith the Lord God." Inasmuch as there is reproach now upon that nation and they are a reproach, and that they have stumbled, we know that these words still await their fulfillment (A.C. Gaebelein, *The Prophet Ezekiel*, New York, Our Hope, 1918, pp, 238-239).

Notice the sequence. Israel returns to their homeland, eventually the "Great Tribulation" occurs, Israel repents, and the Lord returns. When all of this take place, no longer will the nation of Israel be belittled by the people of this world. In fact, their tears will be wiped away. This is their predicted future!

William Kelly, in 1876, states the case about how the Lord has made Israel's future plain for all to see.

> In vain do men apply such glowing words to the return from Babylon, which was but an earnest of what is coming for the entire people. Can anyone who respects Scripture and knows the facts pretend that the Lord multiplied men on the mountains of Israel, "all the house of Israel, even all of it" (Verse 10). Such words seem expressly written to guard souls from such meagre and misleading views. Did Jehovah settle the returned remnant after their old estate and do more good than at the beginning? (Verse 12). Did the land, did the mountains become Israel's inheritance and no more bereave them? (Verse 12) Do we not know that under a fourth empire a still worse destruction came and a longer dispersion, instead of the land devouring no more, neither bereaving its own nations nor bearing the insult of the Gentiles any more? (Verse 15).

> No! The fulfillment of the prophecy is yet to come, but come it will surely as Jehovah lives and has thus sworn through His prophet concerning the land of Israel. To suppose that the gospel or the church is meant by such language is far from simplicity or intelligence (William Kelly, *Notes on Ezekiel*, George Morrish, Paternoster Row, 1876, p. 176).

In other words, the fact that the Lord is not finished with Israel, that they will one day literally return to their own land, could not have been stated any clearer by the Lord Himself.

Commenting upon Zechariah 13:8-9 and 14:1-2, David Baron wrote the following words in 1890.

This is the immediate prospect after restoration to Palestine of the people who rebelled against the Most High, and rejected His Son, and always resisted the Holy Spirit; a furnace seven times heated and anguish as acute as the pangs of a woman in travail. . .

> And although their tribulation and anguish shall be great that there has been none like it, in the midst of wrath God will remember mercy; and, according to His promise, He will not utterly destroy the house of Jacob (David Baron, *The Jewish Problem, Its Solution, or Israel's Present And Future*, 1890, p. 29).

Clearly, God has not forever cast away His ancient people Israel.

J.C. Ryle, in 1879, gives an extended account of why Israel must return to their ancient homeland in the last days.

Out of the sixteen prophets of the Old Testament, there are at least ten in which the gathering and restoration of the Jews in the latter days are expressly mentioned. . .

> Hear what Isaiah says: "In that day the Lord shall reach out his hand a second time to reclaim the remnant that is left of his people from Assyria, from Lower Egypt, from Upper Egypt, from Cush, from Elam, from Babylonia, from Hamath and from the islands of the sea. He will raise a banner for the nations and gather the exiles of Israel: he will assemble the scattered people of Judah from the four quarters of the earth" (Isaiah 11:11,12).

Hear what Ezekiel says: "This is what the Sovereign Lord says: I will take the Israelites out of the nations where they have gone. I will gather them from all around and bring them back into their own land." (Ezekiel 37:21).

Hear what Hosea says: "The people of Judah and the people of Israel will be reunited, and they will appoint one leader and will come up out of the land, for great will be the day of Jezreel." (Hosea 1:11). "For the Israelites will live many days without a king or prince, without sacrifice or sacred stones, without ephod or idol. Afterward the Israelites will return and seek the Lord their God and David their king. They will come trembling to the Lord and to his blessing in the last days" (Hosea 3:4,5).

Hear what Joel says: "Judah will be inhabited forever and Jerusalem through all generation." (Joel 3:20).

Hear what Amos says: "I will bring back my exiled people Israel; they will rebuild the ruined cities and live in them. They will plant vineyards and drink their wine; they will make gardens and eat their fruit. I will plant Israel in their own land, never again to be uprooted from the land I have given them, says the Lord your God." (Amos 9:14,15).

Hear what Obadiah says: "But on Mount Zion will be deliverance; it will be holy, and the house of Jacob will possess its inheritance." (Obadiah 1:17).

Hear what Micah says: "In that day," declares the LORD, "I will gather the lame; I will assemble the exiles and those I have brought to grief I will make the lame a remnant, those driven away a strong nation. The LORD will rule over them in Mount Zion from that day and forever." (Micah 4:6,7).

Hear what Zephaniah says: "Sing, O Daughter of Zion; shout aloud, O Israel! Be glad and rejoice with your heart, O Daughter of Jerusalem! The Lord has taken away your punishment, he has turned back your enemy. The LORD, the King of Israel, is with you; never again will you fear any harm. On that day they will say to Jerusalem, "Do not fear, O Zion; do not let your hands hang limp. The LORD your God is with you, he is mighty to save. He will take great delight in you, he will quiet you with his love, he will rejoice over you with singing. At that time I will deal with all who oppressed you; I will rescue the lame and gather those who have been scattered. I will give them praise and honor in every land where they were put to shame. At that time I will gather you; at that time I will bring you home. I will give you honor and praise among the peoples of the earth when I restore your fortunes before your very eyes, says the Lord." (Zephaniah 3:14-10).

Hear what Zechariah says: "I will strengthen the house of Judah and save the house of Joseph. I will restore them because I have compassion on them. They will be as though I had not rejected them, for I am the Lord their God and I will answer them. The Ephraimites will become like mighty men, and their hearts will be glad with wine. Their children will see it and be joyful; their hearts will rejoice in the Lord. I will signal for them and gather them in. Surely, I will redeem them; they will be as numerous as before. Though I scatter them among the peoples, yet in distant lands they will remember me. They and their children will survive, and they will return. I will bring them back from Egypt, I will gather them from Assyria. I will bring them to Gilead and Lebanon, and there will not be room enough for them (Zechariah 10:6-10).

Hear, lastly, what Jeremiah says. "The days are coming, declares the Lord, when I will bring my people Israel and Judah back from captivity and restore them to the land I gave their forefathers to possess, says the Lord (Jeremiah 30:3). "I am with you and will save you declares the Lord. Though I completely destroy all the nations among which I scatter you, I will not completely destroy you. I will discipline you but only with justice; I will not let you go entirely unpunished (J.C. Ryle, *Coming Events and Present Duties*, Second Edition, London, William Hunt and Company, 1879, pp. 178, 179).

Ryle then asks this question.

> Is there anything improbable about the gathering of Israel? Alas reader, we are poor judges of probabilities. God's ways of carrying into effect His own purposes are not to be judged by man's standard, or measured by the line . . . of what man

calls probable. In the day the children of Israel went forth from Egypt, would anyone have said it was probable that such a nation of serfs would ever produce a book that should turn the world upside down? Yet that nation has done it. From that nation has come the Bible (J.C. Ryle, *Coming Events and Present Duties*, pp. 180,181).

In fact, the God of the Bible does that which is impossible for humans. As the angel Gabriel told Mary so long ago.

For with God nothing shall be impossible (Luke 1:37 KJV).

Nothing indeed!

Furthermore, as the Bible predicted, and as these commentators believed would someday happen, many of the Jewish people miraculously returned to their ancient homeland, and in 1948, the modern state of Israel was reborn.

COMMENTATORS PREDICTING THE JEWS WILL BE RESTORED IN UNBELIEF

We have documented that the Scripture teach that the return to the Promised Land will be in two stages. The first stage will be a return in unbelief. Past commentators have noted this—as David Baron wrote in 1890.

What have we in the last chapters of Zechariah? Israel in their land; not necessarily the entire nation but the bulk of it, evidently, restored in a state of unbelief (David Baron, *The Jewish Problem, Its Solution, Or Israel's Present And Future*, 1890, p. 28).

A.C. Gaebelein wrote the following comments about Ezekiel 37.

The national resuscitation of the whole house of Israel, the restoration to their own land and the accompanying spiritual revival (though the latter does not fully come into view here) is the meaning of the vision. It may be used in application in different ways, to illustrate certain truths, but the true and only interpretation is the one which is given by the Lord in verses 11-14 . . .

Equally bad is that spiritualizing method which takes a vision like this, as well as the hundreds of promises of a coming restoration and applies it to the church, ignoring totally the claims of Israel and their promised future of glory . . .

They say that these visions and promises were exhausted in the return of the remnant from Babylon (less than 43,000 souls) and the spiritual and larger fulfillment is now going on in the church. This method is evil, for it robs the Christian of the true key which unlocks the prophetic word (A.C. Gaebelein, *The Prophet Ezekiel*, New York, Our Hope, 1918, pp. 245, 247)

We find that Gaebelein rightly makes the Biblical distinction between the Jews returning to their land, and their eventual spiritual revival. These two events do NOT happen at the same time.

He also emphasizes the importance of seeing these predictions as having never been fulfilled in the past, nor spiritually fulfilled in the church. In fact, as he pointed out, without understanding this, the believer is robbed of the key to properly interpret Bible prophecy.

Bishop W.R. Nicholson, in the 19th century, made it clear that the return will indeed be in two installments.

Undeniably, both houses of Israel, as one nationality, shall yet be re-established in Palestine, the land of their ancient inheritance. . . The gathering of Israel will be accomplished in two installments . . . But all Israel will not have been gathered back to their land before the Advent; a second and finally complete movement in their restoration will occur subsequently to that great event (Isa. 11:11,12, 15,16). (Bishop W.R. Nicholson "The Gathering of Israel," in Nathaniel West, *Second Coming of Christ, Premillennial Essays of the Prophetic Conference*, Chicago, F.H. Revell, 1879, pp. 228, 230).

He describes it further.

One movement in the process of their restoration will have taken place previously to the Lord's Second Coming. "Behold," saith God in Zechariah (14), "the day of the Lord cometh. For I will gather all nations against Jerusalem to battle; and the city shall be taken, and half of the city shall go forth into captivity, and the residue of the people shall not be cut off from the city." Now, if Israel be not there, why are the nations there to fight against them? For that it is Israel against whom this battle is waged is sufficiently suggested by the word "nations," as designating the attacking party; in fact, however, the whole chapter is express as to the presence of Israel (Bishop W.R. Nicholson "The Gathering of Israel," in Nathaniel West, *Second Coming of Christ, Premillennial Essays of the Prophetic Conference*, Chicago, F.H. Revell, 1879, p. 228).

Again, we find that the return of the Jews will be in two "movements" or two "stages." The first will take place before the Second Coming of Christ, while the second will occur *after* the Lord returns to the earth. At that time, He will supernaturally gather the remaining Jews from all parts of the earth.

Another 19th century writer, J.T. Cooper, also observed that the return of the Jews to their ancient homeland will be in unbelief.

There is a crisis or hour of judgment awaiting both the houses of Israel in the latter days. The ten tribes are at present hidden from view, but under the juridical wrath of God. The awful extent of this wrath, as it hath rested and still continues to rest upon the house of Judah, has been the theme of historians without number. In Hosea 3:4,5, we are told that "the children of Israel shall abide many days without a prince, without a sacrifice, and without an image, and without an ephod, and without teraphim." . . . What a remarkable description of their present condition! The next verse shows us that "afterward shall the children of Israel return and seek the Lord their God, and David their king; and shall fear the Lord and His goodness in the latter days." In harmony with this prophecy of Hosea, Jesus, to whom all judgment has been committed, utters in the midst of His tears the following judgment: "Behold your house is left unto you desolate. For I say unto you, Ye shall not see me henceforth, till ye say, Blessed is he that cometh in the name of the Lord." The probability is that this return will be made by them principally in an unconverted state (J.T. Cooper, "The Judgment of Judgments" in Nathaniel West, *Second Coming of Christ, Premillennial Essays of the Prophetic Conference*, Chicago, F.H. Revell, 1879, pp. 249, 250).

Writing about Zechariah 14, Bishop B.W. Newton made the following observations.

I may now safely appeal to any who have seriously weighed the evidence of the preceding chapters, and ask them to say whether certain great substantive facts touching the future are not conclusively proved by them? It is proved that the vast Gentile nations will again be gathered in siege against Jerusalem; that these hosts are in the land of Israel destroyed; that the Heads of Israel in Jerusalem are delivered and also converted; that consequently they must have returned to their land and city unconverted; and that they are delivered and converted by the personal manifestation of the Lord (B.W. Newton, *Aids To Prophetic Inquiry*, London, James Nisbet and Co., 1848, p. 37).

These statements of Newton cover many of the signs which we have alluded to in this book. Israel, in the last days, not only exists, the nation also returns to its ancient homeland. In addition, the entire city of Jerusalem is under their control. During this final attack by the Gentile nations, the Lord will supernaturally destroy their enemies. The people, realizing the supernatural work of God, then turns to faith in Jesus as their Messiah!

Hence, the logical conclusion is that prior to this, when the nation returns to Israel, and the city of Jerusalem, they do so in an unconverted state.

In sum, we find these ancient commentators recognizing that when Israel does return to their ancient homeland in the "last days," it will be in unbelief of the Lord. This is what they predicted would happen.

Furthermore, as we have shown, the prediction has been fulfilled in 1948—when the modern state of Israel was reborn with the Jewish people still in unbelief of Jesus! Everything is now set for the next stages to occur; the Great Tribulation, the turning of the nation of Israel to faith in Christ, the Second Coming of Christ, and finally, the gathering of all the people of Israel from all parts of the globe.

COMMENTATORS PREDICTING THE REBUILDING OF THE TEMPLE

Many past commentators also looked forward to the time that the Jews would return to their ancient homeland in the "last days" and eventually build a Third Temple. We can cite the following.

The first verse of this chapter [Eleven] under consideration sets forth a sanctuary which can be none other than Israel's. Israel's restoration involves, as we have already seen, the restoration of temple service. The mosque of Omar, which now stands on the temple area of the literal city, shall be thrown down and a Jewish temple shall be erected wherein the daily sacrifices shall be offered when Israel shall again be in possession of her own land (Ford C. Ottman, *The Unfolding of the Ages*, New York, Baker & Taylor Company, 1905, p. 264).

We also read of Bishop W.R. Nicholson predicting a Third Temple will be built and Temple services restored.

They will have rebuilt their temple and re-established their temple services, before the coming of the Lord. For, according to the words of Jesus, in the twenty-fourth of Matthew, they will "see the Son of Man coming into the clouds of Heaven with power and great glory," only after the "abomination of desolation," spoken by Daniel the prophet, shall have stood "in the holy place." (Bishop W.R. Nicholson "The Gathering of Israel," in Nathaniel West, *Second Coming of Christ, Premillennial Essays of the Prophetic Conference*, Chicago, F.H. Revell, 1879, p. 231).

G.H. Pember wrote.

Thus restored and settled in their own land, the Jews will rebuild their Temple and renew the sacrifices and services; but probably, in a proud and atheistical spirit, and certainly in a way very displeasing to God (G.H. Pember, *The Great Prophecies Concerning the Gentiles, the Jews, and the Church of God*, 1881, p. 113).

B.W. Newton wrote about the sign Jesus predicted, "the abomination of desolation."

Although eighteen hundred years have passed since the Lord Jesus uttered these words, the abomination of which He spake has not yet stood in the holy place. But the whole of prophetic Scripture concurs in showing that the Jews again returning to Jerusalem in unbelief   . . . will there re-build their Temple and re-establish their sacrifices, but without God. Accordingly, His hand will be stretched out against them. He will allow them to fall into the hands of the last great king of the Gentiles . . . He will blaspheme God ad Christ; pollute the Temple, take away the daily sacrifice; "and plant the abomination that maketh desolate; and upon the pinnacle of abominations [i.e. the idolatrous pinnacle] shall be the desolator even until the consummation, and that determined shall be poured out on the desolator" (Benjamin Wills Newton, *The Prophecy of the Lord Jesus as contained in Matthew XXIV. & XXV*, Third Edition, London: Houlston and Sons, 1879, pp. 12,13).

Newton also said.

There are two reasons why the "setting up of the abomination of desolation," which is the evidence of the maturity of Anti-christian apostasy in Jerusalem, should be mentioned here. In the first place, the disciples had asked for the sign of His coming. All the events mentioned in the ten preceding verses [Matthew 24:4-14] had been too general in their character, and too prolonged in their duration to be any specific sign of the end. The abounding of iniquity, for example, in the professing Church, has prevailed too long for it to be any definite indication of the end. It is not, therefore, until the second division of the chapter that the Lord speaks of the *definite* sign [italics his] of His coming. That sign is the setting up by the Antichrist of his idol in Jerusalem; the consequent infliction on the land of Israel of a tribulation, "such as was not from the beginning of the creation which God created until this time, nor ever shall be;" and that tribulation immediately followed by the manifestation of the Lord in glory (Benjamin Wills Newton, *The Prophecy of the Lord Jesus as contained in Matthew XXIV. & XXV*, p. 12).

This is merely a small sample of Bible commentators who believed that the Temple would one day be rebuilt and the sacrifices restored.

ONE FINAL POINT: IT IS LOGICAL FOR GOD TO ACT AGAIN IN HISTORY

We will close this section by citing the words of Adolph Saphir. He makes a number of important points about this four-thousand-year-old testimony that the Lord has given to the world through the descendants of Abraham, Isaac, and Jacob.

And why should it be thought a strange thing that Israel's history will be consummated by a direct interference of God ... Was not Israel's history miraculous from the very beginning? The call of Abraham, the birth of Isaac, the Exodus out of Egypt, the preservation of Israel in the wilderness, the entrance into Canaan, the anointing of David by Samuel—in all these facts we see direct interference of divine power. And, last of all, it was not immediately after David and Solomon that the Messiah came, lest Israel's history should be constructed according to the modern ideas of natural evolution; but it was in the time of Judea's lowest condition, when subject to the Roman emperor, that *God* visited and redeemed His people. Angels descended to announce the Messiah's birth. Christ was born of a virgin. Miracle of miracles! And thus the conclusion of Israel's history will be God's act, and manifest to the whole world as supernatural and divine. "Hear the word of the Lord, O ye nations, and declare it in the isles afar off." He that scattereth Israel will gather him and keep him as a shepherd doth his flock" (Adolph Saphir, *Christ and Israel, Lectures on the Jews*, Morgan and Scott, Ltd. London, 1911, pp. 13,14).

This point is hugely important! The God of Scripture is a God who has divinely acted in history. Since the Bible documents how He has miraculously acted in the past, it certainly is not illogical to assume that He will also supernaturally act again in the future. In fact, we should expect it.

SUMMARY OF THE PREDICTIONS BY PAST COMMENTATORS

As we mentioned, these are merely a few of the many predictions that past Bible commentators have made about what to expect in the future. In fact, we could fill an entire book, a huge book, of the specific predictions these ancient commentators of the Scripture made which were based upon their literal understanding of Bible prophecy.

What is abundantly clear is that these people, by faith, believed, that the predictions by the God of the Bible, would eventually take place in the future. As we have documented, they indeed have!

APPENDIX 3

The Consistent Argument Used By Past Commentators: The Miracle Of the Jews!

While almost all of our "Twenty-Five Signs of the End" were not in place during the last nineteen centuries, past students of Scripture did have a continual witness to the truthfulness of the Word of God.

Indeed, it was the miracle of the survival of the Jews. Though scattered to the four corners of the earth, the Jews continued to exist, as well as retaining their national identity without being absorbed into the other nations where they traveled. In fact, this was our first "Sign of the End" in our discussion.

It is fascinating to read what these past Bible commentators have written during their lifetimes while awaiting the fulfillment of the other "end time" prophecies.

Because what they said seemed so interesting, it seemed to be a good idea to read what these past writers had to say about this remarkable sign that the Lord had given to them—the continued existence of the nation of Israel.

As is true with our other citations of past commentators, this is a mere sample of their voluminous material on the subject.

ADOLPH SAPHIR

In the 19th century, when so many predictions had yet to be fulfilled, Adolph Saphir wrote the following words about God's miraculous dealings with Israel:

> And so Jesus Himself predicted to Jerusalem, summing up their whole past history, that they who killed the prophets, and stoned them that were sent to them, were now at last to receive the recompense of their evil deeds, that their house should be left to them desolate because they had not understood the time of their visitation. But yet not for ever did He part with them. He held out the bright and glorious hope that they would see Him again, and not merely with the eyes of the body, but also with the eyes of faith, welcoming Him as the Blessed One in the name of the Lord.
>
> See then, the Old Testament predictions and the New Testament predictions tested most clearly, in the light of the fact, by the history of the last eighteen centuries, that Israel rejected Jesus; that God gave up Israel to banishment and punishment, yet loving them and being faithful to the covenant which He had made; that this nation is preserved in a most wonderful way both physically and spiritually for the fulfillment of those predictions which are interwoven, in the Old Testament, with the predictions of the first advent (Adolph Saphir, *The Divine Unity Of Scripture*, London, Hodder and Stoughton, 1892, p. 107).

This is key. The nation of Israel has been a living witness to the Lord these past two thousand years. They have been miraculously preserved through all these centuries because they are central to the plan of God in the "last days." To understand what the Lord is doing today, people must look at what He has done in the past with this chosen nation.

Saphir also wrote:

The apostle bears witness that the Jews had a zeal for God, though not according to knowledge. If we dwell only on the guilt of Israel, we take a very one-sided view of the nation; for although they rejected Jesus, yet they did not wish to cease being God's covenant people; and it is most touching to notice how, at the destruction of Jerusalem, they clung with all intensity to God and to His service. After the great and unparalleled sufferings which they endured during and after that catastrophe, they still adhered with great service to God. In their dispersion, and notwithstanding all their misery, they established synagogues everywhere, and schools of theology, in which the Scriptures were expounded. True, the holy and righteous judgment of God had come upon them, and they were visited with His displeasure for their sins' sake.

The English poet says: "The wild dove hath its nest, the fox its cave, Mankind its country, *Israel but the grave.*"

But this is not true, sad as is Israel's condition. Israel has the *Word*. The worship of God, the observance of the law, and the exposition of Scripture, were throughout their whole dispersion, and in their lowest condition, the very heart-life consolation and uniting bond of the nation. A spectacle unique in history! (Adolph Saphir, *Christ and Israel, Lectures on the Jews,* Morgan and Scott, Ltd. London, 1911, pp. 4-5).

They are indeed, "a spectacle unique in history."

Since the world has had this objective witness to the truth of Scripture, Saphir made the following plea to Christian ministers.

It is the duty of every minister of Christ to explain the mystery of Israel. It is part of our holy religion. It belongs to the counsel of God. It is inseparably connected with the truth as it is in Jesus (Adolph Saphir, *Christ and Israel, Lectures on the Jews,* Morgan and Scott, Ltd. London, 1911, p. 15).

Indeed, as Saphir continues, Israel is a sign that the Lord has given for all the world to see. In fact, there is no natural way of explaining it.

> There is a *mystery* (italics his) about Israel: there is something that no philosopher will be able to discover. Their present existence, their present dispersion, and their future destiny, have all been revealed to us in the Word; but God's Word can only be apprehended through the teaching of the Holy Ghost. It is quite in accordance with this remark that one of the most astute philosophers—the greatest philosopher that Germany has ever produced—Hegel, a man who was very fond of showing mankind the meaning of history, said, when he came to the history of the Jews, "It is a dark troublesome enigma to me. I am not able to understand it. It does not fit with any of our categories. *It is a riddle.*" (italics his). It is a mysterious nation—just as mysterious as Jesus is mysterious (Adolph Saphir, *Christ and Israel, Lectures on the Jews,* Morgan and Scott, Ltd. London, 1911, p. 17).

Israel is a mystery to those who do not take the Bible seriously. However, for Bible-believers, it is no mystery whatsoever.

F.J. HORSEFIELD

Writing in the early part of the 20th century, F.J. Horsefield made this observation from the evidence of history.

> The history of all the great empires of the Old Testament times bear witness to the fact that the truth of prophecy has, in all ages, been fully vindicated, however, improbable the fulfillment may have seemed whilst the present condition of the Jewish race bears absolutely irrefutable testimony to the same effect. . .
>
> It has been frequently pointed out that the present condition of the Jews, is, in itself, a proof of the fulfillment of

prophecy. Our Lord foretold it when He said, "They shall by the edge of the sword, and shall be led away captive into all the nations: and Jerusalem shall be trodden down of the Gentiles be fulfilled" (Luke 21:24). And in this emphatic statement Christ was only confirming a multitude of Old Testament prophecies which speak of the desolation of the land of Israel; of the people being scattered amongst the heathen; and of the becoming "an astonishment, a proverb, and a by-word amongst all nations whither the Lord should lead them (Deuteronomy 28:37). Yet they were preserved as a separate people, and after the conclusion of the times of the Gentiles, to be brought back to their own land. . . . For the moment we simply notice that after 2,000 years of dispersion the Jews are as distinct as when they were first scattered from Jerusalem. Other races blend and mingle with each other, and in time lose their separate identity, but for twenty centuries that little nation of Israel, scattered all over the world, has been kept separate and distinct from every other nation and race, waiting for the time when they shall be restored in Palestine (F.J. Horsefield, *The Return of the King*, Fifth Edition, Good Books Corporation, Harrisburg, Pa., 1920, pp. 20, 27-28).

The history of the Jews does indeed bear an irrefutable testimony to the truthfulness of the Word of God.

DAVID BARON

In the 19th century, Hebrew/Christian writer David Baron wrote the following about the witness that the nation Israel was to the world:

Israel's present state, and the miracle of their preservation. This is the next item in the divinely dictated message through the prophet Jeremiah. . . The present state of the peculiar people has been foretold with minute exactness in predictions like the following:

"For lo, I will command, and I will sift (lit. *toss* or *shake about*) the house of Israel among the nations, like as corn is tossed in a sieve" (Amos 9:9)

Or in the words of Jeremiah:

"I will even give them up to be tossed to and fro among all the kingdoms of the earth for evil; to be a reproach and a proverb, a taunt and a curse, in all places whither I will drive them" (Jeremiah 24:9).

O ye who doubt the inspiration of the Book of books, compare these prophecies of thousands of years ago with what is going on before your very eyes! How can we account for the repeated dispersions, and the continued, unceasing wanderings and strange restlessness of the Jew apart from these ancient inspired utterances? That Palestine should be vanquished, and that Israel should be cast out of their own land, or even be dispersed among the nations was within the range of human possibility, and mayhap within the power of a shrewd observer to forecast; but that for centuries and centuries, a people vanquished and scattered out of their own country, instead of becoming absorbed among the nations— as has been the case with other peoples; and instead of taking root and finding rest in the new soil to which they have been transplanted, should retain a separate existence, everywhere dwelling alone, and not reckoned among the nations, yet in all places kept in a state of unrest, and continually agitated and tossed about: who, but He whose hand has kept up this standing miracle as His witness among the nations could have foreseen and foretold *that*? (Italics his) (David Baron, *The Jewish Problem, Its Solution, or Israel Present and Future,* 1890, pp. 44-46).

There are some remarkable statements here. For example, "He whose hand has kept up this standing miracle as His witness among the nations" says it all! Israel has been a standing miracle throughout its entire history. This has been particularly so since the time of the destruction of Jerusalem and the Temple in A.D 70, as well as their scattering throughout the entire world. Yet with all of this, they still exist—never having been absorbed into other cultures or losing their national identity. As Baron asked, "Who could have foreseen and foretold that? Indeed, who but God alone?

H. GRATTAN GUINNESS

After thoroughly documenting the history of the Jews, we read the following summation:

> To conclude. The rapid glance which we have taken of twenty-five centuries of Jewish history which have elapsed since the days of Nebuchadnezzar and the beginning of the times of the Gentiles shows that . . . Never since the days when that monarch subdued the Jews have they been independent of Gentile authority, though for five centuries a remnant of them were restored to a tributary condition in their land. That since the rejection of "Messiah the Prince" total dispersion among the Gentiles has been the lot of their whole nation and desolation the portion of their land . . .
>
> We cannot close this section without directing our attention to the bearing of these facts on our faith and hope and duty as Christians. Before such a fulfillment of prophecy as Jewish history exhibits what can all the fiery darts of infidelity do? Their story, extending back as it does through 4000 years of history, forms an impregnable fortress for believers in the inspiration of Scripture. What else but Divine foreknowledge and Divine inspiration *can* [italics his] account for the fact of this strange case? (H. Grattan Guinness, *Light for the last days*, edited and revised by E.P. Cachemaille, Marshall, Morgan and Scott, Ltd. London, 1917, pp. 157, 158).

Indeed, on a purely natural level, how can anyone account for their unique history?

G.H. PEMBER

G.H. Pember, commenting upon Leviticus 26, wrote the following insightful words.

> The second prediction is involved in the statement—thrice repeated in the following verses—that, during the desolation of Palestine, the Israelites should dwell in the land of their enemies; that is, among peoples who would regard them as aliens, and whom they also would feel to be disassociated from themselves . . .

> Commenting on this prediction would be a waste of time. It is known to all men that Israelites are found in every part of the world, and that they have been so dispersed for eighteen centuries, and yet have never been absorbed. Moreover, their case is unique: it has been so with no other nation. Kingdoms, have indeed been broken up, and peoples driven from their own country into other lands; but in such circumstances the people have invariable lost their distinctive national features, and by a gradual assimilation have become incorporated with the strangers in whose land they came to sojourn. There is one exception to this rule, and only one, that of Israel, which has been for so long a time mingled with the vast masses of the world's population, and has, nevertheless, remained a separated and peculiar people; and that for no assignable reason, save that God has willed it. Wherever the Jew is seen, there the arm of the Almighty is revealed, and an assurance given that the portion of His wondrous word which is still unfulfilled must also become history in its appointed season (G.H. Pember, *The Great Prophecies of The Centuries Concerning Israel and the Gentiles*, London: Hodder and Stoughton, 1895, pp. 93,94).

There are many profound truths in what Pember says. As Israel was about to enter the Promised Land, the Lord warned them about what would happen if they disobeyed in the future. Sadly, they still did. Their forecasted future has come to pass precisely as God had warned them. In fact, for eighteen centuries it has been there for all the world to see.

HUGH MCNEILE

Writing early in the 19th century, Hugh McNeile made the following observations about Israel:

> Who, and what are the Jews, and what shall they be? These are questions of lively interest to the Christian. The past history and present condition of the Jewish people, bear witness to the divine inspiration of the Holy Scriptures, and to the immediate personal agency of Almighty God in the management of the affairs of this world, with a power and plainness which no gainsayer can refute. And the Holy Scriptures bear witness to the future pre-eminence of that degraded people, with a reiteration of the prediction which no believer can resist. History is the providence of God. They mutually attest each other, on the subject of the Jewish nation, unto this day. Collusion is manifestly impossible; the inference, therefore, against the sceptic is irresistible. . .
>
> [They were] rooted out [of their land] by the conquering arms of the victorious Romans . . . scattered among the nations to the four winds of heaven . . . preserved as a separate people, not mingling among any people in their dispersion . . . still a separate people in this, and other countries and cities, scattered and peeled, as described by the prophet; a nation wonderful indeed, from their beginning hitherto (Hugh McNeile, *Popular Lectures on the Prophecies relative to the Jewish nation*, London, J. Hatchard and Son, 1840, pp, 1, 11).

McNeile observed that "Collusion is manifestly impossible." Indeed, it is.

ALEXANDER KEITH

In the early part of the 19th century, Alexander Keith wrote a book on Christian evidences. He said the following concerning the Jews:

> Such are the prophecies, and such are the facts, respecting the Jews; and from premises like these, the feeblest logician may draw a moral demonstration. If they had been utterly destroyed, if they had mingled among the nations; if, in space of nearly eighteen centuries after their dispersion, they had become extinct as a people; even if they had been secluded in a single region, and had remained ununited; if their history had been analogous to that of any other nation upon the earth, an attempt might, with some plausibility or reason, have been made to show cause why the prediction of their fate, however, true to the fact, ought not, in such a case, to be sustained as evidence of truth of inspiration. Or if the past history or present state of the Jews were not of a nature so singular or peculiar, as to bear out to the very letter the truth of prophecies concerning them, with what triumph would the infidel have produced these very prophecies concerning them, as fatal to the idea of the inspiration of the Scriptures. And when the Jews have been scattered throughout the whole earth; when they have remained everywhere a distinct race; when they have been despoiled evermore, and yet never destroyed; when the most wonderful and amazing facts, such as never occurred among any people, form the ordinary narrative of their history, and fulfill literally the prophecies concerning them, may not the believer challenge his adversary to the production of such credentials of the faith that is *in him*? They present an unbroken chain of evidence, each link of a prophecy and a fact extending throughout a multitude of generations, and not yet terminated. Though the events, various and singular as they are, have been brought about by the instrumentality of human means, and the agency of

secondary causes, yet they are equally prophetic and miraculous; for the means were as impossible to be foreseen as the end; and the causes were as inscrutable as the event; and they have been, and still in numberless instances are, accomplished by the instrumentality of the enemies of Christianity. Whoever seeks a miracle, may here behold a sign and a wonder, than which there cannot be greater. And the Christian may bid defiance to all the assaults of his enemies from this stronghold of Christianity, impenetrable, and impregnable on every side (Alexander Keith, *Evidence Of The Truth Of The Christian Religion,* New York: Harper and Brothers, 1839, pp. 79,80).

There are many profound truths in Keith's words. Indeed, the Christian can point to the history of the Jewish people as a literal fulfillment of the Word of God. If anyone is looking for the truth, it is there for all to see.

A.C. GAEBELEIN

At the beginning of the 20th century, A.C. Gaebelein wrote these insightful words:

No pen can describe the history of this people and the dark shadows which have been upon them. As the homeless nation they have wandered throughout this age, in fulfillment of the predictions of their own prophets, among the nations of the earth. Awful has been their persecutions, and tribulations upon tribulations have been their lot. Suffering and sorrow, the meat and drink of every generation since they were driven from their God-given land. How dark are the shadows which have come upon the people once more as a result of the world conflict. Millions have lost their all. Hundreds of thousands are homeless wanderers in eastern Europe. Perhaps the story of their suffering in connection with the war will never be written. And the end is not yet (A.C. Gaebelein, *Studies In Prophecy*, Our Hope, 1918, p. 92)

Like these other authors we are citing, Gaebelein saw that the existence of the Jews, and their wanderings across the face of the earth, are vivid examples of the fulfillment of the prophecies of Scripture.

We should not miss the fact that Gaebelein wrote these words right after the First World War had ended. Ironically, he said that the suffering of the Jews, in connection with the War, may never be written. Of course, he had no idea what they would suffer in the Second World War—when six million Jews would be murdered in the death camps.

Yet, as he stated, the end is not yet. In fact, Gaebelein recognized that their worse time of suffering was still to come, just as the Scripture says.

> But do these tremendous events in the East mean that the day will come when the shadows will flee away from the seed of Abraham? Not by any means. The time of Jacob's trouble has not yet been. The last siege of Jerusalem prewritten in Zechariah's prophecy (chapter xiv) still awaits fulfillment. To deliver that nation and that land completely and to bring about the glories promised in God's infallible Word needs more than the conquest of the land. The flag of the British lion now flies over Jerusalem. Some day another flag will be raised above that city—the flag of the Son of Man, the Son of David, the Lion of the tribe of Judah (A.C. Gaebelein, *Studies In Prophecy*, Our Hope, 1918, p. 93).

While the flag of Jesus, the Son of David, is not yet flying over Jerusalem, since 1967, the flag of the state of Israel has been flying over that united city of the Jews.

BISHOP W.R. NICHOLSON

Bishop W.R. Nicholson made the following insightful remarks about the uniqueness of Israel:

And have we not confirmation superabounding, in the miraculous preservation of that people through well nigh a score of centuries of transcendent suffering?

Can the world show anything like it? Twice 1,800 years old, they saw the proud Egyptians perish in the waters of the Red Sea; they heard the fall of the great Babylon's power; they witnessed the ruins of the Syro-Macedonian conquest. And now they have outlived the Caesars, and outlived the dark ages. They have been through all civilizations, shared in all convulsions, and have kept pace with the entire progress of discovery and art. And here they stand to-day, as distinct as ever, occupying no country of their own, scattered through all countries, identical in their physiognomy, earth's men of destiny …

But have they suffered severely? One convulsive groan of agony breathing through eighteen centuries, and heard in every land . . . They gave been fined and fleeced by almost every government known to history. They have been banished from place to place; banished and recalled, and banished again. By the code of Justinian, they were incapable of executing wills, of testifying in courts of justice of having social and public worship (Bishop W.R. Nicholson, "The Gathering of Israel," in Nathaniel West, *Second Coming of Christ, Premillennial Essays of the Prophetic Conference,* Chicago, F.H. Revell, 1879, pp. 237, 238).

Yet with all of this persecution, the Jews still exist, and thrive. Why? Because the Bible says they will!

HORATIUS BONAR

Horatius Bonar made this observation about the continued existence of Israel as compared to ancient empires who no longer exist:

Take again, the prophecies which concern the heathen nations—Babylon, Nineveh, Tyre, Moab, Ammon, Edom

. . . Have not all these been literally fulfilled? Or, *lastly*, take the predictions regarding Israel. Have not all been literally verified? Captivity, dispersion, exile, misery, contempt, and oppression, have been their history to this very hour. And was there one particular of all their wondrous history which prophecy did not foretel? Up to this hour all has been literal fulfillment in their case . . .

Up to this hour, then, everything respecting Israel has been literally accomplished. Nothing in what has hitherto occurred in their strange history gives the slightest countenance to the figurative interpretations for which some so strenuously contend. Why is Israel still an exile, an outcast, a wanderer, if there be no literal curse? Why is Jerusalem laid in heaps, and Mount Zion ploughed as a field? (Jer. 26:18). Why has Moab fled, Idumea become a wilderness, and Mount Seir laid desolate? Why is all this, if there be no *literal* curse? (Horatius Bonar, *Prophetical Landmarks*, London, James Nisbet And Co., Berners Street, 1847, pp. 295, 313, 314).

Why indeed? Why have they been scattered throughout the world yet remain a distinct people? Why have they been treated so badly wherever they do go? Yet, why do they still exist?

He also said:

And was ever a nation so mysteriously indestructible? Plunged into the furnace of Egyptian, Assyrian, Babylonian, Grecian, Roman tyranny, it has come forth unconsumed! Kingdom after kingdom has crumbled down, or been swallowed up, yet Israel has walked secure over the debris of empires, or stood upon fragments of each successive wreck, casting its wistful eye toward Jerusalem, the heritage of its nation, the city of its soul. . .

In them we see the true romance of history. Theirs is, indeed, a strange story oftentimes more like a vision than a reality—yet true, pre-eminently true; not lost in fables or mist, but one entire certainty from the beginning hitherto (Horatius Bonar, *Prophetical Landmarks*, London, James Nisbet And Co., Berners Street, 1847, pp. 333-335).

Again, we find a past commentator of Scripture noting how Israel, as a nation, survives while other nations do not. Indeed, they are indestructible because the Lord has said so!

J.C. RYLE

In the 19th century, the English writer J.C. Ryle wrote the following about the witness of the Jews.

But though Israel has been scattered, Israel has not been destroyed. For eighteen hundred years the Jews have continued as a separate people, without a king, without a land, without a territory—but never lost, never absorbed among the nations. They have been often trampled underfoot—but never shaken from the faith of their fathers. They have been often persecuted—but never destroyed. At this very moment, they are as distinct and peculiar a people as any people upon the earth—an unanswerable argument in the way of the infidel, a puzzling difficulty in the way of politicians, a standing lesson to all the world. Romans, Danes, Saxons, Normans, Belgians, French, Germans have all in turn settled on British soil. All of them in turn have lost their national distinctiveness. All of them in turn have become part and parcel of the English nation, after a lapse of a few hundred years. But it has never been so with the Jews.

Dispersed as they are, there is a principle of cohesion among them which no circumstances have been able to melt. Scattered as they are there is a national vitality which is stronger than that of any nation on the earth. Settle where you please, in hot countries or in cold, you will find the Jews.

But go where you will and settle as you please, this wonderful people is always the same. Scattered as they are, few in number, compared to among those whom they live, the Jews are always the Jews. Three thousand years ago Balaam said, "The people shall dwell alone and not be reckoned among the nations." Eighteen hundred years ago our Lord said, "This generation shall not pass away until all be fulfilled." We have seen these words made good before our eyes (J.C. Ryle, *Coming Events and Present Duties*, Second Edition, London, William Hunt and Company, 1879, pp. 171,172).

Brilliantly said! The world has indeed seen "these words made good before our eyes." Though scattered around the globe, the Jewish people have dwelt alone and have never been absorbed by the various nations to which they have traveled. To this day, they remain Jews.

SUMMING UP THE OBSERVATIONS OF PAST BIBLE COMMENTATORS CONCERNING THE JEWS

We have cited eleven commentators of yesteryear who have pointed to the miracle of the Jews as something all the world should continually observe. Indeed, the Lord had predicted their scattering to the four corners of the earth, their isolation, as well as their constant suffering. Yet, He also predicted their survival!

For almost two thousand years they have been a living witness to the world regarding the truthfulness of God's Word—for all these predictions were literally fulfilled.

As we have also documented in our second "Sign of the End," other nations which attempted to destroy Israel have themselves been wiped off of the face of the earth. Yet the Jew continues to exist.

There is really no explanation that can be given on a "natural level." Indeed, we are not dealing with the natural here—but rather the supernatural! Israel has been, is, and will continue to be, a sign to the world of the existence of the God of the Bible, as well a sign to the truth of His Word.

About the Author

Don Stewart is a graduate of Biola University and Talbot Theological Seminary (with the highest honors).

Don is a best-selling and award-winning author having authored, or co-authored, over seventy books. This includes the best-selling *Answers to Tough Questions*, with Josh McDowell, as well as the award-winning book *Family Handbook of Christian Knowledge: The Bible*. His various writings have been translated into over thirty different languages and have sold over a million copies.

Don has traveled around the world proclaiming and defending the historic Christian faith. He has also taught both Hebrew and Greek at the undergraduate level and Greek at the graduate level.

Look Up Don Stewart

Made in the USA
San Bernardino, CA
31 May 2018